# King John's
Right-Hand Lady

# King John's Right-Hand Lady

## The Story of Nicholaa de la Haye

Sharon Bennett Connolly

First published in Great Britain in 2023 by
Pen & Sword History
An imprint of
Pen & Sword Books Ltd
Yorkshire – Philadelphia

Copyright © Sharon Bennett Connolly 2023

ISBN 978 1 52675 606 0

The right of Sharon Bennett Connolly to be identified as Author of this work has been asserted by her in accordance with the Copyright, Designs and Patents Act 1988.

A CIP catalogue record for this book is available from the British Library.

All rights reserved. No part of this book may be reproduced or transmitted in any form or by any means, electronic or mechanical including photocopying, recording or by any information storage and retrieval system, without permission from the Publisher in writing.

Typeset by Mac Style
Printed in the UK by CPI Group (UK) Ltd, Croydon, CR0 4YY.

Pen & Sword Books Limited incorporates the imprints of Atlas, Archaeology, Aviation, Discovery, Family History, Fiction, History, Maritime, Military, Military Classics, Politics, Select, Transport, True Crime, Air World, Frontline Publishing, Leo Cooper, Remember When, Seaforth Publishing, The Praetorian Press, Wharncliffe Local History, Wharncliffe Transport, Wharncliffe True Crime and White Owl.

For a complete list of Pen & Sword titles please contact

PEN & SWORD BOOKS LIMITED
47 Church Street, Barnsley, South Yorkshire, S70 2AS, England
E-mail: enquiries@pen-and-sword.co.uk
Website: www.pen-and-sword.co.uk

Or

PEN AND SWORD BOOKS
1950 Lawrence Rd, Havertown, PA 19083, USA
E-mail: Uspen-and-sword@casematepublishers.com
Website: www.penandswordbooks.com

*For my old school friends, who all turned the big 50 during the writing of this book, with much love.*
*And to Louise Wilkinson, thank you!*

# Contents

| | | |
|---|---|---|
| *Foreword* | | viii |
| *Acknowledgements* | | x |
| *Introduction* | | xiii |
| Chapter 1 | An Investigation into Nicholaa de la Haye's Family Origins | 1 |
| Chapter 2 | Richard de la Haye | 25 |
| Chapter 3 | Nicholaa and her Sisters | 37 |
| Chapter 4 | Prince John | 45 |
| Chapter 5 | Nicholaa and Gerard de Camville | 54 |
| Chapter 6 | 1191 | 76 |
| Chapter 7 | Lincoln Restored | 91 |
| Chapter 8 | The Magna Carta Crisis | 110 |
| Chapter 9 | 1217 | 125 |
| Chapter 10 | The In-Laws | 139 |
| Chapter 11 | Retirement – Eventually | 152 |
| Chapter 12 | The Legacy of Nicholaa de la Haye | 162 |
| *Appendix A: The 1215 Magna Carta* | | 171 |
| *Appendix B: Enforcers of Magna Carta – The Twenty-Five* | | 185 |
| *Appendix C: The Charter of the Forest 1217* | | 187 |
| *Notes* | | 192 |
| *Bibliography* | | 210 |
| *Index* | | 220 |

# Foreword

Heiress, widow, castellan, sheriff, and war leader – Lady Nicholaa de la Haye, the subject of this welcome new biography by Sharon Bennett Connolly, was one of the most famous women of her day. To her allies, she was the brave, honourable, and loyal lady who stood by King John until his death in October 1216, and who then championed the cause of his young son and heir, King Henry III. To her critics and opponents, she was an evil-hearted and ruthless plunderer of property. This polarization in opinion about her reflected the political divisions of her day, since Nicholaa lived through one of the most momentous periods of English history, an era that witnessed a bitter baronial rebellion provoked by years of misrule under King John and his predecessors. The early stages of the First Barons' War culminated famously in the issue of Magna Carta on 15 June 1215, King John's great charter of liberties that was intended to restore peace. John's subsequent rejection of Magna Carta led to the renewal of civil war in England within a matter of weeks and later compelled the rebels to offer the English throne to Louis, the eldest son of the French king. At Lincoln Castle, one of the few remaining royal strongholds in the East of England that held out against the rebels, Nicholaa was on the front line of the conflict. One of King John's final actions before his death was to appoint Nicholaa, the widowed heiress of the Lincolnshire barony of Brattleby, to the office of sheriff in Lincolnshire, initially alongside one of his most notorious henchmen, Philip Marc.

It was highly unusual for a woman to be appointed to serve as a sheriff, the king's chief local agent in a county in the Middle Ages. This move undoubtedly reflected Nicholaa's experience and renown as a strong local leader. In appointing Nicholaa, John rewarded a long-standing supporter, who had defended Lincoln Castle against other hostile forces in 1191. As a widow, it was Nicholaa who led the defence of Lincoln Castle, when the surrounding city was occupied by rebel forces during the First Barons'

War. She did so, capably, until a great royalist army under William Marshal, King Henry III's regent, successfully came to her relief at the Battle of Lincoln on 20 May 1217. The Battle of Lincoln was one of two great set-piece battles fought in England in 1217; the other was a naval battle fought off the Kentish coast near Sandwich. Second, perhaps, only to the Battle of Hastings in its importance, the Battle of Lincoln helped to set England on the road to peace.

As King John's 'right hand lady' and a figure who played such a pivotal role in safeguarding the English throne for King Henry III in the East Midlands, Nicholaa de la Haye has remained curiously neglected by historians. Although Nicholaa's life has long fascinated academics like me, she has – until now – lacked a book-length study devoted to her family background, life, and legacy. Drawing upon the contents of chronicles, as well as a wealth of medieval records and modern scholarship, this lively and engaging book by Sharon Bennett Connolly fills a significant gap in our literature. Its chapters navigate us from the origins of Nicholaa's family, through her father Richard's career, her marriages, and her involvement in regional government and war, to her later struggles with William Longespée, Earl of Salisbury, her fierce rival for power in Lincolnshire. The book draws to a close with an examination of the shadow that Nicholaa's reputation cast over her descendants, notably Alice (d. 1348), Countess of Lincoln and Salisbury, a later heiress, who as constable of Lincoln Castle and lady of Bolingbroke Castle, found her authority challenged during the turbulent reigns of King Edward II and King Edward III. It is a pleasure to see Nicholaa de la Haye, in this book, finally receive the attention that she deserves.

Louise Wilkinson, Professor of Medieval Studies
Nicola de la Haye Building, University of Lincoln, October 2022.

# Acknowledgements

Writing my sixth book, the third for Pen and Sword, has been an incredible experience and I would like to thank everyone who has helped and encouraged me throughout the process. I would like to thank the staff at Pen and Sword for their continued confidence in me, especially my editors Claire Hopkins, Danna Messer, Lucy May, Sarah-Beth Watkins and Chris Evan Brown, without their support and enthusiasm I would not have been able to write Nicholaa's story. I would also like to give a shout out to the fabulous cover design team, especially Paul Wilkinson, to Laura Hirst and to Rosie Milne, who all played a hand in making the book presentable.

I would particularly like to thank Professor Louise Wilkinson, the academic expert on Nicholaa de la Haye, for lending me her invaluable support and guidance in all stages of the writing of this book. Not only was Louise a sounding-board over coffee, in the shadow of Lincoln Cathedral or in the courtyard of Nicholaa's own castle, but she more than once pointed me in the right direction when I came across a conundrum. I also owe a great deal of thanks to academics Professor Daniel Power, Dr David Stocker, Dr Dean Irwin, Julian Humphrys and Professor Stephanie Moores Christelow, for being generous enough to share their own knowledge and answer my queries on Nicholaa and her family. And, as ever, when it comes to Nicholaa de la Haye and King John, I cannot thank Rich Price enough for all his work on translating the Close Rolls and Letters Patent of the time, and for answering my numerous queries associated with them. Thanks also go to some amazing historians, including Ralph V. Turner, Richard Cassidy, Simon Forder, Michael Jones, James Wright, David Santiuste, Dan Spencer and John Paul Davis for the many little snippets of advice and encouragement.

I would not have written one book, let alone six, were it not for Amy Licence, whose help, advice and friendship has been invaluable to me in my journey to become an author. I am also grateful to my fellow author, Kristie Dean, who has been an amazing friend, offering advice and encouragement throughout my writing career. And thank you to Elizabeth Chadwick for her tireless encouragement over the years. Thanks go to Jayne Smith and Kristie Dean for their kind permission to use their wonderful photos.

Writing can be a lonely experience, you spend your time reading books for research, or sitting, staring at the computer screen, trying to think of something intelligent to write. But social media has changed all that, there are always friends just a 'click' away to give you a diversion or encouragement. I would therefore like to thank the readers of my blog, *History...the Interesting Bits.com* for their wonderful support and feedback. A special thank you goes, too, to my friends in the online community, whose amusing anecdotes and memes have given me that boost when I needed it, particularly Karrie Stone, Tim Byard-Jones, Karen Clark, Geanine Teramani-Cruz, Anne Marie Bouchard, Harry Basnett, Derek Birks and every one of my Facebook friends and Twitter followers. Also, the online author community has proved invaluable to me. So, I would like to extend a special 'thank you' to Darren Baker, Matthew Lewis, Julian Humphreys, Nathen Amin, S.J.A. Turney, Tony Riches, Sarah Bryson, Matthew Harffy, Steven A. McKay, Giles Kristian, Justin Hill, Mary Anne Yard, Paula Lofting, Samantha Wilcoxson, Lynn Dawson, Kim Barton, Jacqueline Reiter, Stephanie Churchill and Prue Batten for all your support and encouragement with this book and the previous ones.

And thank you to the various historical sites I have visited associated with the research of Nicholaa. A special mention must go to the staff and volunteers at Lincoln Castle, especially Helen Woodgate and Malcolm Stainforth, the castle guides who gave up one Saturday in August 2021 to show me around the castle and answer all my queries with regard to Nicholaa and the 1217 Battle of Lincoln. And to the staff and members at Heritage Lincolnshire, the Lincoln branch of the Lincolnshire Family History Association and the Lincoln Civic Trust for all their help and encouragement with this project. Particular thanks have to go to Sasha Drennan and Gill Hart at Lindum Books in Lincoln for hosting my author talks and being a source of huge support and encouragement for this project from the very beginning.

I would like to include some 'thank yous' to those who supported the release of my previous books, *Heroines of the Medieval World*, *Silk, the*

*Sword: The Women of the Norman Conquest*, *Ladies of Magna Carta: Women of Influence in Thirteenth Century England* and *Defenders of the Norman Crown: Rise and Fall of the Warenne Earls of Surrey*. To Gavin Smithies and his wonderful team at 'my local', Conisbrough Castle. And to Nicola – no h – and the staff at Gainsborough Old Hall, for being my 'happy place'.

A thank you must also go to my friends closer to home, particularly Sharon Gleave, Jill Gaskell, Sarah Wildgoose, Helen Walker, Bernadette Blaevoet-Fletcher and all my local friends, for their wonderful support and for dragging me out for a coffee every once in a while. And to Kate Moran – Madame Moran – my French teacher of (quite a few) years ago, who instilled in me a love of the language that has been invaluable to me in my research and who made my day last summer by asking me to sign her copy of *Heroines of the Medieval World*.

I reserve a special thanks to my family, my sister, Suzanne, whose support has been unwavering and very much appreciated, and my brother Stephen. And to my mum and dad for all their love and encouragement, and for their own passion for history. And to my husband, James, thank you for putting up with all the history talks. I could not have done it without all of you.

The biggest thank you of all goes to my research assistant and son, Lewis, who has travelled to various wonderful places with me in the process of making this book a reality and has turned into a fabulous sounding-board for my ideas and arguments. A chip off the old block, if ever there was one, he is turning into quite the historian himself and I really value the many history-related conversations we have on a daily basis. He is my constant inspiration.

I will always owe a debt of gratitude to the great historians throughout history – to the present day – who have gallantly edited and translated the great chronicles of the medieval era, so that they are accessible and readable for all of us who have an interest in the period, but very little understanding of Latin. Every effort has been made to ensure the accuracy of this book. However, any errors that may occur are entirely my own.

# Introduction

In 1217, England was in dire straits. It had lost much of its continental lands, was in the midst of a civil war that had broken out after the failure of Magna Carta, and was enduring its first invasion since the Norman Conquest of 1066. On top of that, it was under the rule of a nine-year-old boy, the son of, arguably, England's most detested king, John.

The reign of King John, from 1199 to 1216, is often seen as one of the most turbulent periods of English history. A time of change and upheaval presided over by a man who is a leading challenger for the title of 'England's worst king'. With John on the throne, the great Plantagenet Empire that had been founded by his father, Henry II, was lost. Normandy and large parts of Aquitaine were claimed by John's erstwhile friend and ally, Philip II, King of France. King Philip's inexorable campaign to unite and expand his kingdom was made at the expense of the Plantagenet dominions in the country. The loss of the ancestral heartlands of Normandy was a particularly harsh blow, both to the king and the Anglo-Norman barons who had, for over a century, held lands on both sides of the English Channel. But more was to follow, with the great duchy of Aquitaine falling piecemeal to the French invaders, so that of all their continental possessions, only Gascony remained by John's death.

John was paranoid and had a reputation for deception, debauchery and outright murder. At one of his lowest points, his own half-brother deserted him for the French invader, Prince Louis, son and heir of King Philip II of France. Following his death in 1216, Matthew Paris provided the epitaph that few would disagree with: 'foul as it is, Hell itself is made fouler by the presence of King John.'[1]

With such a damning indictment of John's life and reign, it is not surprising that so many of his barons deserted him. Given John's actions and reputation, even when he was alive, it is not difficult to understand why so many of his barons rebelled against him. The loss of Normandy, murder of Prince Arthur and persecution of the Braose family is more than enough to justify the mistrust and withdrawn loyalty of the barons.

Indeed, it is harder to understand why some barons remained loyal in spite of everything. The most famous of these, of course, is William Marshal, Earl of Pembroke. Another is Nicholaa de la Haye, hereditary constable of Lincoln Castle. Nicholaa de la Haye is one of those very rare women in English history. She is renowned for her abilities, rather than her family and connections. In a time when men fought and women stayed home, Nicholaa de la Haye held Lincoln Castle against all-comers, defending it in no less than three sieges. Her strength and tenacity saved England at one of the lowest points in its history. She was also the first ever female sheriff in England, when she was created Sheriff of Lincolnshire by King John just hours before his death in 1216. She was not just a figurehead. She took her duties seriously, both for the castle and the county. At his death, John had lost many of his supporters, even family. His half-brother, William Longespée, Earl of Salisbury, and his cousin, William de Warenne, fifth Earl of Warenne and Surrey, had both joined the rebels and allied with the French prince.

However, John still had some powerful, stalwart people on his side. These would provide the backbone and direction to the reign of John's nine-year-old son Henry of Winchester, known as Henry III from the moment of his father's demise. William Marshal, Earl of Pembroke and now popularly known as 'the Greatest Knight' would be the young king's regent, with Hubert de Burgh, King John's justiciar, at his side. And holding Lincoln Castle would be its recently widowed constable, Nicholaa de la Haye, now also Sheriff of Lincolnshire.

Nicholaa had an unbeaten record in the defence of Lincoln Castle. She had been a partisan of John since before he became king, supporting him in his 1191 rebellion against Richard I's hated justiciar, William Longchamp. John had repaid her support with his trust – something not easily won from the paranoid king. And she had never let him down.

Nicholaa's support of King John has often put me into a quandary. There is no doubt that she was a brave, capable woman. She was resolute and stalwart in her support of John, but she must have known of John's ruthless streak. She could not have been ignorant of the accusations the barons laid against him, of the deaths that were laid at the king's door, of his nephew, Arthur, and Matilda de Braose. Which raises the question, what made Nicholaa de la Haye support John to the very end? Why did she remain loyal when everyone else deserted him? And what made her support so valuable? I have often pondered this over the years of researching King John, the emergence of Magna Carta and Nicholaa's story in particular. In studying Nicholaa's career, her relationship with John, and the development of the Magna Carta crisis and subsequent civil war, I hope to answer these questions.

Before we move on to the main part of the book, I just wanted to take a moment to talk about Nicholaa's name. The modern spelling is, of course, Nicola, and this is how it is spelt on the Nicola de la Haye building at Lincoln University. It may also be spelt Nicole or Nichola, but Nicholaa herself, on one of her surviving charters, used Nicholaa, and so that is how I have chosen to refer to her. An interesting anecdote on the city of Lincoln, which may explain how Nicholaa got her name, is that Lincoln, in French, is known as *Nicole*. So maybe she was named after the city in which she received such renown…

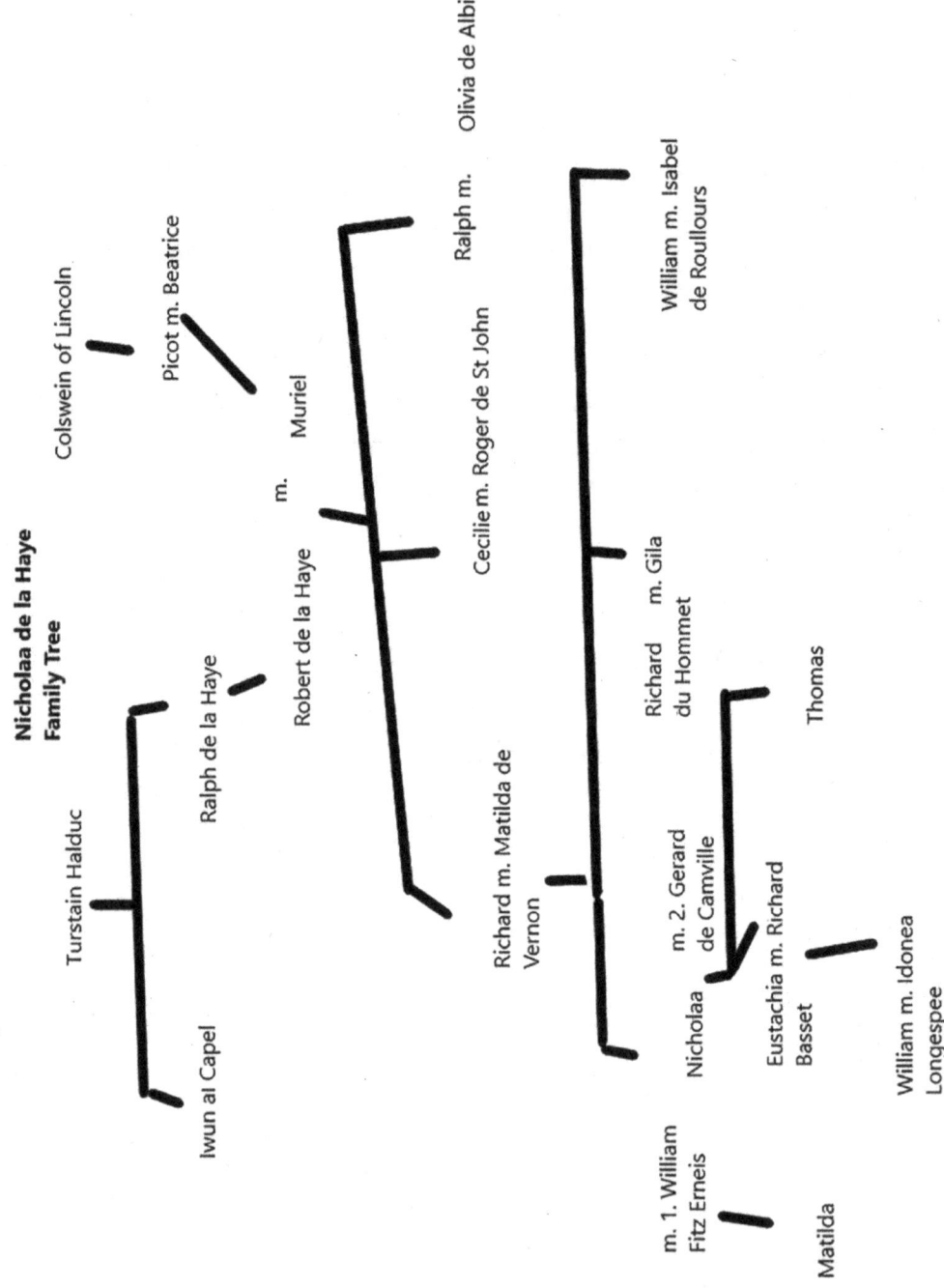

Chapter One

# An Investigation into Nicholaa de la Haye's Family Origins

Through her family history, Nicholaa de la Haye had close links with the city and county of Lincoln, stretching back to before the Norman Conquest of 1066; her heritage was a combination of English and Norman. The eldest daughter and co-heiress of Richard de la Haye and his wife, Matilda de Verdun, Nicholaa was probably born in the early 1150s. As with many of the minor aristocracy of the twelfth century, the La Haye (or La Haie, or Haya) family had their origins in Normandy and took their name from the honour of La Haie-du-Puits in the duchy.[1] The family had also acquired land in England after the Norman Conquest through, especially in Lincoln, a strategic marriage and their continuing service to the Norman and Plantagenet kings. Nicholaa's father, Richard de la Haye was a minor lord, holding the barony of Brattleby in Lincolnshire; in 1166 he was recorded as owing twenty knights' fees, which had been reduced to sixteen by 1172. Brattleby had been inherited from his mother, Muriel, wife of Robert de la Haye and daughter of Picot. Through her father, Muriel was the heir of Colswein (or Colsuan, or Kolsweinn) of Lincoln, an English lord who had found favour with William the Conqueror in the years following the Conquest.

In Lincoln after 1066, Englishmen could be found in the highest levels of urban society. Of the twelve English lawmen with lands and rights in 1066, only two had been replaced by Normans by 1086, five others had been succeeded by their own sons.[2] Although there is no record of Colswein having held land before 1066, he is recorded as holding fifty-six manors in the *Domesday Book* of 1086, either as tenant-in-chief, holding his land directly from the Crown, or as a lord holding the land from his tenant-in-chief. Colswein, along with Thorkell of Warwick, has been identified as one of only two Englishmen holding 'estates of baronial dimensions' in 1086.[3] His substantial holdings were given to him by William the Conqueror, for whom he may have acted in an official capacity, perhaps as the town-reeve of Lincoln.[4] A small number of his holdings were known to have been in the hands of his nephew, Cola, originally, and were inherited by Colswein. Victorian historian E.A. Freeman suggested that Colswein was the son of Alfred de Lincoln, and that he may have been the brother of Thorold of Lincoln, sheriff of Lincoln and the father of Lucy of Bolingbroke, Countess of Chester.[5] If this is the case, Colswein had two further brothers, Alan and Robert de Lincoln. Freeman suggested that Colswein and Thorold were sons of Alfred by his first wife, while Alan and Robert were the sons by a second wife, though neither wife is identified. In this scenario, it was Alan, the oldest son of the second wife, who inherited their father's lands, rather than Thorold or Colswein. This would raise a question mark over whether Colswein was indeed related to Alfred of Lincoln, though Freeman explains it away as Colswein and Thorold having already been settled with considerable lands through their marriages, perhaps to Norman women. It is known that Thorold married around 1066.[6] Thorold was sheriff of Lincoln by the 1070s and was probably also entrusted with the custodianship of Lincoln Castle, the construction of which began in 1068.[7] 166 messuages – houses with land and outbuildings – were levelled to make way for the new castle, while 'the remaining 76 have been destroyed outside the castle boundary, not because of the oppression of the sheriff and his office, but because of misfortune and poverty and the ravages of fire.'[8]

R.E.G. Kirk, suggests that, as Colswein's son Picot, also known as Ansfrid, was recorded as having two grandchildren by 1111, he was possibly sixty years of age, and therefore born around 1050, with Colswein born around 1020. This would make Colswein too old to be the son of Alfred de Lincoln. Kirk suggests that he may have been Alfred's brother.[9] This, however, follows the premise that neither Colswein nor Picot had children before they were thirty, which seems a tad unreasonable to me. If both Colswein and Picot had children in their early twenties, then Picot could still have been in his forties and a grandfather.

Freeman's argument is supported not only by the fact that Colswein bore the name 'de Lincoln' as attested to in a charter to Spalding Priory, but also by the claims of both Thorold's and Colswein's descendants to the constableship of Lincoln Castle.[10] While either theory can be nothing more than conjecture, without further evidence to support it, Freeman's argument certainly would go some way to explain the prominence of Colswein and his family within the county of Lincolnshire, and their extensive links to the city and castle of Lincoln.

Despite his lack of lands before the Conquest, by 1086 Colswein held a sizeable fief, mainly in the Kesteven district of Lincolnshire and to the north of Lincoln itself. Those lands to the north of Lincoln, which amounted to four tofts, had previously belonged to Colswein's nephew, Cola, who Colswein had also succeeded at Barlings, where Ralph de la Haye would later found an abbey. The king also gave Colswein an area of undeveloped land outside the city of Lincoln, on which he had thirty-six houses built, in addition to two churches. One of the churches was St Peter *ad fontem (atte Welles)*, situated to the east of Lincoln.[11] St Peter was later given by Colswein's son, Picot, to St Mary's in York, along with two messuages and four acres of land *in campis et le Hevedland*.[12]

Colswein's son, Picot, succeeded his father in 1101; Colswein's death is recorded as 8 January in the Lincoln Cathedral Obituary.[13] It has been suggested that Picot died without heirs and was succeeded by his sister, Muriel, who was married to Robert de la Haye. However, in a charter issued by Muriel's son, Richard de la Haye, to Spalding Priory, he called Colswein's son, Picot, his grandfather.[14] And in a papal bull of Alexander III, there is confirmation of a gift by Picot, son of Colswein, to Spalding Priory, which also mentions Picot's wife, Beatrice, his grandson Richard, his granddaughter Cecilie, or Cecillia and the rest of his family, who were all admitted into the fraternity of the monastery. The charter grants tithes in Sutton and Lutton and is dated Sunday 14 May 1111, at three o'clock in the afternoon.[15]

It was Colswein's granddaughter, therefore, who married Robert de la Haye, probably in the early years of the twelfth century and certainly before 1111, by which time she already had at least two children by Robert, as demonstrated in the charter granted to Spalding Priory. This charter was issued after the births of Richard and Cecilie, but likely before the birth of their third child, Ralph, given that he is not mentioned. Robert de la Haye had his origins in the Cotentin, in Normandy, where his father, Ralph or Ranulf de la Haye, had been seneschal for William the Conqueror's half-brother, Robert, Count of Mortain. Ralph de la Haye may have been familiar with Lincolnshire through his service to the Count of Mortain, who had been entrusted with the security of

Lincolnshire (the old county of Lindsey) alongside the count of Eu, in 1069 when the Danish landed on its shores and joined with the English rebels. The garrison of Lincoln Castle had already repelled one foraging raid, led by Edgar the Ætheling, the English claimant to the throne seized by William the Conqueror. Mortain was then ordered to remain in Lincolnshire 'to prevent the Danes from breaking out' while the king moved against a rising in Mercia.[16] Mortain was only partially successful in that the Danes did break out of the marshland and received aid from the locals. However, Mortain and the count of Eu were able to drive them off, though could not prevent the Danes from crossing the Humber as the Normans had no ships at their disposal. Given Ralph de la Haye's position as seneschal to the count, it is highly likely that he accompanied his count on this campaign in the county that would later become the home of his son and his descendants.

Robert de la Haye first appears as an official in the service of Henry I; he was one of the king's new men. King Henry made a gift to Robert of Halnac (Hanaker) in Sussex, lands which had been forfeit by William de Ansleville.[17] Robert served as justiciar in Normandy and by 1131 was the king's steward.[18] The founding charter of Boxgrove Priory in Sussex, founded by Robert de la Haye, states that Robert was *consanguineo* (cousin) to King Henry I, though the exact relationship is obscured.[19] An investigation into the history of the La Haye family, from the time of the Conquest, may provide some clarity in this. According to Wace's *Roman de Rou*, at the time of the Norman Conquest, the lord of Robert's ancestral lands, La Haie-du-Puits, was Iwun al Chapel. La Haie-du-Puits lays in the Cotentin, on the coast opposite Jersey. Chapel was married to Muriel, daughter of Herluin de Conteville and his wife, Herleve. Herleve was the mother of William the Conqueror, which would suggest that Muriel was his half-sister, and Iwun al Chapel therefore brother-in-law to the duke of Normandy and future king of England.[20] Wace, however, does go on to say that he 'knows not if children were born to them; I never heard speak of any.'[21]

As a uterine sister of William the Conqueror, Muriel has often been left out of other histories, though Wace clearly explains her relationship. This is supported by the verses, *de capta Bajocensium civitate*, written by Serlon, the canon of Bayeux, which appear to have been addressed to Muriel, then a widow, and sister of Odo of Bayeux, William the Conqueror's half-brother. Muriel's husband, Iwun al Chapel appears to be Eudo de Capello, or Eudes al Capel, meaning du manteau or capuchin, who was the son of Turstin Haldup, also known as Richard, and his wife, Emma. Iwun al Chapel subscribed himself as Eudo Haldub in a charter of 1174. He was dapifer (or steward) to Duke William and head of the house of La Haie-du-Puits; and husband of Muriel, as attested in the charters of the abbey of Lessay, which had been founded by Turstin Haldup.[22] The charter, issued by Robert de la Haye in 1105, clarifies Robert's relationship to both Iwun (Eudo) and Turstin Haldup, stating that:

'...by the counsel and wish of his wife Muriel and his sons Richard and Ralf, he grants to the abbey of Lessay (*Exaquii*) all that Richard, called Turstin Haldup and Eudo his son the founders of that abbey, gave it, etc. ... Moreover he, Robert, grants to the abbey all that his men or others have given it, adding that, by the gift of himself and his wife Muriel and his sons Richard and Ralf, it possesses lands (specified) in Normandy, and that, in England, he has given it the church of Bosgrave with all its appurtenances, and those of Brotebeia and Feligeham and his rights in the church of Rison, and the churches of Berlinges and Subroc and the church of Suavetona, save what [rights] the monks of Acre have in it, also the tithes of the revenue (*denariorum*) from all his manors, namely Brotebeia, Feligeham, Rison, Suavetona, Sutona, Lutona, and Seortona, and one bovate of land at Brotebeia, etc.'[23]

According to Wace, Iwun al Chapel was one of the nobles called upon to advise Duke William at Lillebonne when the duke sought their approval for his proposed invasion of England in 1066.[24] Wace goes on to describe the Sire de la Haie's actions at Hastings, where he 'charged on and neither spared nor pitied any; striking none whom he did not kill, and inflicting wounds such as none could cure.'[25] This may well have been Iwun al Chapel, or possibly Ralph de la Haye, father of Robert de la Haye and seneschal of the count of Mortain, William the Conqueror's half-brother, at the time of the Conquest. Robert, Count of Mortain was the full brother of Odo of Bayeux and Muriel, Iwun al Chapel's wife. A passage in one charter in the *Gallia Christiana* clarifies the relationship of the various members of the La Haye family; Robert de la Haye was the son of Ralph de la Haye, seneschal of Robert, Count of Mortain, and, according to this charter, grandson of Hudonis, dapifer of King William.[26] The foundation charter of Boxgrove Priory, however, names Robert de la Haye as 'son of Ranulf [Ralph] the seneschal of Robert de Mortain' and 'nephew of Eudo dapifer.'[27] The foundation charter is dated to 'before 1105', which would place Robert's birth, given he died in 1050, at between 1175 and 1180.[28] This would explain the relationship between Ralph de la Haye and Iwun al Chapel, as brothers, but does not explain the identity of Hudonis, unless it refers to Turstin Haldup and is a mistranslation or mispronunciation. When he died towards the end of the eleventh century, Iwun al Chapel – also known as Eudo and dapifer to Duke William – was buried at his family's foundation of Lessay and his lands passed to his nephew on his death.[29]

Given the information from the Boxgrove Priory charter, it would appear that Robert de la Haye was nephew and heir to Iwun al Chapel. This familial relationship is borne out by the fact that they both held La Haie-du-Puits at separate times and that Robert's grandfather and Iwun al Chapel were both dapifer to William, Duke of Normandy and later king of England. Such roles were traditionally hereditary. It seems likely, then, that Iwun al Chapel and Ralph de la Haye were brothers, and that Robert de la Haye was Iwun al Chapel's nephew. This would also explain the statement in the charter to Boxgrove Priory, claiming that Robert de la Haye and King Henry I were cousins; this may have been by marriage if it is relating to Iwun al Chapel having married William the Conqueror's half-sister, Muriel, who would therefore be an aunt of Henry I and an aunt by marriage of Robert de la Haye.[30]

What is clear, is that the La Haye family had a tradition of serving William the Conqueror, both when he was duke in Normandy and after he became king of England. They then joined the service of King William's brother, serving the count of Mortain as seneschal. In the early twelfth century, however, Robert de la Haye is found in the service of King Henry I and rewarded with the manor of Hanaker in Sussex. Robert may well have been married twice, as a charter recording the donation to Basselach Priory in Monmouth to Glastonbury Abbey is given with the consent of *Robertus de Haia et sponsa mea Gundrede* ('Robert de la Haye and my bride Gundrada').[31] Gundrada's family parentage is not mentioned, so we know nothing beyond her name. The charter is dated to between 1101 and 1120, but given the charter to Spalding Priory, naming Robert as the husband of Muriel and father to Richard and Cecilie de la Haye, the marriage to Gundrada must have ended in either Gundrada's death or an annulment before 1108 at the latest.

Robert de la Haye's close connection to King Henry I is confirmed by a number of charters. In one, dated to between 1118 and 1135, he appears alongside John, Bishop of Luxembourg, the Earl of Gloucester and Ranulf Earl of Chester, in confirming the privileges of the church of Bayeux.[32] Around 1120, Robert is one of the witnesses to a case involving Thomas de St John, whose actions had brought him in conflict with the monks of St Michael's Mount – Mont St Michel. Thomas was accused of having wasted and destroyed the woodland of Nerun and Crapalt in order to build his castle at St Jean 'and then, eager with greed, proceeded to the wood of Bivia and laid it waste, and likewise occupied and seized (*invadere*) the lands of most of the vavassours in the Honour of St Paternus and the Honour of Geneeium.'[33] When the monks of Mont St Michel, whose lands had been devastated, heard of this, they 'prayed to God to have pity on their house and to avenge them swiftly on such a wrongdoer etc.'[34] On hearing that the monks had called down the wrath of God upon him, a horrified Thomas 'hastened like a madman to the Mount, with his brothers John and Roger and a great company, and enquired of the monks why they were clamouring to God against him and his brethren. On the monks fearlessly replying, because he had wasted their woods and wrongfully seized their lands,' Thomas, counselled by his brothers and advisers, threw himself on the mercy of the abbot, at the foot of abbot Roger and the monks, 'humbly begging them to have pity on his brethren and himself, and allow them to be reconciled on fair terms arranged by friends.'[35]

The abbot, having consulted with his brethren, the monks, asked Thomas what terms he would agree to that would resolve the situation and told him that they could not be reconciled with him, nor cease their complaints, unless he and his cohorts gave up absolutely everything they had seized. Perhaps realising how grievously he had offended the monastery, Thomas offered very generous terms in order to resolve the issue. Thomas promised the abbot; 'I will leave all the demesnes of the church in peace, lovingly, and only ask you to grant me and my brethren the service of those tenants (*homines*) who are our blood-relatives, saving [their watch and] ward at the Mount, and you shall have the multure, and toll, and *tailles*, and aids of their men, and such other services as are due to the over lord (*majori domino*).'[36] Thomas also asked that the knight service (*servitia militum*) of the abbey be granted to him and pledged to perform their service to the abbey himself. Thomas de St Jean then requested that the abbot grant him the service of the lands of Rainald Coquus in the Honour of St Pair, 'on condition that if his heir should call on me to do so, I will restore it him, saving his personal service.'[37] Thomas then turned his attention to the lands of Ralf Malregard, which had been mortgaged to Thomas's nephew, Ralph de Port, for twelve marks of silver, when Ralph Malregard had departed for Apulia. Thomas de St John and his friends agreed, that as Ralph Malregard had received twelve pounds from Thomas for his land, on the agreement that 'when the son of Ralph Malregard is of an age to hold and administer (*regere*) his land, on my pledged faith and that of my brethren, neither by force nor by evil device, will we or any heir of ours detain that land, but will promptly restore it, without question, on the said twelve pounds being repaid to us or our heirs, and, for further security, I and my brethren swear of our own accord, on the Holy Gospels that we and our heirs will keep this undertaking.'[38]

Another land which Thomas de St Jean had in wardship was that of Roger de Grandivilla, who had been his squire, but had recently become a knight and in the presence of the abbot and all those attending the case, both monks and laymen, Thomas restored Roger's lands to him, knowing that, 'like the other barons of the abbey, he ought to serve the abbots.'[39] In consideration of this Thomas requested that the abbot grant him the service of Robert son of Ivo, allowing that the abbot retain for the abbey the dues of all his men. Two men, William de Pomeria and Stephen de Tabula had made submission, as traitors to his brother Roger, and Thomas now counselled his brother to do the abbot 'homage for their service and to become the abbey's man, on the terms that their vavassors, shall go and carry, wherever required, for you and your monks the wallets (*manticas*) and clothes (*pannos*) of the monks and pay you tithe, multure, tolls, [and] aids, because we would not diminish the dues payable to this abbey to which we owe our bringing up and subsistence.'[40] At this point, Roger de St Jean arose and did homage to the abbot, and, on the Holy Gospels, swore to be faithful to the abbey, and in no way to deprive it of its dues or seize its lands. Thomas then mortgaged the land of Getho and Poterel, in the honour of Genecium, on the terms that if the abbot and monks should repay him four pounds in money of Le Mans, they would enjoy it in peace. Thomas went on to return lands and rights to the abbey that appear to have been acquired by him unjustly, for the most part. He listed several transactions, such as that of 'Niel the priest, when leaving for Jerusalem (*habiens jer'm*) mortgaged his vineyard to me for one marc of silver on the terms that if the monks of the abbey were willing to redeem it from me or any of my heirs they should enjoy it in peace, and while it is in my hands or those of my heirs, the land-due (*terrageum*) shall be most fully and lawfully paid both from it and the other vineyards of my tenants (*rusticorum*), nor shall the wine ever be removed till the land-due has been brought to St Michael's winepress (*thorcular*), I restore to you the toll of Dune which I had unjustly usurped and seek your pardon for my wrongdoing therein; also the land of Rainald de Monastero having learnt that I was persuaded by perfidy to accept (*reciperem*) it; also the land of Garonbert, having learnt for certain that Robert FitzHaymon gave it to the abbey for the weal of his soul when he became a monk (*ad monachatum venit*).'[41] Thomas then requested that the abbey grant him the land of Theobald 'liber', which Hugh de Inferno held of him, because he received an income of ten shillings annually from him, an amount he was not willing to lose. He did, however, relinquish to the abbey certain meadows, below the vineyards of Briun, which that Hugh wrongfully had placed under Thomas's protection and which now Thomas had ascertained rightfully belonged to St Michael's demesne.[42]

All was not as yet resolved and Thomas returned to the Mount another day, accompanied by the bishop of Avranches and many other barons, approaching the abbot and monks and asking that they would kindly receive his homage, which they did. Thomas admitted that he owed the abbey 'twenty shillings in money of Le Mans, yearly, for the land of Lambert the goldsmith, and that of Rainald son of Serlo, at the fair (*nundinos*) of Montmartin.'[43] He offered an alteration to the deal in that if the abbey would admit his father and mother, as well as himself and his brothers into their confraternity, he would 'most faithfully guard, without any claim to inheritance for myself or my heirs, your wood, which, at present, is wholly destroyed, and would grant you instead the land of Doblellus which renders me eight quarters of wheat, and all the wheat round about the wood, as is accustomed, and from the men who dwell round the wood, and from the lands if ever they should be cultivated and from the mill of Haie to your granary.'[44] The abbot and monks accepted the offer and agreed to the exchange of these twenty shillings, saying to Thomas 'as you desire, and would lovingly grant you all you ask in death and in life, if we did not believe that we are being deceived by your false and fraudulent words.'[45]

With the agreement finally reached, Thomas and his brethren rose from their knees and, in the presence of the bishop and the whole convent, 'received the benefits of monks at the abbot's hands, with the gospels and promised with a kiss faithfully to observe all this agreement, and Thomas quit-claimed absolutely the land on which the wood stood and declared that neither his heirs nor his brethren should seek to regain possession. This he testified (*testamentum factum est*) in the chapter house of the abbey, in the time of abbot Roger and, afterwards, when he returned from captivity at Gorram, before the most pious and glorious king Henry at Argentan, Richard being abbot.'[46] Thomas's testament was given among notable witnesses, including Robert de la Haye. Robert's presence can be explained for a number of reasons. He may have been acting in the service of King Henry I, or in his family's interests; Robert de la Haye's daughter Cecilie married Roger de St John, who was probably one of the brothers of Thomas, and present throughout the proceedings to support his brother and help to appease the monks of Mont St Michel.

In 1126, Henry I also confirmed the possessions of the abbey of Holy Trinity at Lessay, including donations by Robert de la Haye, with the approval of his wife, Muriel, and his sons Richard and Ralph.[47] The Benedictine abbey of Holy Trinity at Lessay had been founded by Robert's grandfather, Turstin Haldup in 1056 and was confirmed in a charter by Turstin's son, Iwun al Chapel, in 1080.[48] Robert's marriage to Muriel, granddaughter of Colswein of Lincoln, brought him extensive lands and responsibilities in Lincolnshire. He inherited the barony of Brattleby, just north of Lincoln, by right of his wife, as well as the constableship of Lincoln Castle, following the death of his father-in-law Picot sometime in the second decade of the twelfth century; Picot was still living at the time of the charter to Spalding Priory in 1111, but had been succeeded by Robert by the time of the completion of the Lincoln Survey, which was compiled no later than 1119.[49] The obituary of Lincoln Cathedral records the death on 'VIII Kal Mai' of 'Ansfridus qui cognominatur Picotus' [Ansfrid known as Picot], but fails to record the year.[50] Historian J.C. Holt puts Picot's death at around 1115.[51] An 1100 charter of Henry I, to Tewkesbury Abbey, demonstrates the links between the de la Haye family and the Lincoln family. The charter mentions grants by both Robert de la Haye and Alfred de Lincoln.[52] Robert also made grants to Montacute Priory, again alongside Alfred de Lincoln, and it was suggested by historian R.E.G. Kirk that this Alfred was a younger son of Colswein, and therefore a relation by marriage to Robert de la Haye.[53]

Robert and Muriel were generous patrons of the abbey of Lessay in Normandy, to which they donated various parts of their lands, including the churches of Boxgrove and Brattleby. Donations also included tithes from various parishes, tithes from woods, for mast and sale, pasturage for cattle and the measure of wheat, called cherchet, 'issuing out of his lordships, churches and tithes.'[54] They also gave the church of the manor of Swaton to Lessay, excepting the interest there that was already held by Castle Acre Priory in Norfolk, a Cluniac monastery found by William de Warenne, first Earl of Warenne and Surrey, and his wife, Gundrada. Although most of Robert's donations went to Lessay, he also patronised various abbeys including Tewkesbury and Montacute. At Boxgrove, Robert de la Haye founded the priory with three monks from the abbey of Lessay, giving the priory the rest of his lands in Boxgrove, 'so that they were owners of the whole town.'[55]

Robert de la Haye and his wife, Muriel, had at least three children, two sons and a daughter. There is the suggestion of another child, whose name is lost but had a son named Ralph, in some genealogies, but I suspect he is spurious and has been confused with Robert and Muriel's youngest son, who was named Ralph. This may have resulted from a mistranslation of the Latin term 'nepos' to mean nephew, rather than its actual meaning of grandson. The confusion arises in an 1157 charter to Blanchelande Abbey, in which is mentioned *'Radulfus de Haya Ricardi nepos'*. The mistranslation would make him a nephew of Richard de la Haye, rather than the grandson of Turstin Haldup (also known as Richard de la Haye).[56] Their daughter was named Cecilie, or Ceclia, and married Roger de St John. Orderic Vitalis relates that in 1118 Roger de St John defended the castle of La Motte Gautier for Henry I, against Fullk V, Count of Anjou.[57] Cecilie and Roger had three children together,

William, Robert and Muriel, before Roger's death in or before 1130. The de la Haye lands at Halnaker, in Sussex, were given to Cecilie, probably as her marriage portion, and these descended through the St John line thereafter and eventually to the Poynings family.[58] Cecilie survived her husband and died sometime between 1162 and 1177.[59]

The youngest child of Robert and Muriel was Ralph de la Haye. Ralph is not mentioned in the 1111 charter to Spalding Priory issued by Picot, which suggests he was born in the years after the charter was issued. Ralph founded the great Lincolnshire abbey of St Mary at Barlings, with permission from his older brother Richard, on whose land it was built.[60] Founded in 1154, the abbey was given to the relatively new, and little-known, order of Prémontré (the Premonstratensians), whose first statute was as recent as 1131.[61] The order was patronised and promoted by Empress Matilda, who had known its founder, St Norbert, personally when she was empress in Germany.[62] Given that Ralph de la Haye founded the abbey for the Premonstratensian order so favoured by Empress Matilda, and in the year 1154, when Matilda's son, Henry II succeeded his mother's rival, King Stephen, to the throne of England, the abbey's foundation clearly demonstrates Ralph's political leanings in favour of the new Plantagenet regime. Ralph granted property at Riseholme to Barlings Abbey in its foundation charter of 1154.[63] In their initial grants to Barlings, the de la Haye family reserved a large hunting park for their own personal use. It was located in the parish, to the north of the new monastery. The park was probably a part of the original manorial complex once owned by Colswein, and its proximity to Lincoln would have made it a convenience the family would not want to lose, as well as allowing them to maintain a secular influence close to the abbey.[64] Although the abbey was founded by Ralph, it was his older brother, Richard, who donated the church at Barlings, St Edward's, to the new foundation. The church had originally been donated to the abbey of Lessay, which had been founded by Turstin Haldup, Richard and Ralph's grandfather. There must have been some negotiation between the de la Haye brothers and the Benedictine abbey at Lessay, for the abbey to relinquish its possession of St Edward's church so that it could be re-gifted to the abbey at Barlings, with Lessay getting an annual payment of one silver mark in compensation.[65] Moreover, it was Richard's descendants, rather than Ralph's, who continued to patronise the abbey in subsequent generations, so that it eventually passed from

Nicholaa, via her granddaughter, to the earls of Salisbury, and through Margaret of Salisbury to Alice de Lacey, Countess of Lincoln. Both Nicholaa de la Haye and Alice de Lacey were considerably generous benefactors to the abbey at Barlings.[66]

Ralph was married to Olivia d'Aubigny, the daughter of William d'Aubigny and Maud le Bigod; her father had distinguished himself fighting for the king at the Battle of Tinchebrai in 1106. Olivia was therefore the sister of William d'Aubigny, first earl of Arundel and second husband of Queen Adeliza of Louvain, the second wife and widow of King Henry I. Olivia's brother settled a dower on her in Sussex and donated property to Boxgrove Priory, in an undated charter, for the souls of *'Adelizæ reginæ...Olivæ sororis meæ, et Olyvæ filiæ meæ, et Agathæ, quæ ibi iacent'*, ('Queen Adeliza...my sister Olivia, and my daughter Olivia, and Agatha, who rests there').[67] It is probably through this marriage that the de la Haye family name survived into the next generation. A charter of 1150 confirms this. In it 'Ralf de la Haia, son of Ralf de la Haia' confirms 'all the endowments (*helemosinas*) which his father's predecessors (*antecessores*) and his father himself gave at Burwell, to St Mary of La Sauve Majeure and the monks dwelling at Burwell, also a certain *costa*, near their grange, to which he laid claim, and which he now releases to them, also the ditch between their orchard and the road and a certain parcel of land. This charter was executed in the time of Gislebert the prior, and Girard the monk and Eudo the priest.'[68]

Ralph had his own lordship at Burwell, a medieval market town in the Lincolnshire Wolds.[69] Burwell had originally been in the hands of Ansgot, who founded a priory there in 1110, but a charter of Robert de la Haye clearly demonstrates that the land passed to him. The charter was addressed to 'Rainal de Landa and all his other lieges (*fidelibus*) of Lincolnshire. One of the monks of Burwell (*Borawellis*) has sought him out in Norm[andy]. He enjoins on them [at his request] to secure to the monks all their possessions in tithes, in chattels, and all things as they held them in the time of Ansgot de Borewelle; and as to the church of Carleton which was built after Ansgot lost the land, they are to support the monks; and as to the land which William d'Aubigny lent them after his crops were gathered in, it is to be placed in [Robert's] demesne, and land is to be assigned them which Robert's ploughs cannot work till it is restocked, and they are to help the monks in every way they can.'[70]

That Ralph de la Haye succeeded his father at Burwell is confirmed by a charter, dated to between 1155 and 1158, in which Ralph confirmed gifts, made by Ansgot, to the abbey of St-Marie-la-Sauve-Majeure in Gascony.[71]

Ralph de la Haye is recorded as holding one and a half knights' fees in Branton, as well as a third of a knights' fee on land in Kent which he held from the king.[72] Ralph is known to have joined in rebellion with the earl of Chester, on the side of Henry the Young King, against Henry II in 1173. He was taken prisoner at Dol, in Brittany, and incarcerated until the end of the year. When he recovered his freedom, he joined Philip, Count of Flanders, who promised his assistance, but the rebellion ultimately failed and Henry II and his son were reconciled, to some extent. Ralph is said to have been a 'general of the forces of the same young Henry.'[73] Given that Ralph de la Haye was probably born sometime after 1111, it seems likely that he was in his fifties at the time of the Young King's rebellion, perhaps a little old to be going off to war. It is not unfeasible, therefore, that this Ralph de la Haye was younger and likely his son. Although, the elder Ralph is mentioned in the *Red Book of the Exchequer* records of enfeoffments in the duchy of Normandy in 1172, '*Radulfus de Haia*' with two knights and one half '*de honore de Plaiseisio*' (the honour of Plaiseisio), one knight '*de honore Mortolii, de feodo de Crienciis*' (the honour of Mortolii, the fee of Criensiis) and six knights and one half '*in Constantino*' (in Constantine) in his own service, suggesting that he was still living and active at that point in time.[74] Ralph's date or year of death have been lost to history; he was, however, buried at his own foundation, Barlings Abbey, in Lincolnshire.

Ralph's older brother, and the son and heir of Robert de la Haye and his wife, Muriel, was Richard de la Haye. From his father, Richard would inherit the family's Norman lands at La Haie-du-Puits in the Cotentin, in Normandy. Through his mother, Richard would inherit the barony of Brattleby and the extensive lands throughout Lincolnshire that had once belonged to his great-grandfather, Colswein of Lincoln. From his father, Richard also inherited the position of constable of Lincoln Castle. Although there is no evidence from Robert's lifetime that he held the post, a charter dated to between 1155 and 1158, issued by Henry II, confirms Richard's succession to his father in all of his father's lands in Lincolnshire and in the constableship of Lincoln Castle.[75] The charter was issued at

Nottingham, probably in 1155, before Thomas Becket became archbishop of Canterbury, as he witnesses the charter as 'Thomas, Chancellor'.[76] As further confirmation that Robert was also constable of Lincoln Castle, father and son appear in a grant of land in the Bail of Lincoln – the area in which the castle stands – which is witnessed by 'Robert the constable and Richard de Haia'.[77] According to the historian of medieval Lincoln, J.W.F. Hill, the family held Lincoln Castle by service of castle guard.[78] This system arose following the Norman Conquest, suggesting that the knight service owed by the de la Hayes to the castle had also been owed by Picot and his father, Colswein, alongside the bishop of Lincoln. This is supported by the fact that, although a royal castle, several people had an interest in the running of the fortress. The bishop of Lincoln had a hall within the castle bailey and the sheriff of Lincolnshire also had an interest. In fact, in 1116 when a charter was granted by Henry I to Bishop Robert Bloet, giving permission to make an exit in the wall of the castle, several individuals were required to be notified of the grant. These individuals included Osbert the sheriff, Picot son of Colswein, and Ranulf le Meschin, the third and final husband of Countess Lucy of Bolingbroke, daughter and heir to Thurold of Lincoln.[79] One third of the bishop of Lincoln's knights performed duty as castle guard at Lincoln castle; the bishop owed a total service of sixty knights.[80] However, the bishop gained permission from Henry I to withdraw his troops sometime between 1123 and 1133, when they were reassigned to duties at the new castle that the bishop was building at Newark.[81] According to the *Anglo-Saxon Chronicle*, 1123 was a desperate year for the people of Lincoln. The E manuscript of the chronicle states, 'before the bishop of Lincoln came to his bishopric, almost the whole of Lincoln burned down, and a countless host of people, men and women, burned to death, and such great damage was done there that no-one could describe it to another. That was the day of 19 May.'[82] With the bishop's departure, control of the castle was shared between the king, through his constable, on one side, and Countess Lucy and her two sons, Ranulf, Earl of Chester, and William de Roumare, on the other.

In their book, *Custodians of Continuity*, Paul Everson and David Stocker suggest that the de la Haye family were 'typical lesser men made rich by the conquest of England.'[83] Robert de la Haye's marriage to Muriel, granddaughter of Colswein of Lincoln, certainly established Robert, not only in his barony of Brattleby, but also in his position as constable of Lincoln Castle, a position made all the more powerful by the removal of the bishop of Lincoln's interest by 1133 at the latest. Everson and Stocker also assert that the de la Haye family are likely to have been adherents of the brothers William de Roumare and Ranulf, Earl of Chester, possibly acting as lieutenants of William de Roumare, who had inherited the majority of their mother's lands in Lincolnshire.[84] Given the possible familial connection between the two families, if Thurold of Lincoln and Colswein were indeed brothers, this would not be surprising; Robert de la Haye's wife, Muriel, would be a second cousin to William and Ranulf.

As we have seen in the foundation of Barlings Abbey, the de la Haye family were associated with Empress Matilda and both Richard and Ralph de la Haye, Robert's sons, may have fought for the empress in her struggle for the English throne against her cousin, King Stephen, the period known to history as the Anarchy. This would explain the suggestion by both Stocker and Everson, and J.W.F. Hill, that Robert was dispossessed of Lincoln Castle at some point during the Anarchy.[85] The castle was, after all, a royal castle and the constable served the king, Stephen. Unfortunately, there is no clear evidence as to when Robert de la Haye was stripped of his constableship of the castle, or for how long. It seems likely that he was removed before the castle fell into the hands of Ranulf of Chester and William de Roumare, who took the stronghold by a clever ruse.

William de Roumare and Ranulf of Chester had submitted to Stephen as king in 1137. William was even made earl of Lincoln by Stephen, probably in 1140, although it seems Stephen stopped short at including Lincoln Castle in the gift. This disappointment, or the failure by Stephen to offer other expected rewards, may have caused the disillusionment in the brothers that led them to rebel against the king before the year was out. As a consequence, the brothers contrived to gain possession of Lincoln Castle by subterfuge. As Orderic Vitalis tells it, 'they cunningly found a time when the household troops of the garrison were widely dispersed, and then sent their wives ahead to the castle under the pretext of a friendly visit. While the two countesses were passing the time there, laughing and talking with the wife of the knight who ought to have been defending the castle, the earl of Chester arrived, unarmed and without his cloak, as though to escort his wife home, and three knights followed him without arousing any suspicion. Once inside the castle they suddenly snatched crowbars and weapons which lay to hand and violently expelled the king's guards.'[86] Once the guards were overpowered, William de Roumare then 'burst in with a force of armed knights, according to a prearranged plan, and in this way the two brothers took control of the castle and the whole city.'[87]

If Robert de la Haye were still in charge of the castle at this point, the ruse by which William and Ranulf's wives contrived to visit the castle would make sense, in that they were visiting relatives, given that Robert's wife, Muriel, was probably a cousin to Ranulf of Chester and William de Roumare. However, what does not make sense in this scenario is that they waited for the constable of the castle to be out of the way, especially if Robert de la Haye was of William de Roumare's affinity. If Robert were the constable, William de Roumare could have reasonably expected a warm and friendly welcome, and not needed to resort to subterfuge. This would suggest, therefore, that Robert de la Haye had been replaced as constable before 1141, possibly by another Lincolnshire baron, given that William and Ranulf's wives were also familiar with the new constable's wife. It is entirely plausible, however, given his intimate knowledge of the castle, that Robert de la Haye was among the knights who accompanied William de Roumare in the taking of the castle.

Whatever the circumstances by which the half-brothers gained control of Lincoln Castle, the event was a turning point in the civil war and would herald the empress's most successful year of the conflict. It also serves to demonstrate how the earls of the time relied on their wives, not just to produce children and look after hearth and home, but to take an active part in operations, when the situation called for it. Alexander, Bishop of Lincoln, and the citizens of the city, sent word of events to the king, who 'was very angry at the news and astounded that his close friends, on whom he had heaped lands and honours, should have committed such a crime.'[88]

When the appeal for help arrived from the citizens of Lincoln, the king wasted no time and had promptly arrived outside the castle walls. According to Orderic Vitalis, the king 'hurried to Lincoln and, one night, without warning, aided by the citizens, captured seventeen knights who were quartered in the town. The two earls were in the castle with their wives and close friends, and were alarmed and uncertain what course to take when they found themselves suddenly surrounded.'[89]

Earl Ranulf, 'the younger of the two as well as being the more resourceful and particularly daring', managed to escape from the castle, with a handful of knights, and returned to his lands in Chester in order to raise more troops.[90] He also took the opportunity to appeal to his father-in-law, Robert of Gloucester, for aid. A very capable soldier, Earl Robert commanded Empress Matilda's military forces and his daughter, Matilda of Gloucester, was still trapped within Lincoln Castle. If the need to rescue his daughter was not enough motivation to persuade Robert of Gloucester to intercede at Lincoln, Ranulf also promised to switch his allegiance, and his considerable resources, to Empress Matilda.[91] Earl Ranulf appealed to kinsmen, friends and those disinherited by the king, for aid, according to Orderic Vitalis who also claimed that 'one of the first to whom he [Ranulf] applied was Matilda, countess of Anjou; he urgently demanded help from her, promised her his fealty and won her favour as he wished.'[92] Earl Robert gathered as many men as he could and marched to Lincoln, meeting up with his son-in-law along the way. The earls' combined forces arrived on the outskirts of Lincoln on 1 February, crossed the Fossdyke and the River Witham and formed up to offer battle, most likely at the bottom of the hill on which the castle stood, near to modern-day Carrholme. Their rapid approach caught Stephen unawares. According to Orderic Vitalis, the king did not believe his enemies 'capable of risking any great enterprise.'[93] Outnumbered, Stephen was advised to withdraw his men, until he could muster enough forces to make an even fight of it.

Stephen, perhaps remembering the destruction of his father's reputation after his flight from Antioch during the First Crusade, refused to withdraw. He would stand and fight. Before battle, King Stephen attended a solemn mass in the cathedral; according to Henry of Huntingdon, a canon at Lincoln Cathedral who claimed Bishop Alexander of Lincoln as his patron and may well have been present, the service was replete with ill omens. As the king 'placed in the hands of Bishop Alexander the taper of wax, the usual royal offering, it broke, betokening the rupture of the kings. The pix [pyx] also, which contained Christ's body snapt its fastening, and fell on the altar while the bishop was celebrating; a sign of the king's fall from power.'[94] After mass, the king led his forces through

Lincoln's West Gate, deploying them either on the slope leading down to the Fossdyke, or at the base of the hill. He formed his army into three divisions, with mounted troops on each flank and the infantry in the centre. On the right flank were the forces of Waleran de Meulan, William de Warenne, Simon de Senlis, Gilbert of Hertford, Alan of Richmond and Hugh Bigod, Earl of Norfolk. The left was commanded by William of Aumale and William of Ypres, Stephen's trusted mercenary captain, who led a force of Flemish and Breton troops. The centre comprised the shire levy, which included citizens of Lincoln, and Stephen's own men-at-arms, fighting on foot around the royal standard.[95]

The opposing army also deployed in three divisions, with 'the disinherited', those deprived of their lands by King Stephen, on the left. The infantry, comprising of Earl Ranulf's Cheshire tenants and other levies, and dismounted knights were in the centre under Earl Ranulf himself. The cavalry, under the command of Earl Robert of Gloucester formed the right flank. The Welsh mercenaries, 'ill armed but full of spirits' were arrayed on the wings of the army.[96] Before the battle, Earl Ranulf addressed his father-in-law and fellow barons, saying, 'Receive my hearty thanks, most puissant earl, and you, my noble fellow-soldiers, for that you are prepared to risk your lives in testimony of your devotion to me. But since it is through me you are called to encounter this peril, it is fitting that I should myself bear the brunt of it, and be foremost in the attack on this faithless king, who has broken the peace to which he is pledged. While I, therefore, animated by my own valour, and the remembrance of the king's perfidy, throw myself on the king's troops...I have a strong presage that we shall put the king's troops to the rout, trample under foot his nobles, and strike himself with the sword.'[97]

Chronicler Henry of Huntingdon, reports speeches from both sides, exhorting the men to battle and insulting the opposing commanders. As his voice 'was not clear' Baldwin fitz Gilbert was deputed to speak for King Stephen. According to Huntingdon, the armies were mobilising before Baldwin fitz Gilbert's speech ended. The rebels were the first to advance, 'the shouts of the advancing enemy were heard, mingled with the blasts of their trumpets, and the trampling of the horses, making the ground to quake.'[98] The ranks of the 'disinherited' moved forward with swords drawn, rather than lowered lances, intent on close quarter combat. This left flank of the rebel army fell upon Stephen's right flank, 'in which were Earl Alan, the Earl of Mellent [Meulan], with Hugh, the Earl of East Anglia [Norfolk], and Earl Symon, and the Earl of Warenne, with so much impetuosity that it was routed in the twinkling of an eye, one part being slain, another taken prisoner and the third put to flight.'[99] Orderic Vitalis was less tactful and reported that 'Count Waleran and his brother, William de Warenne, Gilbert of Clare and other distinguished Norman and English knights, gave way to panic when they saw the first squadron in flight and themselves turned tail.'[100] Faced with the ferocity of the assault and the very real prospect of death, rather than being taken prisoner and held for ransom, the earls fled the field with the remnants of their men. It was every man for himself as Stephen's right wing disintegrated in panic.

The left wing of the royal army appeared to have greater success, at least initially. The men of William of Aumale, Earl of York, and William of Ypres, Stephen's mercenary captain, rode down the Earl of Chester's Welsh mercenaries and sent them running, but 'the followers of the Earl of Chester attacked this body of horse, and it was scattered in a moment like the rest.'[101] Other sources suggest that William of Ypres and William of Aumale fled before coming to close quarters with the enemy.[102] Orderic Vitalis recorded that, 'in that battle treachery ran wild' and that 'William of Ypres with the Flemings and Alan with the Bretons [Aumale] were the first to turn in flight, thereby encouraging the enemy and leaving their allies in a state bordering on panic.'[103] Either way, William of Ypres' men were routed and he was in no position to support the king and so fled the field, no doubt aware that he would not be well-treated were he to be captured. Stephen's centre, the infantry, including the Lincolnshire levies and the king's own men-at-arms, were left isolated and surrounded, but continued to fight. Stephen himself was prominent in the vicious hand-to-hand fighting that followed. Henry of Huntingdon vividly describes the desperate scene as 'the battle raged terribly round this circle; helmets and swords gleamed as they clashed, and the fearful screams and shouts re-echoed from the neighbouring hill and city walls.'[104] The rebel cavalry charged into the royalist forces killing many, trampling others and capturing some. King Stephen was deep in the midst of the fighting:

> 'No respite, no breathing time was allowed, except in the quarter in which the king himself had taken his stand, where the assailants

recoiled from the unmatched force of his terrible arm. The Earl of Chester seeing this, and envious of the glory the king was gaining, threw himself upon him with the whole weight of his men-at-arms. Even then the king's courage did not fail, but his heavy battle-axe gleamed like lightning, striking down some, bearing back others. At length it was shattered by repeated blows, then he drew his well-tried sword, with which he wrought wonders until that, too, was broken.' [105]

According to Orderic Vitalis and the *Gesta Stephani*, it was the king's sword that broke first, before he was passed a battle-axe by one of the fighting citizens of Lincoln, in order to continue the fight.[106] Whatever the order, the king's weapons were now useless and the king 'fell to the ground by a blow from a stone.'[107] Stephen was stunned and a soldier named William de Cahaignes then rushed at him, seized him by his helmet and shouted, 'Here! Here! I have taken the king!'[108] The king's forces being completely surrounded, flight was impossible; the king 'surrendered to Earl Robert his kinsman and was taken prisoner.'[109] All were killed or taken prisoner, including Baldwin fitz Gilbert, the man who had given the rousing pre-battle speech to the king's forces. In the immediate aftermath of the fighting, Lincoln was sacked, buildings set alight, valuables pillaged, and its citizens slaughtered by the victorious rebels. According to William of Malmesbury, it was just punishment for 'they had been the origin and fomenters of this calamity' by summoning Stephen to their aid.[110] Defeated, Stephen was 'handed...over to the Countess Matilda shortly afterwards.'[111] The king was first taken to Empress Matilda and then to imprisonment at Bristol Castle; 'thus then at a turn of the fickle wheel of fortune the king was hurled from the royal throne and imprisoned, alas! wretched and languishing, in the mighty castle of Bristol.'[112]

Following the victory of her forces at the Battle of Lincoln, Empress Matilda's cause was in the ascendancy. With Stephen imprisoned and the church behind her, Empress Matilda was now in command of England. It was at a council in Oxford that Henry of Blois, Bishop of Winchester and Stephen's brother, first proclaimed Matilda *domina Anglorum*, 'lady of the English'.[113] She was, however, still waiting for Stephen's supporters to come over to her side in greater numbers. By May, the empress was at Wilton, where Theobald, Archbishop of Canterbury came to meet her: 'Here such crowds of people flocked to meet her, that the gates of the town hardly allowed their entrance. After celebrating there the feast of Easter, she came in the Rogation days [4th May] to Reading, where she was received with honours; the chief men and the people pouring in from all quarters to tender their allegiance.'[114] On first meeting with the empress at Winchester, the archbishop had refused to offer fealty until he had consulted with King Stephen, It was only after he had visited the deposed king in Bristol that he pledged his fealty to the empress as Lady of the English; if Stephen did, indeed, give his permission to the archbishop, to change his fealty, it is a mark, perhaps, of Stephen accepting his current predicament.

By mid-June, the empress was at Westminster. Empress Matilda was now at the height of her success. Her rival was in her custody, the church was on her side, she had the keys to the royal treasury and was about to make a ceremonial entry into London, her capital: 'The empress, as we have already said, having treated with the Londoners, lost no time in entering the city with a great attendance of bishops and nobles: and being received at Westminster with a magnificent procession, took up her abode there for some days to set in order the affairs of the kingdom.'[115] However, the empress now had Stephen's queen, Matilda of Boulogne, to reckon with. The queen took on the reins of the regency in her husband's absence. When pleas for her husband's freedom fell on deaf ears, she established a secure base in Kent, from where she raised an army to march on London, burning and ravaging the countryside surrounding the capital. When the queen moved up William of Ypres and his Flemish mercenaries, to threaten London, this induced the Londoners to turn against the empress. On the eve of the empress's ceremonial entrance into the capital, the city's church bells rang out, a prearranged signal for the citizens to rise against the empress and open the gates to the queen's approaching army. With Westminster being indefensible, the empress had no choice but to flee the approaching forces, 'being, however, forewarned by some of them, she fled shamefully with her retinue, leaving all her own and their apparel behind.'[116]

The two armies met once again at Winchester, where the empress was besieging the bishop of Winchester's palace. Queen Matilda encircled the besieging army, who were forced to withdraw. In the hectic retreat, the empress managed to get away but her half-brother and most trusted

## An Investigation into Nicholaa de la Haye's Family Origins 23

general, Robert of Gloucester, was captured whilst trying to cover his sister's retreat. With Gloucester as a bargaining chip, the queen was eventually able to secure King Stephen's release. By the end of the year, Stephen was back on the throne; war was resumed and 'it came to pass that they parted without any pacification, and during the whole of the ensuing year, in all parts of the kingdom and country, pillage of the poor, slaughter of men, and violation of churches cruelly.'[117]

With Stephen back on the throne, William de Roumare reconciled with the king and, if he had not been given the earldom of Lincoln in 1140, he was certainly in possession of it in 1142, when he relinquished the title of earl of Cambridge, given to him by Stephen in 1139.[118] In the spring of this year, William was also given a grant of Kirton-in-Lindsey and confirmation of the right to hold Gainsborough Castle and the Trent Bridge, just eighteen miles north of Lincoln, 'with all rights enjoyed by an English earl in respect of his castles.'[119] William's brother Ranulf, Earl of Chester had remained with the empress and only defected from her cause in 1146, though he was distrusted by the king and his refusal to surrender Lincoln Castle to Stephen saw him arrested at Northampton and forced to surrender his castles in order to gain his freedom. Once freed, unsurprisingly, the earl immediately defected back to Empress Matilda and remained in her camp until his death in 1153. Ranulf tried to recapture Lincoln, but his forces were repulsed, his commander killed attacking the north gate of the city; after losing many men he was forced to retire. In 1149, on the invasion of Henry of Anjou, Stephen came to agreement with Ranulf by which, in return for his support, the king granted to Ranulf the city and castle of Lincoln, to be held until the king could restore the earl's lands and castles in Normandy. By this same agreement, Ranulf was allowed to fortify one of his towers in the castle, and hold it until the king gave him custody of Tickhill Castle. Once he obtained Tickhill, the new tower – probably the one now known as the Observatory Tower, now largely rebuilt – was to be returned to the king, though Earl Ranulf would retain a second tower (the Lucy Tower), built by his mother, Countess Lucy, as well as the constableship of Lincoln and the county.[120]

King Stephen came to an agreement with Henry of Anjou the empress's son and heir, in 1153. It was by this agreement, the treaty of Winchester, that Henry was formally established as Stephen's heir 'by hereditary right'.¹²¹ A clause in the 1153 treaty stipulated that Lincoln was to be held by Jordan de Bussey, who would yield it to Henry on Stephen's death. It may have been after William de Roumare's reconciliation with Stephen that Robert de la Haye was reinstated as constable at Lincoln Castle, but this clause suggests that Robert was not reinstated in his lifetime. However, a letter from Richard de la Haye, dated to 1150, confirms that Stephen did reinstate Richard in all his father's lands in Lincolnshire; 'Letter of R. de Haia to the *dapifer* of Borawelle [Burwell] and his ministers, and all his men French and English. He has granted in almoin to the monks of Borawella all that they held, and of which he found them possessed on the day he came to Borowelia when king Stephen restored him all his father's land in Lincolnshire. They are to hold all in peace, and no one is to wrong them.'¹²² This confirms that by the end of the Anarchy, the de la Haye family were back in possession of their Lincolnshire lands, though possibly not Lincoln Castle itself, after a tumultuous nineteen years, a period which the *Anglo-Saxon Chronicle* described as:

Wherever men tilled, the earth bore no corn because the land was all done for by such doings; they said openly that Christ and His saints slept. Such things, and more than we know how to tell, we suffered 19 years for our sins.'¹²³

## Chapter Two

# Richard de la Haye

After the turbulent years of the Anarchy, the accession of Henry II in 1154 must have held much promise for those who had suffered a reversal of fortunes or lingering distrust under Stephen's regime. The crown had returned to the direct line of Henry I. The new king and his wife, Eleanor of Aquitaine, with their young family, were now in possession of a great Plantagenet Empire that stretched from the Scottish border in the north to the Pyrenees in southern France. Henry was King of England, Duke of Normandy and Count of Anjou; through his wife he was also Duke of Aquitaine. Almost twenty years of civil conflict was now over and with the new reign began a new era and a dynasty that would last for over 300 years.

For the de la Haye family, the new reign would see a confirmation of their rights and position with regard to Lincoln Castle. The end of Stephen's reign was not without upheaval, however. Robert de la Haye died sometime in the early 1150s. The obituary of Lincoln Cathedral commemorates his death but does not record the date. Rather, it records the date of grant made by '*Robertus de Heia et Muriel uxor eius*' ('Robert de la Haye and Muriel his wife'), on '*IV Id Sep*'.[1] The letter which Richard de la Haye issued to Burwell Priory confirms that Stephen had restored the de la Haye lands in Lincolnshire before his death, but that they were restored to Richard, suggesting that Robert de la Haye had not been reinstated as constable of Lincoln Castle before his own death in 1150/1.

Following the death of Earl Ranulf of Chester in 1153, the royal demesne which he held reverted to the crown. Lincoln Castle came wholly under the king's possession, the claims held by the descendants of Lucy of Bolingbroke were ignored, leaving the castle solely in the hands of the de la Haye family. A charter dated between 1155 and 1158, issued by Henry II, confirmed the succession to his father in all of his father's lands in Lincolnshire and in the constableship of Lincoln Castle.[2] As the Pipe Roll clearly demonstrates that Richard de la Haye was in favour with the king in 1156, and one of the witnesses to the charter, Richard de St Remi, was known to be in Nottingham in 1155, but not later, it seems likely that this charter confirming Richard in his father's possessions was issued in 1155, rather than later.

Richard de la Haye was the oldest son of Robert de la Haye and his wife, Muriel, granddaughter of Colswein of Lincoln, as confirmed by the charter to Spalding Priory, issued by Richard's grandfather, Picot in 1111.³ In it, Picot mentions his grandson, Richard, and his granddaughter, Cecilie. The omission of Richard and Cecilie's younger brother, Ralph, suggests that Ralph was born after the charter was issued. From that, we can also surmise that Richard and Cecilie were very young, probably no more than toddlers, in 1111. The date of the charter also suggests that Robert and Cecilie were born in the first decade of the twelfth century, though we cannot narrow down the date of birth of either any further.

Richard de la Haye's early career can be traced through the various charters in which he is mentioned. In 1130, Richard appears in a writ of Henry I, 'addressed to John bishop of Lisieux, [Robert] earl of Gloucester, Ranulf, earl of Chester, Richard de Haia, and all officers in whose bailiwicks the canons of Bayeux hold lands. The canons are to enjoy all their possessions etc. as freely as ever they did in the time of his father and brother and of bishop Odo, and like other land held in almoin in England and Normandy.'⁴ Another writ of Henry I, from the same year, was witnessed by Richard de la Haye. Addressed to his justices of Normandy, and William of Glastonbury, Eudo of Bayeux, and Guy de Sablé, it dictated that 'The canons of Bayeux are to enjoy their prebends etc. as freely as in the time of his father and brother, and in his own since, and to have from the forests of St Mary [of Bayeux] what they need for repairs of their buildings and for firing, as before.'⁵ Richard de la Haye was only in his early twenties at this point and probably working in Normandy as his father's deputy. Interestingly, the county of Mortain, which Richard de la Haye's father had served as seneschal, had been given to Stephen of Blois – the future King Stephen – by his uncle, King Henry, in 1112. It seems likely that, given their support for the empress during the Anarchy, the position of seneschal was no longer held by Robert de la Haye or his son, Richard, when Stephen was granted the title.

A writ of between 1144 and 1150, when the Anarchy was raging across England and Geoffrey, Count of Anjou, had invaded and conquered

Normandy in support of his wife's claims, clearly demonstrates that Richard de la Haye was firmly in the empress's camp, acting as a justice for the duke of Normandy. Geoffrey had claimed the title of duke of Normandy in 1144 and relinquished it in 1150, when he passed it on to his son and heir, Henry – the future King Henry II. In the writ, issued to Enjuger de Buhun, Geoffrey ordered that the 'bishop of Bayeux is to enjoy in peace the knights' fee which Robert Marmion held of him at Witevill, and his fee which William de Moiun ought to hold of him at Munmartin. Unless Enjuger sees to this, his justice R[ichard] de Haia is to ascertain in accordance with his assize (*secundum assisiam meam recognosci faciat*) how the said fee of the bishop was held by his predecessors in the time of King Henry, and to see that the bishop enjoys it accordingly (*sicut recognitum fuerit*). And Enjuger is entreated not to trouble the bishop wrongfully in future, as the duke will not suffer him to lose wrongfully any of his rights. And Richard de Haia is to ascertain, in accordance with his assize, the fief of the bishop of Bayeux throughout his bailiwick, and to see that he enjoys it in peace as it is ascertained in accordance with the duke's assize.'[6]

In 1154, after agreement had been reached with King Stephen, but before Stephen's death on 25 October of that year, Henry, as duke of Normandy, issued a charter to Arnulf, bishop of Lisieux, in which he refers to Richard de la Haye as his dapifer, or steward; 'Charter of Henry, duke of Normandy and Aquitaine and count of Anjou, addressed to Arnulf bishop of Lisieux, Richard de Haia, *dapifer*, and all his other justices. Geoffrey de Clinton has acknowledged before him, at the siege (*in exercitu*) of Torigny, that he has mortgaged his land at Douvres (*Dovera*) to Philip bishop of Bayeux for thirty pounds of Anjou until Geoffrey or his rightful heir shall restore those thirty pounds to the bishop. He has also acknowledged that the land at Conion is to remain the property of the treasurer of Bayeux for three years from Michaelmas in the year that the king of the French and the duke of the Normans made peace.'[7]

This charter demonstrates that Henry of Anjou and Richard de la Haye enjoyed a good working relationship, even before Henry became king of England. It may explain why Henry was so quick to confirm Richard in his father's lands, and as constable of Lincoln Castle, once he became king. As constable of Lincoln Castle, Richard de la Haye may well have been in attendance on the king in 1157, when he kept Christmas at Lincoln and even took part in a crown-wearing ceremony. In deference to an old tradition in Lincoln, that a king wearing his crown within the city walls was unlucky, Henry caused himself to be crowned at Wigford, outside the city walls. The celebrations within the city, however, were extravagant. Venison was sent to Lincoln from the sheriffs of Nottingham and Derby, Worcester, Essex and Hertford, and Warwick. The sheriffs of London 'despatched 20 tuns of wine, 100 wooden cups, 1,000 pounds of wax, 60 pounds of pepper and a great number of scullions.'[8] Entertaining a king required much organisation and it fell to the sheriff of Lincoln to repair the king's house, 'to find quarters for the royal huntsmen and squires, and pay other expenses of the king's sojourn in the city.'[9]

*The Red Book of the Exchequer* records Richard's brother Ralph as 'Radulfus filius Roberti de Haia, j militem' ('Ralph, brother of Richard de la Hay, 1 knights' fee').[10] Richard de la Haye appears in the Red Book in a list of scutage payments of 1190/91, which recorded Ricardus de Haia as owing scutage in Lincolnshire of 'viij*l*. – xvi milites' ('£8 – 16 knights' fee').[11] Despite the fact Richard de la Haye died in 1169, this does appear to be a reference to his holdings, as he is known to have originally held 20 knights' fees which had been reduced to 16 by the time of his death. By 1190/91, the responsibility for this scutage would have passed to Richard's daughter, Nicholaa. Richard and Ralph de la Haye can often be seen working together in the historical record. When Ralph de la Haye founded Barlings Abbey in Lincolnshire in 1154, he could not have done it without the help and cooperation of his older brother. Indeed, the land at Oxney that Barlings was built on belonged to Richard, not Ralph, and the founding charter of the abbey affirms that it was founded with the permission of Richard de la Haye.[12] Both Ralph and Richard continue to appear in royal charters, particularly in Normandy. Sometime in the decade before his death in 1164, William of Anjou, also known as William fitzEmpress, issued a charter which was witnessed by Ralph de la Haye: 'Charter of William, brother of [Henry II] the king of England. He gives the nuns of St Mary of Mortain, for his father's soul and his own, 40 shillings of Anjou a year from his manor of Ste. Mère Eglise (*Sancte Marie Ecclesia*).'[13]

In the same year that Ralph had founded Barlings Abbey, Richard de la Haye, as baron of La Haye-du-Puits, and his wife Matilda de Vernon, founded the abbey of Blanchelande at Neufmesnil in Normandy. As with Barlings Abbey, the abbey at Blanchelande was also dedicated to the

Premonstratensians, also known as the White Canons, in 1161. Sometime between 1151 and 1157, Richard de la Haye was witness to a number of charters, one involving his own foundation of Blanchelande Abbey in which a 'Charter of R[ichard] Avenel, giving to the abbey (*ecclesie*) of Blanchelande by consent of his brother William and his [William's] son Richard the church of St Georges-en-Bauptois (*de Bauteis*) etc.... This gift he makes by the hand of Richard bishop of Coutances. The charter is sealed by William de Vernon, because Richard has no seal.'[14] Richard de la Haye's own vassals also donated to Blancheland, as demonstrated by a charter of 1168, in which Joslen de Englesby, granted 'to the canons of Blanchelande his mill at Weletun held of his lord Richard de Haia, to be held in inheritance of him and his heirs at the annual rent of 12 shillings, 10 to his lord, and 2 to himself; and, on account of his necessity, he receives at the outset his [own] rent for eight years, that is, 16 shillings.'[15]

We see the continuation of family connections throughout the charter evidence. As in 1162, when Richard and Ralph de la Haye both acted as witnesses to a grant involving the family of their sister, Cecilie. In the charter issued by William de St John, his brother Robert and his sister Olive, at the 'inspiration of God, by the counsel of Hugh archbishop of Rouen, Achard bishop of Avranches, and Richard bishop of Coutances, and with the consent of king Henry, they, for remission of their sins and of those of their predecessors and successors, give the abbey of the Holy Trinity, Luzerne (*Lucerna*) and the canons regular there serving God, the site of the abbey, and the church of St Jean etc... and the tithe of hens at St Jean and a place for a fishery at the sea and the whole tithe of their fisheries and their cuttlefish from boats (*sepiarum de batellis*) etc.... They also grant the gift of six quarters of wheat which Robert Heriz gave the abbot, by consent of his sons Robert and Andrew, for the weal of his soul and that of Agnes his wife. In England, they grant a third part of the manor of Mundreham, with all its appurtenances in exchange for the tithe of the rents of that manor and of Berneham and of Wauburguetone. All this they give the abbey in almoin, free accordingly, partly in exchange for the tithe of their rents, which they used to pay it, partly in augmentation, for their weal and that of their predecessors, successors, and heirs.'[16]

In the same decade, we see continued evidence of the trust placed in Richard by the king in that Richard de la Haye witnessed a charter issued by Henry II to the abbey of St Sauveur in the Cotentin, granting it, among other things, 'freedom [from toll] on all its property throughout his land of England and Normandy etc....'[17] Ralph de la Haye is mentioned in a charter of Henry II dated to between 1184 and 1187, though given the lateness in the century that the charter was issued, this Ralph is likely to be the son of Ralph de la Haye, nephew of Richard and cousin to Nicholaa:

> 'Charter of Henry II addressed generally. He gives to the abbey (*ecclesia*) of St Lo of Countances and the canons regular there serving God, in alms for ever, a fair for one day on the octave of Easter, etc....And he grants them the gifts of Algar and Richard bishops of Countances confirmed by Hugh, Rotrou, and Walter, archbishops of Rouen...the church of Champrépus (*Campus Repulsus*) etc....that share of the church of St Ermeland which belonged to the fee of John de Campellis; the church of St Thomas the Martyr at St Lo; of the gift of Ralf de Haia fourteen acres of land etc. of the gift of William de Tracy the tithe of his mills of Humeel of that of Gerard de Bruis twenty — four quarters of wheat and five shillings annually from his mill of Londa...of that of William de Moyon his right of advowson in the church of Mesnil (*Maisnillum*) Opac, and the church itself with its appurtenances...of that of William de Haia a sextary of wheat from (*in*) the church of St Martin de Mesons...of that of Philip de Croilleio the messuage of Popelina at Monfai...of that of Corbin de Agnell is a measure (*mina*) of wheat at Leville; of that of William earl of Arundel a sextary of wheat from the mill of Roard at Aubuigni (*sic*)...of that of William de Diva twelve quarters of wheat from (*in*) the church of Fleury (*Flureium*), according to the compromise made between the abbot of St Lo and Enguerrand de Humeto concerning the mill of Martinvilla, and a moiety of that mill;...of that of William de Siccavilla the church of St Peter of Grismesnil; of that of Richard de Lucy St Croix "de Vasto".'[18]

It was in 1188, after Richard de la Haye's death, that Henry II issued a charter to the abbey at Lessay, founded by Richard's great-grandfather, Turstain Halduc, confirming Richard's gifts to the abbey: King Henry 'confirms to the abbey of l'Essay, and the monks there serving God, Richard de Haia's gift of the church of St John of Haye (Haia) with all its appurtenances and the tithe of the toll of Haye and the tithe of the park, and ten shillings of accustomed (*usualis*) money for the light of that church from his toll, of the gift of his mother and himself, and a carucate of land in Onsgovilla, and some thirty acres round about Haia in the parish of St Symphorian, and the tithe of five watermills [named]; of the gift of Reginald de Maisnillo a measure of wheat in the mill of Montaign (*Mons acutus*); the tithe of four pounds, given by Richard de Haia, according to his charter.'[19]

A surviving source that shows the extent of Richard de la Haye's influence over the county of Lincolnshire is the *Carta of Richard de la Haye*. Taken from the 1166 enquiry into military service, it helps to demonstrate the continuity of the de la Haye barony from the time of Colswein. It clearly shows that the barony 'was almost entirely made up of the fee which Colswein held at the time of the Domesday Survey. This was itself a creation of the Conquest. Hence the link is not with a subject of King Edward, but with a vassal of King William, albeit, on the evidence of his name, an English one.'[20] Not all of the lands belonging to Richard de la Haye in 1166 had been part of those held by Colswein at the time of the Domesday Survey, or not held by Colswein in chief. On many others no undertenant was recorded in the Survey; apparently they were still held by Colswein in chief.[21]

I will not bore you with a whole list of which knights held what, but it may be an idea to give you an example of the way in which knights held lands, and how these fees were often shared between a number of knights:

'These are the knights of Richard de La Haye, and they serve in the service of the king by carucates. And five carucates make a knight, and the knights hold them, some more, some less: Philip of Kyme and Jocelyn of Ingleby owe two knights, Roger of Stixwould, one knight, Richard of Faldingworth, Robert of Hanworth and Roger of Sudbrooke, half a knight, Thomas of Pickworth and Jionec of Flintham, two knights, Reginald of Newton and Alan Pescanis, one knight, Roger Burnel and Robert son of Julian, two knights, Gerard of Kirkby, Jordan of Ashby and Richard of Croxton, two knights, Walter de Amundeville, half a knight. These are the knights of the old enfeoffment'[22]

The knights are often divided between those of the old enfeoffment and those of the new, so that for Richard, 'these are of the new enfeoffment: Hugh Bardulf, two knights, Doun Bardolf, one knight, William de La Launde, one knight, And five knights are on the demesne.'[23]

Alongside his responsibility to his estates and his knights and tenants, Richard de la Haye's primary duty was as constable of Lincoln Castle. The precise duties of a constable were wide-ranging and described in a study of Windsor constables as 'Primarily, the office is…ill-defined, military in origin, but overlaid by other administrative and fiscal duties.'[24] The constable's most urgent military duties involved the maintenance of buildings within the castle, the acquiring and storing of provisions and commanding the troops stationed there. Although the constable had to be prepared for war, few constables in England experienced it, although Lincoln was one of those castles which did. In peacetime, a constable was responsible for raising revenues from the shire farms and maintaining the castle's preparedness for war.[25] In Lincoln, 'with the construction of the new castle in the 11th century, the appointed constable is known to have been Coleswein or Coleswegen.'[26] The constable was often also the sheriff of the county, although this does not seem to be the case with Lincoln and although the constable administered the castle on a day-to-day basis, a sheriff was appointed to administer the city and much of the county with responsibilities for the collection of taxes and the enforcement of law; some of the money collected in tax by the sheriff would have been used for maintaining, repairing and for construction works to the castle.[27]

Although the records are sketchy for the sheriffs of Lincoln, neither Richard nor his father are mentioned as sheriff in the surviving evidence. Shortly after the Conquest, but not before, the position had been in the hands of Thorold of Lincoln, who is recorded as Thorold the sheriff in Domesday.[28] From Thorold it passed through Lucy of Bolingbroke, who is believed to have been Thorold's daughter, to her first husband, Ivo Taillebois, who is recorded as Ivo the sheriff in Domesday. However, it seems that towards the end of the century, a move was made to prevent shrievalties from becoming hereditary and Ivo was replaced by Osbert, often referred to as Osbert 'the priest', who was sheriff from 1093.[29] As the sheriff of Lincoln, Thorold certainly held an interest in Lincoln Castle; he was probably sheriff when the site was cleared, and the castle built. Lucy of Bolingbroke built a tower at the castle, which still stands today and is known as the Lucy Tower. At the time of the Anarchy, William de Roumare, oldest son of Lucy of Bolingbroke and the successor to her lands in Lincolnshire, revived his family's hereditary claims to the castle and the shrievalty of Lincoln, as a useful weapon and bargaining chip with King Stephen.[30] However, while the hereditary aspect of the position of sheriff of Lincoln was removed, that does not seem to be the case with the position of constable of Lincoln Castle.

Although we do not know for certain whether Colswein passed the position of constable to his son, Picot, we do know, as a result of the 1155 charter issued by Henry II, that it was held by Picot's son-in-law, Robert de la Haye who passed the position to his son, Richard, who would, in turn, pass it on to his eldest daughter, Nicholaa de la Haye, highlighting the hereditary aspect of the position. As the twelfth century progressed, control of Lincoln Castle came firmly into royal hands, and under the sole control of the constable, with the interests of both the earl of Lincoln and the bishop of Lincoln being removed; the bishop relinquishing his interests around 1123–33 and the death of Ranulf, Earl of Chester, in 1153 allowing Henry II to take full control on his accession in 1154.[31]

Richard de la Haye's life and career appears to have been one guided by a sense of duty, both to the king and the castle of Lincoln. The charter evidence demonstrates that he had responsibilities on both sides of the English Channel, in England and Normandy, and that he fulfilled them diligently. Having been born in the first decade of the twelfth century, it is perhaps surprising that a wife does not appear on the scene until around 1150. It may be that Richard was married earlier, but that the identity of the first wife had been lost, and no children were born to the marriage. Or, it could be that Richard de la Haye had been busy holding his family estates together during the tumultuous Anarchy, and active in Normandy, to the extent that he had no time to find a wife. As the conflict waned towards the end of the 1140s, however, Richard may have had the time to consider the future and look for a wife. The influence of the family's connections to William de Roumare, Earl of Lincoln, can be seen in Richard's choice, Matilda de Vernon. Matilda was the daughter of William de Vernon and his wife Lucy de Tancarville; Matilda's paternal aunt, Hawise, was the wife of William de Roumare.[32] Matilda's paternal uncle was Baldwin de Redvers, Earl of Devon, who was the first magnate to rebel against King Stephen and the only one to never accept Stephen's rule. Baldwin was a staunch supporter of Empress Matilda during the Anarchy, seizing Exeter in her name and turning to piracy in her cause. It was the empress who made him earl of Devon. Matilda's brother, Richard de Vernon, issued a charter 'granting to the Abbey "de Voto" at Cherbourg, saving the service due to the king and to himself, the mill of Guerevilla etc.'[33]

In another charter, issued by Henry II, a William de Vernon appears alongside Richard de la Haye in the witness list. Although it is not clear who this William was – Matilda's father was dead by the time the charter was issued – it clearly demonstrates that the two families were well acquainted and served the king together. The charter was a notification from the king, sometime between 1160 and 1170 ' that the abbey of St Sauveur of the Côtentin, with all its property and possessions, is under his protection, and he grants to it freedom [from toll] on all its property throughout his land of England and Normandy etc....and from pontage at Hanton and Sorham etc....also [freedom from] pannage in all his woods and enclosures (*haiis*) etc....and a market (*forum*) at St Mary Des Pieux (*de Podiis*) on Friday's, and a fair (*nundinas*) on St George's day, and on Rogation Wednesday etc....[gifts in Normandy]...also all the churches which the abbey holds in the island of Gersey, namely the whole church of St Brelades (*Broelarii*) with five parts of the tithe, and the land appurtenant....'[34]

The Haye family in Normandy is very well documented, even though a lot of the records were destroyed during the Second World War. Records survive for the Premonstratensian abbey founded by Richard and Matilda at Blanchelande, and the older Benedictine abbey of Lessay, founded by Turstain Halduc and patronised by many generations of the de la Haye family. There is also abundant evidence for the Vernon family, evidence which records where their lands were and their pious gifts, rather than personal relationships, unfortunately. Such evidence is in the form of charters, such as that of Matilda's uncle Baldwin, Earl of Devon, in which he 'gives to St Mary of Montebourg, with the permission of his sons Richard, Henry, and his brothers William de Vernone and Robert de Sancte Marie Ecclesia, for the weal of his soul, and for the souls of his father and mother, his predecessors and successors, a certain manor in Berkshire, Ouelay, by name, with all its appurtenances.'[35] Matilda's father, William de Vernon, is mentioned in the charter. Her brother,

Richard, confirmed his father's donations to the abbey at Montebourg, and added some of his own, as stipulated in a charter 'confirming his father William de Vernon's gift to Montebourg abbey of St Maglorius in the island of Serc with its whole enclosure and with the site of the mill. He adds also, of his own gift, for the love of God and the weal of his soul, that the monks there serving God and St Maglorius shall, for ever, have thirty shillings of Anjou out of the four pounds of Anjou of rent that he has been in the habit of receiving from that island to be paid yearly on the feast of St Christopher, by his officer, to the monk of Montebourg resident in the island. To secure that residence he confirms this endowment by his charter.'[36]

Another charter relating to the Vernons was issued not by King Henry II but by his son, Henry the Young King. Issued in 1171, it was a 'Charter of Henry king of the English, duke of the Normans and count of the Angevins, son of king Henry, addressed to the archbishops, etc. of England. He confirms to the abbey of Montebourg the manor of Wuelay, with its appurtenances, which Alice de Revereiis (Redvers), mother of earl Baldwin gave them, of her marriage portion, for ever, and which William de Vernon the younger confirmed.'[37]

Richard de la Haye, 'having married Maude the daughter of William de Vernun, departed this life before the thirty second year of King Henry the Second's reign, leaving her surviving, with the lordship of Swaton for her dowrie (dower); as also three daughters, his heirs.'[38] Though whether Richard de la Haye's death was in 1169, as reported by Robert de Torigny, or 1171 is uncertain. Torigny reports the death of 'Ricardus de Haia' in 1169, saying that he left 'filias tres' (three daughters).[39] However, the *Red Book of the Exchequer* records scutage from 'Ricardus de Haya xx*l*' in Lincolnshire in 1171/1172.[40] This is a conundrum, but one suspects that the *Red Book* may be the more accurate source, given that this is a record of payments to the Exchequer, as opposed to Robert de Torigny's chronicle, which is not an official record. Unfortunately, the obituary of Lincoln Cathedral does not act as arbiter, as it merely records the death of 'Ricardus de Heia' as being 'VIII Kal. April.'[41]

Richard de la Haye's career had been one of service to the crown in both Normandy and England. His service to Henry II when he was just duke of Normandy had stood him in good stead so that on Henry's accession to the crown in 1154, he confirmed Richard de la Haye in all his lands in

England, and in his position as constable of Lincoln Castle, as had been held by his father before him. As with many Anglo-Norman nobles of the time, Richard de la Haye also had an eye to the patronage of religious institutions, helping his brother found Barlings Abbey, on the outskirts of Lincoln, by donating land and revenues to the new foundation. He and his wife, Matilda de Vernon, also founded the abbey of Blanchelande in Normandy, where he would be buried on his death. The notes in Wace's *Roman de Rou* sum up Richard's career in one succinct sentence; 'Richard was taken by pirates and his estates went to daughters.'[42]

Chapter Three

# Nicholaa and her Sisters

Richard de la Haye and Matilda de Vernon had three children together, all daughters. Nicholaa de la Haye was the eldest of the three sisters and, when her father died in 1169, she inherited his barony of Brattleby in Lincolnshire. Like her father and grandfather before her, she also inherited the position of castellan of Lincoln Castle; a post which she brought to both her marriages and in which Nicholaa herself would play an active role for over fifty years. As she inherited her father's hereditary right to the constableship of Lincoln Castle, we know that Nicholaa was the eldest of the three sisters. Nicholaa had two younger sisters, Gila (Gille) and Isabel, though their birth order is unknown.

Gila, whose name appears as Gille in French but appears on charters in the Latin, Gila, was married to Richard du Hommet, who died around 1199/1200. Richard was the eldest son and heir of William du Hommet (or Hummez), constable of Normandy, who died around 1204 and his wife, Lucy. According to a charter dated 1232, recording donations to the monks of Saint-Sauveur-le-vicomte, Lucy was the granddaughter and heir of Adam de Bruys.[1] As constable, William du Hommet appeared as a witness to a charter of 1 March 1190 in which King Richard I 'confirms to the archbishop and church of Rouen and all the bishops and mother churches of Normandy, concerning those who break the *trêve de Dieu* (a truce organised by the church).'[2]

Gila was probably born sometime in the 1150s, so will have married Richard du Hommet in the late 1160s or early 1170s. She died in the 1190s and her husband remarried before his own death at the turn of the century. Gila and Richard had at least three sons and two or more daughters; two of these sons were the last two constables of Normandy from the Hommet family. Richard du Hommet had married Gila by the mid-1170s at the latest, when his grandfather, another Richard du Hommet, was still constable of Normandy, but Richard was still underage then; their first child was born around 1180.[3]

Richard du Hommet predeceased his father by four or five years, so never became constable of Normandy in his own name, though he does appear to have assisted his father in his duties. In June 1190, Richard appears as a witness, alongside his father, to a charter of Richard I in which he 'confirms to St Martin's, Troarn and the monks there serving God the vill and island of Reimberhome etc., with the right of presentation to the church of St Mary there, as given, with his assent, by John son of William count of Ponthieu, etc.' Father and son are recorded as 'Willelmo de Humeto constabulario; Richardo de Humeto' in the witness list.[4]

Richard and Gila are the subjects of a unique charter, issued by King Richard I in June 1190. The charter was preserved by the Abbey of Aunai, which had been founded by the du Hommet family. It conferred the manors of Varreville and Pouppeville upon the couple, naming both Ricardo de Humetis and 'Gila, uxor sue' (his wife) in the grant.[5] And it has very famous laces by which the seal was attached, which are made of silk and fifty centimetres in length each; one of the laces is green, now turning yellow, and the other is blue, speckled with brown.[6] An Old French poem was embroidered on the laces: 'Je suis gage d'amour. Ne me donnez pas. Que celui qui sépare notre amour puisse recevoir la mort' ('I am a pledge of love. Do not give me away. May whoever separates our love receive death'). For this reason, the charter is known as the *charte aux lacs d'amour* (the charter with the laces of love). And while the idea of a love poem being attached to a charter issued in relation to a royal land grant is charming, the reasons behind it remain elusive. At first glance, the grant appears to have no special significance that would justify such a declaration of love, nor such careful detail and precision work, being undertaken on its creation. Unfortunately, while the laces are still attached to the document, the words, which were still visible in the nineteenth century, have faded away.[7]

Under Henry I the lands of Varreville and Pouppeville had been in the hands of Roger, Bishop of Salisbury, and had returned to the crown on his death. King Henry II had granted the lands to Richard de la Haye, but they had reverted to the crown on his death in 1169, and were accounted for in the Exchequer accounts of 1180.[8] So, it seems that in granting Varreville and Pouppeville to Gila and Richard du Hommet, Richard I was returning them to their former owners. This may explain why Gila is specifically mentioned in the charter and the grant specifies that the lands pass to Richard's children by Gila.[9] According to Léopold De Lisle, in his study of the charter, the two manors formed Gila's dowry, though she and her husband were unable to take possession of the lands immediately after the marriage.[10] In the charter King Richard 'gives, renderes and confirms to Richard du Hommet, and to Gila his wife, and to their heirs, Pouppeville and Varreville with all their dependencies, for them to hold from the king with their barony, by right of the said Gila.'[11] De Lisle goes on to suggest that the laces used, with the accompanying love poem, were once a love token, given by Gila to Richard, and that Richard du Hommet persuaded the king to attach them to the charter that gave him possession of Gila's lands.[12] If so, the fact that they have survived the centuries is particularly poignant.

When Gila died in the 1190s, she was buried in Blanchelande Abbey, the foundation of her parents, and the abbey in which her father, Richard de la Haye, had already been interred. On her death, her mother, Matilda de Vernon, with the approval of her son-in-law, Richard du Hommet, made a donation to the abbey in Gila's name. After a short period as a widower, Richard du Hommet married for a second time, to Alienor, widow of Robert de la Haie, who may have been a distant cousin of Gila.[13]

Gila's sister Isabel was married to William de Rollos, or Roullours, though very little is known of William's origins and family and he hasn't yet been positively identified from the historical record. The majority of their English lands appear to have been in Yorkshire. The family held the manor of Stanwick St John, in the north Riding of Yorkshire, by whom it was held until King Stephen disseised (dispossessed) Richard de Rollos for serving the empress and gave his lands to Roald the Constable. Henry II made an arrangement between the two by which Roald was to hold the manor for life with reversion to Richard de Rollos and his heirs. The Rollos returned to Normandy in the reign of John and their English lands were forfeited and confirmed by the king to Roald the Constable.[13] Elsewhere in Yorkshire, the Rollos were in dispute with Roald the Constable over the manors of Brompton-on-Swale and Skeeby. Henry II 'by his will and without judgment' disseised Roald the Constable, and gave Brompton and Skeeby Manors, among others, to Richard de Rollos, son of Richard de Rollos, who was a tenant-in-chief in Leicestershire at the time of the Domesday Survey and brother of William lord of Bourne in Lincolnshire in the time of Henry I. Brompton and

Skeeby after the death of Richard de Rollos descended to his son William, 'who held them "till the Normans returned to Normandy", when they were seized by the king and restored to Roald the Constable, grandson of the above Roald, on his payment of £100 and two palfreys, although they were claimed by Robert Cotele son of an aunt of William de Rollos.'[15] In 1177, Richard de Rollos II, son of Richard de Rollos paid £30 to the king for having seisin of the lordship of Saddington in Leicestershire.[16]

From the evidence of these manors, we have two candidates for the William de Rollos who married Isabel de la Haye. The first candidate is through Richard II de Rollos, who held land in Yorkshire and Leicestershire and had a son named William. However, given the proximity to the de la Haye lands, it seems more likely, that the William de Rollos who married Isabel de la Haye was the brother of Richard II de Rollos, who was lord of Bourne, in Lincolnshire, in the time of Henry I, or maybe a son of this William. Without further research, it is impossible to say. However, given the information that the Rollos family returned to Normandy in the reign of King John, this is almost certainly the family that Isabel de la Haye married into.

Nicholaa de la Haye was the eldest of the three sisters. She was probably born in the early 1150s and would not have been considered as her father's heir until it was apparent that no sons would be born in the marriage of Richard de la Haye and Matilda de Vernon. As with most medieval women, we have no knowledge of her childhood. She probably grew up on the family's estates in and around Lincoln, possibly at Swaton, which would later form her mother's dower lands, or at Brattleby, just a few miles to the north of Lincoln and the seat of the family's barony. Nicholaa was married twice. Her first husband was William Fitz Erneis. The Fitz Erneis family originated in Normandy and came to England at the time of Norman Conquest. A Robert Fitz Erneis is mentioned in Wace's *Roman de Rou*.

> 'Robert Fitz Erneis fixed his lance, took his shield and galloping towards the standard with his keen-edged sword, struck an Englishman who was in front, killed him, and then drawing back his sword attacked many others, and pushed straight for the standard, trying to beat it down; but the English surrounded it and killed him

with their bills. He was found on the spot, when they afterwards sought for him, dead, and lying at the standard's foot.'[17]

After Robert Fitz Erneis was killed at Hastings, he was succeeded by his son – another Robert. According to the notes attached to the 1837 edition of the *Roman de Rou*, edited by Edgar Taylor, Robert Fitz Erneis was nephew of Raoul Taisson I, who had fought for William the Conqueror when he was duke of Normandy, at the battle of Val-ès-Dunes in 1047. Fitz Erneis was the cousin of Raoul Taisson II, who was also counted among the barons at Hastings. According to Taylor, Robert was son of Erneis and Hawise his wife, sister to Fulk d'Aujou. His fall in the battle is mentioned in a charter of his son Robert Fitz Erneis, containing much information as to the family pedigree. The charter of Robert II Fitz Erneis states that his father Robert I was 'killed in England' ('eodem vero patre meo in Anglia occiso'), and it explains that William the Conqueror ordered Robert I's brother, Ralph Fitz Erneis, to escort his brother's body back to the family monastery of Fontenay near Caen.

Professor Daniel Power has looked into the family origins and suggests that the Robert Fitz Erneis killed at Hastings was Robert I Fitz Erneis. His father was actually called Erneis and was the younger brother of the leading Norman noble Raoul (I) Taisson. Through Professor Power's research, we can trace the family line tentatively from Robert I Fitz Erneis, who was married to Hathemudis and killed at Hastings in 1066, to their son, Robert II, who married Gersendis Marmion. This Robert had a son, Robert III, who appears in the historical record in 1106, but whose wife is unidentified. Robert IV Fitz Erneis was probably their son. He married Rohese de Courcy but died before 1173. Their eldest son was another Robert, who died around 1189, and it is likely that William was this Robert's brother. This theory is supported by the fact William was a Courcy family name.[18] If this line of descent is correct, it would make Nicholaa's husband the great-great-grandson of the Robert Fitz Erneis who was killed at Hastings.

The family does not appear to have formed an establishment in England at Domesday, this may be because Robert fell at Hastings and his son was not yet old enough, or not in England, to claim his father's due. Though the family must have gained land in England at some point, as we subsequently find King John confiscating lands in Essex as 'terra Rob.

fil. Hernisii'.[19] Several members of the Fitz Erneis family appear in the *Red Book of the Exchequer*. The scutage records of 1166 for the *Red Book* show 'Eudo filius Ernisii' as owing 'dimidium militem' (half a knights' fees) in Suffolk and 'j militem' (one knights' fee) in Shropshire.[20] In the *Red Book* records for 1190–91 there is a scutage recorded for 'Eudoni filius Ernisii' as 'xx*s*' in Essex and Herfordshire.[21] Also in the *Red Book* 'Robertus filius Ernisii' is shown as owing 'ij militibus' (two knights' fee) for 1201–1202 and 'Robertus filius Ernisii, j militem de honore Gloucestriæ' (one knights' fee of honour for Gloucestershire) for the same period.[22] Interestingly, one 'Robertus filius Ernulfi [Ernisii]' is recorded as owing scutage of two knights' fees, in Lincolnshire in 1166.[23] Given the timing, it seems likely that William Fitz Erneis, the first husband of Nicholaa de la Haye, was the son of this Robert Fitz Erneis, who was paying scutage in Lincolnshire at the time Nicholaa was entering her teens.

It is likely that William and Nicholaa married in the late 1160s, possibly before the death of Richard de la Haye in 1169. It may also be that Nicholaa's parents still had hopes of having a son to succeed Richard when the marriage occurred. This would explain why Nicholaa, heiress to a large estate in Lincolnshire and the constableship of Lincoln Castle, was married to the younger son of a minor lord. This would also explain why Nicholaa's younger sister, Gila, made a more prestigious marriage, to the son of the constable of Normandy, if she was co-heiress to her father's estates by the time of the marriage. On Richard's death, his hereditary position as constable of Lincoln Castle passed to Nicholaa and, through her, to William. Unfortunately, William is very much in the shadows of history. He does not appear to be mentioned in any of the chronicles and is barely mentioned in the government business of the day. There are a few references to him in the Pipe Rolls of Henry II, starting in 1173–74, when he is recorded in the assize for Sutton as 'Willi fil Ernisi'.[24] William appears alongside his father-in-law, Richard de la Haye. In 1174–75, in the 'de scutagio Hybernie', the estate of Richard de la Haye rendered account of '20*l.*' (£20) while William Fitz Erneis was assessed for 'LXX*s.*' (70 shillings).[25] In the 1175–76 Pipe Rolls William appears in two entries alongside his father-in-law. The first is in a special tax levied for the marriage of the king's daughter, Joanna, who married William, King of Sicily, in February 1177. William was assessed as owing the same that would have been owed by Richard de la Haye, which amounted to 'iiij*s. Et* iiij*d*' (4s. and 4d.).[26] The second mention in that year was for scutage payments of 'lxx*s*. De feodo Ricardi de Haia quod idem Willelmus habet' ('70 shillings of Richard's fee which the same William has').[27] This is the last mention of Richard de la Haye in the Pipe Rolls, who had died in 1169. In the 1176–77 Pipe Roll, William Fitz Erneis is accounted for 'xxiij *m.*' 'in perdona per breve regis Willelmo filioi Ernisi' ('in pardon by the king's writ').[28] The last mention of William in the Pipe Rolls comes in that of 1177–78 when Joscelin de Engleby rendered account for 'xiij*l.* and xix*s*. de exitu terre quit fuit Willelmi filii Ernisi. In thesauro liberavit per manum vicecomitis' ('13s. 19d. for land that beloinged to William Fitz Erneis. Given into the treasury of the sheriff').[29]

William Fitz Erneis died in 1178, leaving Nicholaa a young widow with one child, a daughter named Matilda. The young girl was probably named after Nicholaa's mother, who was still living into the 1190s. It is often stated that Matilda was the daughter of Nicholaa's second husband, Gerard de Camville. However, it was Nicholaa who was fined 300 marks by the king in 1194, for an agreement that she could marry her daughter to whomever she wished except, of course, to an enemy of the king. The fact the debt was solely attributed to Nicholaa, and that the fine would not have been necessary, had Matilda's father still been alive, is evidence that Matilda was Nicholaa's daughter by her first husband, William Fitz Erneis. Nicholaa was still accounting for this debt until 1212 and had renegotiated the amount with King John in 1200; in 1201 she still owed £20, 40 marks and one palfrey (a horse).[30]

Matilda was married to William de Gisnei or de Gidnei, who had lands in Kent, as well as in Norfolk, Suffolk, and possibly Rutland. It is possible that some of the Norfolk lands were Matilda's inheritance from her father, being his sole heir, since the Fitz Erneis family had land in that county up to 1204. They recovered some of that during the civil war at the end of John's reign. The Gisnei, or Gidnei name may come from Gînai in southern Normandy, though this is just speculative. Matilda appears as *Matildis Erneisia* in a court case concerning her chattels in Suffolk in 1201, with her husband William de Gisney as her attorney. Elsewhere, she appears mostly as Matilda de Gisnei. In 1207, Matilda had to take on a debt that her father William Fitz Erneis owed to the Jewish moneylender Aaron of Lincoln. This was still due in King John's reign, since the Crown took over Jewish debts after the death of a money-lender, and it had been settled by William Fitz Erneis on Nicholaa's manor of Brattleby. In 1208, the debt was transferred to another Jewish moneylender called Eliàs, but nothing more is heard after that. Interestingly, in a list of escheats taken in 1226–28, Aaron is recorded as living in the Bail, neighbouring the castle. His house was worth 6s. yearly. The house had been escheated to the king and it was held by none other than Nicholaa de la Haye.[31] Matilda appears several times in court cases up to 1214, and may be the Matilda de Gisnay who had land at Dowsby in Lincolnshire in 1226.[32] It seems likely that her husband was still alive in 1228, when he appears with his son Roger, who was probably Matilda's son. A Roger de Gisney also appears in a case in the reign of King John, when 'an assise was brought to show if Walter de Evermow had disseised Roger de Gisney of lands' in Norfolk.[33]

Matilda's marriage to William de Gisnei was to a man of fairly humble status, which probably means that it happened after the birth of Matilda's half-brother, Richard de Camville, and that therefore, Matilda's value as a bride had lessened. Unlike her mother, with a brother to inherit, Matilda would not be bringing the great prize of the constableship of Lincoln Castle, nor the barony of Brattleby, as her dowry. Professor Power also argues that, as Matilda does not appear to have inherited any of the Norman lands of the Fitz Erneis family, this is further evidence that Matilda's father, William Fitz Erneis, was most likely a younger son.[34] Matilda's fortunes in her relatively humble marriage contrast starkly with those of her niece, Idonea de Camville, Richard's daughter, who would marry King Henry III's cousin William Longespée, whose father was the illegitimate son of King Henry II. He was the son and heir of the earl and countess of Salisbury. As the heir of Nicholaa de la Haye, Idonea would have both the constableship of Lincoln Castle and the barony of Brattleby as her dowry, eventually.

With William Fitz Erneis' death in 1178, Nicholaa de la Haye would not have expected to remain a widow for long. She controlled one of the most important medieval strongholds in England at the time. Lincoln Castle was a military base right at the heart of the east Midlands and as such could not be left in the care of a woman. Before 1185, she was married to Gerard de Camville, a man whose family had a proven track record of administrative and military service to the crown.

Chapter Four

# Prince John

Nicholaa's story is irrevocably interwoven with that of the youngest son of King Henry II and Eleanor of Aquitaine: John. As we shall see, her fortunes rose and fell with those of Richard the Lionheart's youngest brother. In turn, John's own story has been framed by the emergence of Magna Carta and the checks and balances that this great charter imposed on the crown. The names of King John and Magna Carta are inextricably linked in history and the story of the thirteenth century. Magna Carta was a product not only of John's reign, but of John's actions and personality, from his early years onwards. Medieval government in England was led by the king, its style determined by the character of the individual monarch. William the Conqueror imposed autocratic Norman rule on England. His youngest son, Henry I, continued this tradition, which was slightly derailed by the accession of King Stephen and the contest that raged for almost twenty years, with Empress Matilda's determination to recover the crown that was, as she saw it, hers by right. Henry II, succeeding Stephen and achieving what his mother could not, imposed his rule on a vast empire, from the Scottish border to the Pyrenees. Henry's eldest surviving son, Richard the Lionheart, was a warrior king who spent his ten-year reign in almost constant warfare, trying to hold together a vast empire against the ambitions and incursions of the king of France, determined to erode and destroy English – or, rather Anglo-Norman – influence within the lands of which he was overlord, particularly Normandy and Aquitaine.

John's own distrustful nature and paranoia led to a domineering government and John himself coming down through history to be judged as a tyrant. He is still, and has always been seen as, 'Bad King John'. However, the story of a man – or king – is never so cut-and-dried that we can give him one label which explains the entirety of his life, career, and personality. John was just as complex an individual as any of us are. His nature was not just determined by his birth and family, but also by his life experiences; from being the youngest, favoured, son of a reigning monarch, Henry II, to seeing his mother, Eleanor of Aquitaine, imprisoned, and the rebellions and deaths of his three surviving older brothers, John's experiences helped create the king he would become.

John, as the youngest son, was never expected to inherit the crown. He was probably born on Christmas Eve 1166, or maybe 1167, at Beaumont Palace in Oxfordshire – the confusion appears to be due to the slack recording of the chroniclers, who had little interest in noting the birth of this younger son. His mother was in her early forties by this time, and he was the last of his parents' eight children, seven of whom survived into adulthood. The eldest son of Henry and Eleanor, William, had died in his third year. Of the three other boys, Henry, the Young King, was born in 1155, Richard, later King Richard I and known by the soubriquet 'the Lionheart', was born in 1157 and Geoffrey, later Duke of Brittany, was born in 1158. Following a continental tradition that would not catch on in England, Henry was crowned in his father's lifetime and was known as Henry the Young King. He would, however, die in 1183, at the age of twenty-eight, and while campaigning against his father. Geoffrey would become duke of Brittany by right of his wife, Constance, but was tragically killed in August 1186 when he was trampled to death when taking part in a jousting tournament in Paris. He was twenty-seven years old and his son, Arthur of Brittany, was born posthumously in March 1187.

John's oldest sister, Matilda, born in 1156, may already have left England before her little brother was born, in preparation for her marriage to Henry V, known as the 'Lion', Duke of Saxony and Bavaria, which took place in Minden Cathedral, Germany on 1 February 1168. Another sister, Eleanor (Leonor in her adoptive country of Castile) was born in October 1162 and married Alfonso VIII of Castile at Burgos Cathedral in 1174. Of all his siblings, John was closest in age to Joanna, born in 1165. Given that there were nine years between John and the youngest of his older brothers, he probably had little to do with them growing up, nor they with him.[1]

John's lack of importance as a younger son was ably demonstrated by a peace treaty with King Louis VII of France, just a year after John's birth. In it, Henry II set out the division of his lands, should he die. His eldest surviving son Henry, the Young King, would inherit Henry's principal domains of England, Normandy and Anjou; Richard would have his mother's duchy of Aquitaine and Geoffrey would receive Brittany, which Henry had taken by force in 1166. There was nothing for John, earning him the nickname – which contemporaries believed had been given by his father – of Lackland, a name that has followed him doggedly down through the centuries. It is possible that John had been initially intended for the church; as a child he and Joanna were educated, for a time, at the great abbey of Fontevrault in France. As a consequence, John was literate and developed a love of books, his library included works in both French and Latin. However, little else is known of John's early childhood and education. His sister, Joanna, spent some time with their mother in Poitou, but John appears to have remained at Fontevrault until brought back to England by his father in 1174. The world surrounding John was far from stable, however; in 1173, when John was seven years old, a family rift arose that would see the young prince's parents pitted against each other.

The argument arose from Henry II's desire to provide for his youngest son by marrying him to the daughter of Humbert, Count of Maurienne. Humbert had no sons, so by marrying John to his eldest daughter, Henry was securing John's future as Humbert's heir. The king agreed to give John the castles of Chinon, Loudun and Mirebeau, to finalise the marriage agreement. This move spurred John's oldest brother Henry, who held those castles, into rebellion. The Young King was encouraged by his father-in-law Louis VII, King of France, who was always happy to foment trouble in the family of his biggest rival for control of France and the current husband of his former wife; the marriage of Eleanor and Louis had been annulled in 1152 after fifteen years and only two daughters, no son. Louis welcomed the disaffected Angevin prince to his court. Eleanor of Aquitaine, whose relationship with Henry II was strained by this time, to say the least, sided with her sons against her husband and sent fifteen-year-old Richard and fourteen-year-old Geoffrey to join their older brother at the French court, while she rallied her barons in Poitou.[2]

When the rebellion failed, Henry accepted the submission of his sons, but Eleanor, who was captured as she rode towards safety in France, dressed in men's clothing, was not so fortunate. While it was not encouraged for sons to rebel against their father, it was seen primarily as a case of boys flexing their muscles. For a wife to rebel against her husband was practically unheard of, and went against the natural order of society, and therefore deserved harsher punishment. Unforgiven and defeated, Eleanor was sent to imprisonment in various castles throughout southern England. In October 1175 Henry II tried to obtain an annulment of his marriage to Eleanor, intending to send her into seclusion at Fontevrault and thus allowing him to remarry. He claimed they were related within the fifth degree, the same relationship claimed for the queen's 'divorce' from Louis VII. The papal legate, who was visiting England on other business refused to countenance the idea, however.[3] Although the terms of her imprisonment would be relaxed in later years, Eleanor's freedom would only come with Henry II's death and Richard's accession in 1189.

With the revolt suppressed, John was granted the castles that had been the cause of the insurrection, plus substantial revenues. In September 1174 John was given £1,000 in annual revenues from England, as well as the castle and county of Nottingham, and the castle and lordship of Marlborough.[4] He was also given 1,000 livres in revenues from Normandy and Anjou, and two Norman castles.[5] In addition, the death of William, Earl of Gloucester, in 1176, gave Henry II the perfect opportunity to provide for his youngest son, by betrothing him to the late earl's daughter and co-heiress, Isabella of Gloucester. While an earldom would ordinarily pass intact to the eldest son, when the earl left only daughters the inheritance was usually shared equally among all the surviving sisters, with the title itself passing through the eldest daughter, as happens with Nicholaa de la Haye. With the Gloucester earldom, this did not happen. Henry effectively disinherited Isabella's older sisters and their husbands, in order that the earldom should pass, intact, through Isabella, to John. Although the wedding did not take place immediately – in fact, it did not happen in Henry's lifetime – John was allowed to enjoy the use of his betrothed's lands and money, in anticipation of the marriage.

In May 1177 Henry had John named King of Ireland, and even asked the pope, Alexander III, to provide a crown for the occasion. It was, by all accounts, an empty gesture; John was still very much subject to his father's authority, being styled in charters as *filius regis* – 'the king's son'.[6] King Henry seems to have made a habit of promising lands and titles to his sons, without relinquishing to them any actual authority. Henry also had a habit of changing and rearranging the domains he allowed his sons to possess. The death of the Young King, John's oldest brother, in 1183, prompted one such redistribution of lands and launched John, now about fifteen, on his first political mission: to wrest Aquitaine from his brother Richard. Richard had been groomed to be duke of Aquitaine from a young age, but Henry wanted it transferred to John, now that Richard was heir to Henry's entire empire. With the help of his only other surviving brother, Geoffrey, John launched an attack on Aquitaine, which failed; unsurprising, given that Richard was already an accomplished warrior, while John was an untested youth. Richard kept his mother's beloved Aquitaine and John remained landless, for the moment.

In order to rectify this, John was sent to claim his kingdom of Ireland, despite his own request to be sent to help Jerusalem.[7] The Anglo-Norman lord, Hugh de Lacy, Lord of Meath, Henry's representative in Ireland, was enjoying a greater degree of independence than Henry wished, and it was decided that John would mount an expedition to curb Lacy's ambitions. The young prince was knighted in March 1185, before embarking for the crossing to Ireland. He was accompanied by Ranulf de Glanville, who was appointed as John's *magister* in 1183 and may have encouraged and developed John's later interest in the law. John's well-equipped and substantial force arrived in Waterford on 25 April.[8] The prince was also accompanied by the chronicler Gerald of Wales (also known as Giraldus Cambrensis), who recorded that the 'undertaking…auspiciously commenced' when the princes of Ireland made 'voluntary submission without delay, did homage to the king, and indisputably confirmed his right.'[9] However, it was not to last. According to Gerald:

> '…the Irish people, who were so astounded and thrown into such consternation at the arrival of the first adventurers, by the novelty of the thing, and so terrified by flights of arrows shot by the English archers, and the might of the men-at-arms, soon took heart, through delays, which are always dangerous, the slow and feeble progress at the work of conquest and the ignorance and cowardice of the governors and others in command.'[10]

According to Gerald, the Irish became experts with bow and arrow and 'practised in stratagems and ambuscades by their frequent conflicts with our troops,' which enabled them to mount a 'stout resistance'.[11] On arrival in Ireland, John built and garrisoned three castles, at Tibrach, Archfinan and Lismore. Unfortunately for John, this did nothing to alleviate the unrest and a series of ambushes followed. The garrison of Archfinan were set upon when out raiding, with nineteen of their number killed, while the men of Meath 'put one hundred of the invaders to the sword.'[12] John de Courcy lost thirteen men-at-arms as they returned to Connacht. Gerald of Wales lamented, 'that time, the state of the land was such, in all places was weeping and crying and much sorrow.'[13] Moreover, the Irish kings of Limerick, Connacht and Cork, apparently encouraged by Hugh de Lacy, soon took up arms again, as John started rewarding land grants to his own followers, with complete disregard for existing Irish rights.

This catalogue of disasters is explained by Gerald of Wales, who blames Henry II's failure to answer the pleas of Heraclius, Patriarch of Jerusalem, who sought Henry's assistance for the beleaguered Holy Land. Instead of launching a crusade, the king sent John to Ireland 'with a retinue and outfit more sumptuous than profitable...for his own aggrandisement, not for the cause of Christ'.[14] Further blame is attached to John who, when Irishmen loyal to England came to congratulate him, treated them not only with 'contempt and derision, but even rudely pulled them by their beards.'[15] The Irish judgement of John was not very flattering, Gerald of Wales reports that they 'found him to be a mere boy, surrounded by others almost as young as himself; and that the young prince abandoned himself to juvenile pursuits.'[16] Although Holingshed, in his *Chronicles of Ireland*, claims John was only twelve years old, he was, in fact, approaching his nineteenth birthday. Still young and experiencing his first real chance to exercise his authority, it seems he was not as mature or sensible as the Irish lords would have liked. Roger of Howden adds that John's own greed, and failure to pay his troops their due, led to their deserting to the Irish.[17]

In the end Henry II 'discarding the new-comers as totally incapable, if not cowardly and resolving to employ men who from the first had acquired experience in the conquest of the island,' sent John de Courcy to take overall command of the Irish expedition as John returned home.[18] A year later the death of Hugh de Lacy, who was 'treacherously slain and decapitated by the axes of the Irish under his dominion' saw Henry planning a new expedition to Ireland.[19] He was encouraged by an accord with Pope Urban III, who had come to agreement with Henry over a number of things his predecessor, Pope Lucius, had refused; 'one of which was that such one of his sons as he should think fit should be crowned king of Ireland. This was acceded to by our lord pope who confirmed the same by his bull. and, as a proof of his assent and confirmation thereof, sent him a crown made of peacock's feathers, embroidered with gold.'[20]

However, the death of John's brother Geoffrey, Duke of Brittany, in August 1186, meant the new Irish enterprise was postponed indefinitely and the crown left unused, as Henry saw the opportunity for a far-reaching redistribution of the family domains. John remained 'lord of Ireland', a title held by all subsequent monarchs until Henry VIII, but the focus of all interest now rested on the inheritance of King Henry's vast empire. Henry II had only two living sons remaining: Richard and John. The fact John was widely perceived as the king's favourite son led to rumours, fuelled by Philip II Augustus, King of France, that Henry planned to disinherit Richard, his oldest surviving son, in favour of John. The fact that Henry refused to allow John to take the cross, when he, Richard and Philip Augustus did so in 1187, and Henry's own refusal to name Richard as his heir, further added to the speculation that John would supplant his older brother in the succession.

The refusal to name Richard as his heir finally pushed the warrior prince into the welcoming arms of Philip Augustus, and open revolt against his father in 1188. Henry II's position rapidly became desperate, and with the fall of Le Mans, on 12 June 1189, John deserted his father to join the winning side. Many contemporaries believed that the news of John's betrayal was the final straw for Henry II, who died, defeated and all-but deserted, at Chinon Castle on 6 July 1189, apparently crying 'Shame, shame on a conquered king' before breathing his last. He was buried at the great abbey of Fontevrault in his native Anjou.[21] Richard was now king of England and ruler of the vast Angevin Empire that had been built by his father, with lands stretching 1,000 miles, from the Scottish border in the north to the Pyrenees in southern France. He had also, already, acquired a formidable reputation as a soldier, with one contemporary saying he cared 'for no success that was not reached by a path cut by his own sword and stained with the blood of his adversaries'.[22] Richard was crowned in Westminster Abbey on 3 September 1189, and immediately set about planning his crusade to the Holy Land in earnest.

Richard's accession saw John given possession of those lands and castles long promised to him by their father; the county of Mortain in Normandy and the honours and castles of Peverel, Lancaster, Marlborough and

Ludgershall in England. He was also given the English honours of Tickhill and Wallingford and the counties of Derby and Nottingham, though not their castles. Even before Richard's coronation, John's long-proposed marriage to Isabella of Gloucester was finally solemnised, the wedding taking place on 29 August 1189, at John's castle at Marlborough.[23] It was not without controversy, however, as the Archbishop of Canterbury categorically opposed the match on the grounds of consanguinity; John and Isabella were both descended from King Henry I of England. John's grandmother, Empress Matilda was half-sister to Isabella's grandfather, Robert, Earl of Gloucester, illegitimate son of Henry I. The archbishop stipulated that the couple should not sleep together. A papal legate recognised the marriage as lawful, pending John's appeal to Rome against the archbishop's prohibition; however, the fact that John never actively pursued the appeal meant the legality of the marriage remained conveniently ambiguous, therefore both lawful and voidable at any time.[24]

The Gloucester estates included Bristol and the marcher lordships of Glamorgan and Newport. As a result, Richard provided John with an army and sent him to relieve the Welsh castle of Carmarthen, besieged by the Welsh prince Rhys ap Gruffudd, known as the Lord Rhys. Although John came to terms with Rhys and brought him to Oxford in October, Richard refused to meet him, which may suggest that he found the outcome of John's campaign unsatisfactory. However, Richard's generosity continued towards his baby brother and in December 1189, John was given the counties of Cornwall, Devon, Somerset and Dorset, bringing his English revenues to somewhere within the region of £4,000 a year. John now had considerable landholdings, both in Normandy and England, and managed them efficiently from Marlborough.[25] The chronicler William of Newburgh suggests that Richard's love for his brother had led to such generosity, though Richard obviously did not trust his brother completely and took steps to curb John's activities before he left England to lead the Third Crusade. In March 1190 the king extracted oaths from not only John, but also their illegitimate half-brother, Geoffrey, Archbishop of York, making them both swear to stay out of England for three years, the expected duration of the king's crusade to the Holy Land. It is possible that Richard also recognised John as heir to the duchy of Normandy at the same time, though not England; and he did later lighten the restriction by allowing that his justiciar, William de

Longchamp, could choose to release John from the oath if he saw fit to do so. Within just a few months of his departure, before he had even arrived in the Holy Land, Richard's concerns would prove justified. Nicholaa de la Haye, and her husband, Gerard de Camville, would endure a decade of fluctuating fortunes as a consequence.

Chapter Five

# Nicholaa and Gerard de Camville

Having been widowed, with one young daughter, in 1178, Nicholaa de la Haye was a valuable marriage prize for any man seeking to improve his fortunes. Not only was she in possession of the large barony of Brattleby, with lands throughout Lincolnshire, Nicholaa also brought to her marriage the hereditary constableship of Lincoln Castle, the vast medieval fortress in the heart of the Midlands. With this in mind, Nicholaa would have known that she would not be allowed to remain a widow. Before 1185 she was married to Gerard de Camville, son of Richard de Camville, lord of Middleton Stoney in Oxfordshire, and his first wife, Adelice. Like the de la Haye family, the Camville's had a long record of service to the crown. Gerard's father, Richard, was a loyal supporter of King Stephen and then served Henry II.

Dugdale reports that, during the reign of King Stephen, a Gerard de Camville 'gave two parts of the tithes of Cherleton-Camville, in Somerset', to the monks of Bermondsey Abbey.[1] This Gerard de Camville had his family seat at Lilburne in Northamptonshire, where a castle used to stand. He was succeeded by his son, Richard de Camville – Gerard's father – who founded Combe Abbey in Warwickshire. The founding charter of the abbey is undated, though it was sometime in the reign of King Stephen and founded with the consent of '*uxoris meæ et filii mei et hæredis Gerardi*' ('my wife and my son and heir Gerard').[2] Towards the end of Stephen's reign Richard de Camville was 'one of the witnesses to that accord then made betwixt the king and Henry Duke of Normandy, touching the succession of the same Henry to the crown of England.'[3] Richard de Camville appears to have successfully negotiated the change in regimes, from Stephen to Henry, and by 1155 had been created sheriff of Berkshire. In the same year, he received a grant from King Henry II of the lordship of Sutton in Northamptonshire. In 1159 he accounted 'xv*l*' (15 livres) for the rent of Cornberie Forest in Oxfordshire for five years.[4] In the following year, Richard was sent 'beyond-sea, with the king's austringers and falconers.'[5] Demonstrating early links to Lincolnshire, Richard de Camville is mentioned in the *Red Book of the Exchequer* in 1161–2 in relation to William de Roumare and the forgiving of a king's writ.[6]

Richard de Camville appears to have been an integral part of Henry II's administration. In 1164, he witnessed the charter issued by the king that recognised the peoples' rights and liberties. Central government had been enfeebled by the almost twenty-year civil war of Stephen's reign and the accession of Henry offered a promise of peace and stability:

> '…after the miseries they had endured people hoped for better things from their new monarch, especially as he gave signs of prudence, resolution, and a strict regard for justice, and from the very outset bore himself like a great prince.…In the early days he gave serious attention to public order and exerted himself to revive the vigour of the laws of England, which seemed under King Stephen to be dead and buried.'[7]

In the twelfth year of King Henry's reign, 1166, Richard de Camville was assessed for aid for the marriage of the king's daughter – a tax to help pay for the princess's wedding and trousseau – he certified that he held one knights' fee of the king of the old enfeoffment.[8] The princess in question would have been the king's eldest daughter, Matilda, who was married to Henry V the 'Lion', Duke of Saxony. The first of her parents' daughters to be married, Matilda's dowry and send-off cost was around £4,500 (about a quarter of England's annual revenue). The money was raised by taxes specifically levied for the occasion. The twelve-year-old princess was given a trousseau worth £63, including saddles with gilt fittings, 'two large silken cloths, and two tapestries and one cloth of samite and twelve sable skins'.[9] Thirty-four packhorses were needed to transport all her belongings. In July 1166 the emperor's envoys arrived in England, to escort Matilda to Germany. Her mother accompanied her to Dover, where she embarked on a German ship; and the wedding to Henry V the 'Lion', Duke of Saxony and Bavaria, finally took place in Minden Cathedral, Germany, on 1 February 1168.

Richard de Camville's final service to King Henry was to form part of the escort for the king's youngest daughter, Joanna, when she left England in 1176 to marry King William II of Sicily. The king of Sicily's ambassadors, the bishops of Troia and Capaccio and the count of Camerota, had arrived at Henry's court in April 1176, along with Rotrou of Rouen, a kinsman of the king of Sicily, seeking a betrothal with Joanna. The ambassadors were answered:

> '...after deliberation, on 20 May. The mention and promise of a future marriage were turned, with oaths on each king's soul, into a definite wedding. In order to bring about the alliance with the king of Sicily effectively and enter more closely and solemnly into it, the king of England sent ambassadors to Sicily who, after settling what gifts were to be made on account of the marriage, hurried back.'[10]

Joanna was provided with a magnificent trousseau, similar to that of her sister Matilda, which was worth £63 and had included saddles with gilt fittings, 'two large silken cloths, and two tapestries and one cloth of samite and twelve sable skins'.[11] Having been permitted to say goodbye to her mother, who was still a prisoner, Joanna left England's shores on 27 August 1176, sailing for Normandy; 'There Henry the Younger came to meet his sister, conducting her with the greatest honour to the County of Poitiers of his brother, Richard. Thenceforth, Richard escorted Joanna through the lands he held [Aquitaine]. Then the girl traveled to Saint-Gilles with Richard of Canterbury, Geoffrey of Ely, Giles of Evreux, Hugh of Beauchamp, and Hamelin of Warenne, her father's half-brother.'[12] Some of the escort arrived back in England in December 1176, although Bishop John of Norwich reported 'to Henry that during his voyage from Messina to Saint-Gilles he had encountered a storm, and two fine galleys carrying various, precious gifts from William had sunk.'[13] Other nobles accompanying the English princess had been ordered not to return home until they had seen 'the King of Sicily and Joanna crowned in wedlock'.[14] They remained in Sicily until after the wedding in February 1177. Roger of Hoveden (or Howden) described Joanna's entry into Palermo and subsequent wedding:

> 'When she had arrived at Palermo, in Sicily, together with Giles, bishop of Evreux, and the other envoys of our lord, the King, the whole city welcomed them, and lamps, so many and so large, were

lighted up, that the city almost seemed to be on fire, and the rays of the stars could in no way bear comparison with the brilliancy of such a light: for it was by night that they entered the city of Palermo. The said daughter of the King of England was then escorted, mounted on one of the King's horses, and resplendent with regal garments, to a certain place that there she might in becoming state await the day of her marriage and coronation. After the expiration of a few days from this time, the before-named daughter of the King of England was married to William, King of Sicily, and solemnly crowned at Palermo, in the royal chapel there, in the presence of Giles, bishop of Evreux, and the envoys of the King of England, who had been sent for that purpose. She was married and crowned on the Lord's day before the beginning of Septuagesima, being the ides of February....'[15]

Unfortunately, Richard de Camville did not see the wedding, nor did he return to England. He died in Apulia, in southern Italy, in 1176, having made numerous gifts to religious houses, including the Cistercian abbey of Combe in Warwickshire, which he had founded during the reign of King Stephen.[16] A charter dated to c.1200, recounting the history of a donation of land to Eynsham Abbey, records that King Henry I granted the Stanton to Robert Marmion and his wife Millicent, and that 'post Robert Marmion' the king granted 'predictam Milisent' ('the aforesaid Millicent') to Richard de Camville who died 'in terra de Pulle' ('in the land of Apulia') after which 'Ricardus Ruffus precepto regis' ('by order of the king') took Stanton '...in manu regis' ('into the king's hands').[17] It was held in custody by Richard Rufus until 1190, when Richard I restored it to Richard de Camville's younger son, Richard, who would die on crusade in 1191. Before 1176 a small undertenancy was created in the manor, when Millicent and the elder Richard de Camville granted lands there to Leger Pipard to be held for one third of a knight's fee; in 1190 the fee was held of the younger Richard de Camville by Leger's son Robert, who transferred it to his brother Richard.[18]

Richard de Camville had married, firstly, Adelice, or Alice, whose origins are unknown. She is mentioned in a charter to the abbey of Jumièges, in which Richard de Camville made a donation of the third part of the tithe at Hottoth, for the souls of 'uxoris mee Adelicie et sequentis uxoris mee Milesente...Rogeri fratris mei' ('my wife Adelice and my subsequent wife Millicent...and Roger my brother.')[19] The charter is dated to between 5 Apr 1170 and 27 Mar 1171, and is witnessed by Richard's younger son, Richard de Camville. Gerard was the son of Richard and Adelice and, as a consequence, inherited the majority of his father's estates. Gerard's half-brother, Richard was the son of their father's second wife, Millicent, or Melisende. Richard de Camville also had a daughter, Matilda, who is described as 'Matildis de Ros que fuit filia Ricardi de Kaunville et soror Gerardi de Kaunville' ('Matilda de Ros who was the daughter of Richard de Camville and the sister of Gerard de Camville').[20] This may suggest that Matilda was a full sister to Gerard and therefore the daughter of Richard and his first wife, Adelice. The *Rotuli de Dominabus* of 1185 records that Matilda was married to William de Ros and held land 'in Heldrinham...de feodo Gerardi de Kaunville' ('of Gerard de Camville's fee'). It goes on to say that she and William had 'iii filios et iv filias, primogenitus est xx annorum' ('three sons and four daughters, the oldest is twenty years old').[22]

Millicent was a cousin of Henry I's second wife, Adeliza of Louvain. She was the daughter of Gervase de Rethel and his wife, Elizabeth de Namur. The Chronicle of Alberic de Trois-Fontaines records that her stepfather, Clarenbaldus de Roseto, alienated, or sold off, the lands of 'filiastram suam Gervasii filiam' ('his daughter, the daughter of Gervase') and married her to 'cuidam nobili Roberto Marmioni de Normannia' ('one noble Robert de Marmion'), without giving her name.[21] White Kennett quotes the charter under which 'A...regina' ('Queen Adeliza') granted 'manerium meum de Stanton' ('my manor of Stanton') in four parts to Reading convent, to the Knights Templars, to 'Milisendi cognatæ meæ uxori Roberti Marmium' ('Millicent my kinswoman, wife of Robert Marmion'), and to 'Willielmo de Harestactu;' the charter is undated.[23] Millicent was therefore married first to Robert Marmion of Tamworth, and later to Richard de Camville. Her second marriage and her relationship to Queen Adeliza, is mentioned in a charter dated 1154 under which Henry Duke of Normandy (the future King Henry II) confirmed Stanton Harcourt, Oxfordshire, to 'Milicenti uxori Ricardi de Camvilla in feodo et hereditate sibi...sicut regina Adelisia...in maritagium dedit' (to 'Millicent, wife of Richard de Camville in fee and inheritance...like Queen Adeliza...gave into marriage').[24]

Richard de Camville inherited his father's land at Stretton and his mother's interest in the manor at Stanton Harcourt. This Richard, as lord of the manor of Erdinton in Oxfordshire, gave one messuage there to the canons of Osney, 'with liberty to gather the tithes of his demesnes of that place, and in Berncestre (Bicester).'[25] In 1176, he was sent to Paris, France, on the king's behalf, though we seem to be lacking the details of the mission.[26] Richard de Camville attended the coronation of King Richard I and in 1190, Richard was appointed as one of the five admirals for the king's expedition to the Holy Land; the others were the archbishop of Auxienne, the bishop of Bayonne, the Templar Robert de Sablé and William de Forts (Forz).[27] Robert de Sablé, the future grandmaster of the Knights Templar, and Richard de Camville, were in command of the fleet's transport ships, carrying the crusade's supplies. According to Roger of Howden who was accompanying the crusading army, the fleet set out, on its way to Jerusalem, immediately after Easter from various ports in England, Normandy, Brittany and Poitou. En route to the Holy Land, Richard negotiated a truce at Lisbon with the king of Portugal, before rejoining the crusading fleet with his ships at Marseilles. According to Howden, part of the fleet, ten ships which had departed from Dartmouth, was caught up in a 'mighty and dreadful tempest...and in the twinkling of an eye they were separated from each other.'[28] Nine of the ten ships eventually made it to Lisbon, where they heard of the plight of King Sancho of Portugal, who was facing an invading Muslim army led by Botac El Emir Amimoli, emperor of Africa and Saracenic Spain, seeking revenge for the death of his father six years before 'while besieging Santa Erena, a castle of king Alphonso, father of the said Sancho, king of Portugal.'[29]

As the nine ships arrived at Lisbon, the Almohads besieged the Portuguese king's castle at Torresnovas. Sancho pleaded with the crusaders for help and, according to Howden, 500 of the English army – 'the bravest and most courageous' – elected to go to the king's aid. On their arrival, they discovered the castle had been taken and the king of Portugal was 'utterly destitute both of resources and counsel, for he had few soldiers and nearly all of those without arms.'[30] The king of Portugal then experienced a stroke of luck, as he and his new allies were preparing to defend Santa Erena, news arrived that the emir had died. The crusaders were returning to their ships, to continue their journey, when Richard de Camville and Robert de Sablé arrived at Lisbon with 'sixty-three great store-ships [transports] of the king of England'.[31] Roger of Howden continues the story:

> 'Some, however, of the men who had come under the command of Robert de Sablé and Richard de Camville were evil-doers and vicious persons; for, on disembarking from the ships, they made their way into the city of Lisbon, and as they went through the streets and lanes, talked to the people of the city giving themselves airs, and then committed violence upon the wives and daughters of the citizens.'[32]

The crusaders also attacked the Muslims and Jews, who were servants of the king, plundered their property and burned their houses, going so far as stripping the vineyards of every grape. A furious King Sancho hurried to Lisbon to confront the crusaders. The king:

> '...came with all haste with a powerful hand; but on finding there Robert de Sablé and Richard de Camville, with the fleet of the king of England, he manifested towards them a cheerful countenance and a peaceful disposition, bearing with patience the injuries done to himself and his people. On the day after the king's arrival, the commanders of the fleet exacted an oath from all the men of the fleet that they would faithfully keep and inviolably observe the before-mentioned statutes enacted by the king of England.'[33]

Perhaps inevitably, however, within three days of the oath, being given, more confrontations occurred between the people of Lisbon and the crusaders. Numerous people on both sides were killed in an ensuing skirmish. When the king heard of it, he closed the gates to the city and arrested all the crusaders still within the city, gathering provisions. According to Roger of Howden 700 men – crusaders – were imprisoned on the king of Portugal's orders. The chronicler continues:

> 'Before they were released from the custody of the king, the king of Portugal made peace with Robert de Sablé and Richard de Camville on such terms as he pleased, that is to say, to the following

effect: that past injuries should be mutually overlooked, and that they should strictly keep the peace towards the pilgrims throughout all his territories; and it was further agreed that the arms and all other things which had been lost in the affray should be given up on either side.

This having been done, Robert de Sablé and Richard de Camville left the city of Lisbon with the fleet of the king of England, on the vigil of Saint James the Apostle, being the fourth day of the week, and, on the same day, came to the inlet of the Tagus falls into the sea. On the same day also, William de Forts de Oleron arrived there with thirty great ships of the fleet of the king of England; in consequence of which, there were together at the same place one hundred store-ships of the king of England, and six great ships laden with warriors, provisions and arms'[34]

The following day, their forces combined, the crusading fleet left the port of Lisbon. The fleet sailed down the Portuguese post, sailing past Cape St Vincent and Cadiz and passing through the Straits of Gibraltar (referred to as the Straits of Africa by Roger of Howden) and into the Mediterranean Sea on the first day of August 1190.[35] Roger of Howden gives a detailed description of their itinerary, naming the mountains and cities that they passed as the crusading fleet sailed along the coastline, until they finally arrived in Marseilles:

'Accordingly, Robert de Sablé, Richard de Camville, and William de Fortz de Oleron, passing with the fleet of Richard, king of England, between Africa and Spain, after many tempests which they suffered on the voyage, arrived at Marseilles on the octave of the Assumption of Saint Mary, being the fourth day of the week. Not finding their master the king there, they made a stay of eight days, for some necessary repairs to the fleet; after which they set out in pursuit of the king, and the feast of the Exaltation of the Holy Cross, being the sixth day of the week, arrived at Messina in Sicily.'[36]

The king's sister, Joanna, as the wife of William II, had been queen of Sicily for thirteen years. And when William died without an heir in November 1189, Joanna became a pawn in the race for the succession.

William's aunt, Constance was the rightful heir, but she was married to Henry VI, Holy Roman Emperor and many feared being absorbed into his empire. William II's illegitimate nephew, Tancred of Lecce, seized the initiative. He claimed the throne and, in need of money, imprisoned Joanna and stole her dowry and the treasures left to her by her husband. Who knows how long Joanna would have remained imprisoned, if it had not been for her brother's eagerness to go on Crusade? Having gained the English throne in 1189 Richard I – the Lionheart – had wasted no time in organising the Third Crusade and arrived at Messina in Sicily in September 1190.

Richard demanded Joanna's release; and fearing the Crusader king's anger Tancred capitulated and freed Joanna, paying 40,000 ounces of gold towards the Crusade in fulfilment of William II's promise of aid. Described as beautiful and spirited, Joanna was now in her mid-twenties it seems that, while at her brother's court, she caught the eye of Richard's co-Crusader, King Philip II of France. Richard was having none of it and moved Joanna to the Priory of Bagnara on the mainland, out of sight and hopefully out of mind. Richard stayed in Sicily for some time, negotiating a treaty with Tancred which would recognise him as rightful king of Sicily in return for the remainder of Joanna's dowry and nineteen ships to support the Crusade. In his chronicle, Roger of Howden copies out the entire text of the treaty between the kings:

> 'To Tancred, by the grace of God the illustrious king of Sicily, and of the dukedom of Apulia and the principality of Capua, Richard, by the same grace, king of England, duke of Normandy and Aquitaine, and earl of Anjou, health to Him who bestows health upon kings. Whereas, while on our pilgrimage, the Lord inspiring us thereto, we were passing through your lands for the purpose of aiding the land of Jerusalem, which, its sins so demanding, the incursions of the pagans have in a great measure overrun, and the sword of the enemies of Christ laid waste, we were compelled to make some stay at your city of Messina, the inclemency of the winds, and of the sea, and of the season, preventing us from setting sail, on which, a dissension chancing to arise between our people and the citizens of the said city, great loss resulted to both parties both in property and men: in consequence whereof, it seemed probable to many that

our brotherly love and affection might receive some check: we have therefore taken due care to observe the purpose and intention of our pilgrimage, and resolved that both by ourselves, and by our dearly-beloved and faithful friends, as also by your venerable archbishops, to wit, Richard, archbishop of Messina, William, archbishop of Montreal, William, archbishop of Risa, and Richard, son of the venerable man Walter, your chancellor, and other excellent men delegated on your behalf, the bonds of inviolate peace should be drawn still closer between us; the tenor of which should be preserved to last to future ages by being reduced to writing. Therefore, we have promised to you, and to your realm, and to all lands under your dominion, that we will, both by land and sea, both of ourselves and our people, observe a lasting peace, all questions whatsoever being set at rest, which, by our envoys to you, we had raised, both as to the dower of the queen, our sister, as also other matters; this, also, being added thereto, that, so long as we shall stay in your kingdom, we will be everywhere in readiness for the defence of your territories, and give you our assistance, whoever may wish to invade the same, or wage war against you. To the tenor and form of this treaty of peace, which it is our wish and our purpose, with unbroken faith, to observe towards you and your people, we have, by Walter, archbishop of Rouen, Gerard, archbishop of Auxienne, John, bishop of Evreux, Bernard, bishop of Bayonne, Jordan de Humez, our constable, William de Courcy, Richard de Camville, Gerard Talbot, Robert de Sablé...and many others of our household, made oath, upon our soul, in presence of the before-named archbishops appointed by you for the said purpose, and others of your illustrious men, to confirm and ratify the same, according to the tenor of the articles therein contained. And further, to the end that this peace and brotherly love may be knit together by bonds as multiplied as stringent, the before-named principal men of your court treating thereon on your behalf, and the Lord so disposing, we have agreed that a marriage shall be contracted, in the name of Christ, between Arthur, the excellent duke of Brittany, our nephew, and, if we shall chance to die without issue, our heir, and your daughter; so that when she shall, by the will of God, have arrived at marriageable years, and you shall have sent her to such place as shall have been agreed upon by either side, our said nephew shall, within fifteen days from the time of his meeting her, be espoused to her as his lawful wife; or if it shall please your highness that she shall be married before she arrives at marriageable years, our said nephew shall do so according to your pleasure therein, if the Supreme Pontiff shall grant a dispensation for the same. And it is our wish that such a dower shall be assigned to her as shall befit an illustrious lady and the daughter of a mighty king, we do engage, on behalf of our said nephew, that such a dower shall be provided for her out of the dukedom of our said nephew, and the same we have caused to be sworn at the present time by our faithful servants before named, and do engage that the same shall be given by our said nephew; and we admit that we have received for the use of our nephew, from your mightiness, a sum for the said marriage, that is to say, twenty thousand ounces of gold; this also being a part of the agreement, that if, which may heaven prevent, either shall die in the meantime, or if, through the fault of our nephew, or of ourselves, or of his people, the said marriage shall not take place, then, in such case, we or our heirs will, without any demur thereto, repay to you or to your heirs the above-mentioned sum of money in full. Moreover, as to the said matters, that is to say, the treaty of peace which we have ratified and confirmed with you, and as to the repayment of the said sums of money, in case from the before-named causes intervening the said marriage shall not take place, we do give our lord the pope and the Church of Rome as our sureties; to the end that if, which may God forbid, the said peace should chance to be violated on our part, the Church of Rome shall have power by stringent measures, to coerce both ourselves and our territories. In like manner, also, he shall have full power to compel ourselves and our nephew to contract the said marriage, or in case, by reason of the causes before-mentioned, the said marriage should not take place, to compel us, or our heirs, or territories, to repay the said sum of money. That this, also, we will do the Roman church being our surety, we have bound ourselves by the oaths of the persons above named, according to the tenor of the words contained in the instrument which we have sent to you, sealed with our seal. Moreover, if, in case of our dying without heirs [issue], he shall succeed to our throne by hereditary right, then we do assign to her from our kingdom the following dower, that is to say, the ancient and customary dower of the queens of England.'[37]

It is notable that such treaties have a specific hierarchy in the list of witnesses, with the named in order of seniority. The fact that Richard de Camville's names comes so high in the list of witnesses – he is only the second secular lord to be named – attests to his importance and seniority in the crusading army's hierarchy. Perhaps I should also note here that it is this treaty which incites Richard's brother John to rebellion in England in 1191, a rebellion in which Richard de Camville's sister-in-law, Nicholaa de la Haye, will play a significant role. But more of that later...

King Richard was also waiting in Sicily for his mother to catch up with him. Eleanor of Aquitaine had collected Richard's bride, Berengaria, from her native Navarre and escorted her to Sicily, enjoying a brief reunion with her youngest daughter, Joanna, before returning to the Plantagenet domains. Joanna became Berengaria's chaperone, and they were lodged together at Bagnara, like 'two doves in a cage'. Unable to marry in the Lenten season, Richard sent Joanna and Berengaria on ahead of the main army and, in April 1191, departed Sicily for the Holy Land.

The fleet of 150 large ships and 53 well-armed galleys were dispersed by a dreadful storm. Richard's ship, with a portion of his fleet, made land at Crete before moving on to Rhodes to await the arrival of his scattered fleet. Caught in the same storm, the royal ladies' ship was driven ashore at Limassol on Cyprus. Their ship, or buss, survived the storm but two busses accompanying them were wrecked, with many knights and men-at-arms lost to the sea. The survivors were seized by the ruler of Cyprus, Isaac Comnenus, and he appropriated all the property from the wrecks, from the living and the dead. On top of this, Comnenus refused to allow the buss carrying Queen Joanna and Berengaria to enter the harbour. On hearing of the perilous state of his womenfolk, Richard came 'with all haste to their assistance, with a great number of galleys and a vast fleet of ships'.[38] On recovering Joanna and Berengaria, Richard then appealed to Comnenus to respect the cross and release his men, who were being kept captive in chains, according to Roger of Howden. Comnenus did nothing, so Richard resolved to facilitate the release of his men by force of arms. The Cypriots defended their shores, but the lightly armed civilians were no match against Richard's men, trained and armed for war. The king forced a landing and 'the emperor and his people took flight'.[39] Richard pursued the emperor of Cyprus and his men, but was hampered by a lack of knowledge of the landscape. According to Howden, Comnenus escaped from one attack on his camp, 'made his escape in a state of nudity, leaving behind him his treasures.'[40]

On the third day of the campaign, Isaac Comnenus sent envoys to King Richard to sue for peace, offering to free the prisoners and release the property he had seized, and 20,000 marks to replace the money lost when the ships were wrecked. He also offered the services of himself and 1,000 of his men to join the crusade, offering fealty to the king, and offering up his daughter and sole heir as a hostage to his good faith. However, barely hours after agreeing to the terms, and swearing fealty to Richard in front of the king of England's leading barons, Comnenus had a change of heart and he snuck out of the camp and sent word to King Richard that he renounced his fealty. Richard systematically seized the castles and major cities of Cyprus, forcing Comnenus and his men to seek shelter in the mountains. The Cypriot emperor was advised to seek peace with Richard before his whole nation was destroyed, but apparently cut off the nose of the man giving him the advice. King Richard then took a day off, to marry Berengaria of Navarre, the service performed by Nicholas, the king's chaplain. Immediately after the wedding, Berengaria was crowned queen of England by John, Bishop of Evreux. The king then returned to war, taking Nicosia. He proceeded to take castle after castle, and the emperor's daughter, who surrendered to him. The emperor had sheltered in the fortified abbey of Cap Saint Andrew but came out to meet the king when his army arrived at the gates. Comnenus offered unconditional surrender, only eliciting a promise from the king that he not be 'placed in fetters and manacles of iron.'[41]

King Richard had reduced Cyprus in three weeks. Adhering to Isaac Comnenus' request, the king ordered that the defeated emperor be chained in fetters and manacles of silver and gold: 'All these matters being brought to a conclusion, the king of England sent the emperor, with his guards, to the city of Tripoli, and gave the island of Cyprus into the charge of Richard de Camville and Robert de Turnham.'[42] With Cyprus subdued and his own governors in place, the king could continue his journey to the Holy Land to join the Third Crusade, arriving at Acre on Saturday in the week of Pentecost, 8 June 1191. Richard de Camville was only in command of Cyprus for a matter of weeks, however, for 'in the same month of June, Richard de Camville, whom the king of England had appointed one of his justiciaries in the island of Cyprus, was taken ill, and, without asking leave, came to the siege of Acre, where he died.'[43]

News of Richard de Camville's death would have taken time to reach his family in England. Richard was married, though his wife's name has gone unrecorded, and fathered two children. A writ dated to 56 Hen III, 1372, the last year of Henry III's reign, reported that, after the death of Hugh, son of James Wake, 'King Richard enfeoffed Richard de Kaunville [Camville] of Benham manor [Berkshire], who died in the Holy Land and John his son died in England without heir of his body' but that 'Gerard the elder brother of the said Richard intruded upon the manor, but the king…delivered it to Hugh Wake.'[44] With his son John's death, Richard's sole heir was his daughter, named Isabel in secondary sources, who was married to Robert de Harcourt of Bosworth, who is recorded in the 1192/93 Pipe Rolls as holding Stanton, Horton and Sutton, Richard's lands, by right of his wife – the name of Stanton was thus changed to Stanton Harcourt.[45] Isabel and Robert had four children; William de Harcourt, who is buried in Worcester Cathedral, Alice de Harcourt, whose second marriage was to Waleran, Earl of Warwick, Robert de Harcourt, who married the widow of Guy de Dive, and Ivo de Harcourt.

The Camville family originated from Camville-les-Deux-Églises in Normandy, in the same region as the de la Haye honour of La Haie-du-Puits. The leper hospital of Bolleville, near to La Haie-du-Puits, records grants from both families in its cartulary.[46] Since the Norman Conquest, the Camville family had held lands spread across the Midlands and south-west England, including King's Sutton in Northamptonshire, Middleton Stoney in Oxfordshire and the manors of Charlton and Henstridge in Somerset, which were held by Nicholaa as her dower after Gerard's death.[47] Despite also holding various lands in Bedfordshire and Wiltshire, Gerard's marriage to Nicholaa de la Haye gave him a concentrated power base in Lincolnshire, and possession of one of the greatest fortresses in England. We do not know the precise date of Nicholaa and Gerard's marriage, but we do know that it had taken place by 1185. Gerard had followed in his father's footsteps and become a 'successful servant in Henry II's entourage'.[48] According to Stephen Church, it was for this service that he was richly rewarded with Nicholaa de la Haye's hand in marriage, giving him her inheritance in England and Normandy and, of course, custody of Lincoln Castle.⁴⁹

The de la Haye family connections to the Camvilles, and others, are evidenced by a charter, dating to between 1184 and 1187, of a grant involving Nicholaa's uncle, or more likely her cousin, Ralph de la Haye. The charter, issued by Henry II, lists the donations of the king and confirms the gifts of others, including Ralph de la Haye:

> 'He gives to the abbey of St Lo of Countances and the canons regular there serving God, in alms for ever, a fair for one day on the octave of Easter, etc.... And he grants them the gifts of Algar and Richard bishops of Countances confirmed by Hugh, Rotrou, and Walter, archbishops of Rouen...the church of Champrépus etc....that share of the church of St Ermeland which belonged to the fee of John de Campellis; the church of St Thomas the Martyr at St Lo; of the gift of Ralf de Haia [Ralph de la Haye] fourteen acres of land etc. of the gift of William de Tracy the tithe of his mills of Humeel of that of Gerard de Bruis twenty-four quarters of wheat and five shillings annually from his mill of Londa...of that of William de Moyon his right of advowson in the church of Mesnil Opac, and the church itself with its appurtenances...of that of William de Haia a sextary of wheat from (*in*) the church of St Martin de Mesons....of that of Philip de Croilleio the messuage of Popelina at Monfai.... of that of Corbin de Agnell a measure of wheat at Leville; of that of William earl of Arundel a sextary of wheat from the mill of Roard at Aubuigni (*sic*)....of that of William de Diva twelve quarters of wheat from (*in*) the church of Fleury, according to the compromise made between the abbot of St Lo and Enguerrand de Humeto concerning the mill of Martinvilla, and a moiety of that mill;...of that of William de Siccavilla the church of St Peter of Grismesnil; of that of Richard de Lucy St Croix de Vasto.'⁵⁰

The witness list includes several people related to the de la Haye family through marriage, including the constable of Normandy, William du Hommet, William d'Aubigny, the Earl of Arundel (Sussex), William de Saint John, Bertrand de Verdun and Richard de Camville, Gerard's half-brother, suggesting that Nicholaa and Gerard were married by the time the charter was issued. Gerard is also mentioned in an undated charter to Wells Cathedral, issued in the time of his father, Richard de Camville, who died in Apulia in 1176. It is a 'Notification by Richard, archbishop of Canterbury, John, bishop of Norwich, Baldwin, bishop of Worcester and Seffrid II, bishop of Chichester, that Richard de Camville granted to Wells Cathedral the church of Henstridge (Somerset) as a perpetual prebend, and that Gerard de Camville, his son and heir, confirmed this placing it in the hand of Bishop Reginald of Bath to be collated by him to whomever he wished as with the other prebends of Wells.'[51] A confirmation of this charter was issued at Westminster in early 1182, which stated: 'Notification by archbishop Richard of Canterbury and bishops John of Norwich, Baldwin of Worcester and Seffrid of Chichester that Gerard de Camville, son and heir of Richard de Camville, has confirmed in their presence and that of Rannulf de Glanville, the king's justiciar, and of Roger FitzReinfrid and many others of the Exchequer, the grant which his father made and confirmed by charter of the church of Henstridge, to be a perpetual prebend of the church of Wells. Gerard placed the church in the hands of Bishop Reginald of Bath to be collated by him to whomsoever he wished, like other prebends as Wells. The bishops were present and have recorded the grant by this charter with their seals.'[52]

Given that the witnesses are the same for each charter, they are both recording the same incident, that whereby Gerard de Camville confirms his father's gift to Wells Cathedral. Although the first charter is undated, the second is dated to 1182. There is no mention of Nicholaa, which may suggest that this confirmation was made by Gerard after his father's death in 1176, but before his marriage to Nicholaa; or it may simply mean that Nicholaa was not involved as the charter referred to a gift made before Nicholaa's marriage to Gerard.

Nicholaa's husbands each claimed the position of constable of Lincoln Castle by right of his wife. However, Nicholaa seems to have been far from the traditional subservient wife. When her husband was not in the castle, Nicholaa was left in charge rather than an alternative, male deputy. On the accession of King Richard I in 1189, perhaps anticipating the wholesale redistribution of offices that Richard would introduce, Nicholaa and Gerard travelled to Normandy to meet with the king and to receive confirmation of their inherited lands 'with the [service of] castle-ward and the constableship of the castle of Lincoln'.[53] The king issued a confirmation to 'Gerard de Camville and Nicholaa his wife, of all her inheritance in England and Normandy, with the constableship of Lincoln Castle, as held by her father, Richard, and Grandfather, Robert de Haye, and grant to the same parties of lands at Poupeville and Varreville.'[54] The charter excluded 300 librates of land in Poupeville and Varreville, which, it said, were granted to Richard du Hommet, the husband of Nicholaa's younger sister, Gila. As we have already seen, this was later confirmed by Richard I in the *charte aux lacs d'amour*. The charter was executed at Barfleur before 13 August 1189, and before King Richard left Normandy for his coronation, which took place at Westminster Abbey on 3 September.

In the Pipe Roll for 1189/90, Gerard de Camville was assessed for scutage of Sutton, in Northamptonshire, inherited from his father, at 'xxx li' (30 livres).[55] In the same county, William du Hommet was assessed 'xv li' for land at Duddington, attesting to the close relations, both in geography and family, of the de la Haye, Camville and Hommet families.[56] The Pipe Roll for Michaelmas 1190 records that Gerard paid 700 marks for the possession of Lincoln Castle and the shrievalty of Lincolnshire.[57] Possession of the castle and the shrievalty of Lincolnshire had not previously been held together; there is no record of Nicholaa's father, nor her grandfather, being appointed sheriff of Lincolnshire. It is significant, therefore, and a testament to Gerard's reputation, that he was allowed to hold both at the same time.

As constable of Lincoln Castle, Gerard had a rather prominent role in the local politics of Lincolnshire. Gerard also supported the men of Holland, in the same county, in their long-running marshland dispute with Crowland Abbey, also known as Croyland. In early 1189, when Henry II was still on the throne, Gerard was drawn into a dispute involving the monks at Crowland Abbey, in the south of the county. Problems arose during their annual maintenance of the surrounding marshland, which was done each year around the time of the Rogation Days (the sixth Sunday of Easter and first three days of the following week). The monks had informed the neighbouring settlements that they should prevent their cattle from entering the marsh, in order that the crop of hay could grow freely. It seems that the prior of Spalding, in a dispute with the abbey of Crowland over ownership of the marshland, used this annual practice as an excuse to advance his claims and encouraged the locals to ignore the monks and, as a result, according to the Crowland Chronicle, even more cattle than before could be found grazing in the marshes. The abbot impounded the cattle, as the monks had done in former years. However, the men of Holland took exception to this and they 'came to the marsh of Crowland, armed, all of them, with all kinds of weapons; just as though in array for battle, and exceeding in number three thousand men.'[58]

The abbot met with the men and pleaded for peace, fearing the abbey would be attacked and levelled to the ground. The crowd calmed a little but did not disperse, rather they went into the marsh and divided it amongst themselves, 'according to the situation of their respective vills, although located at a considerable distance around the marsh'.[59] The men also camped around the abbey, erecting tents and setting sentries and 'they dug up turf, cut down the greater part of the wood and alder-beds of Crowland, and depastured upon the meadowland; while they carried off firewood and committed other acts of violence for fifteen days, just like so many armed men in camp.'[60] Crowland Abbey was, effectively, under siege, the monks hardly daring to venture beyond the church gates.

The abbot appealed for help from the king's justices and one of them, Geoffrey Fitz-Peter, sent six knights from Northampton to find out what was going on. These knights 'first met with the tents and quarters of the men of Sutton, the liegemen of Gerard de Camville, and found them provided with all kinds of arms. Upon being questioned by them, these men answered, that they were there by the orders of their lord.'[61] Each encampment named their lord as their authority to be there. The abbot appealed to the king and one of the king's justiciar's, Hubert FitzWalter ordered Geoffrey Fitz Peter to summon the prior of Spalding and all the men of Holland to appear before the king's justices. At Deeping, in the week of Pentecost, the men of Holland and prior of Spalding met with Geoffrey Fitz Peter, who 'arrived, bringing with him many men of rank, and members of the king's household.'[62] Abbot Robert charged the prior and men of Holland with breaking the king's peace and with causing violence and injuries. Some of those charged were imprisoned and the judge ordered the case to be heard before the chief justice at Westminster. The case of ownership of the marsh dragged on even beyond the deaths of Henry II and Abbot Robert of Crowland. With the election of Henry, a monk of Evesham, as the new abbot, the monks of Spalding 'made no mention of any claim upon Crowland.'63 Abbot Henry was the brother of William Longchamp, Bishop of Ely and chancellor of King Richard. They would raise the issue again, when the king's brother, John, Count of Mortain, led the opposition against Longchamp.

In 1191, as John was in the ascendancy against William Longchamp, William de Roumare, who had succeeded his grandfather, the son of Countess Lucy, as earl of Lincoln, caused the abbot to be summoned by the justices on the king's writ, so that the dispute over the marsh could finally be settled. On the day he was supposed to appear, the abbot claimed he was ill. On hearing this, 'orders were sent from the king's court by the justices to Gerard de Camville, the sheriff of Lincoln, an enemy of the chancellor, and the especial leader of the opposition faction, immediately to send four lawful knights of the county to make view of the abbat [sic] on a certain day named.'64 The abbot, though not yet recovered from his illness, had left for court before the knights arrived at Crowland. The abbot arrived in London on the day of Ascension where he found 'gathered together against him, the princes of the land, namely earl John, archbishop Walter of Rouen, Hugh de Novant, bishop of Chester [it was actually Hugh de Nonant, bishop of Coventry], William de Roumar and his accomplice Gerard de Camville and Roger de Stikelwald, his under-sheriff, and the abbat [sic] of Angers, together with others innumerable, who took part against him through hatred of his brothers.'65

The abbot lost the case, despite producing charters issued by both Henry II and Richard I, confirming the abbey's ownership of the marsh. As a result, 'the sheriff of Lincoln [Gerard de Camville] received seisin of the whole marsh of Crowland below Munechelade, to which they had never laid claim, as well as two leagues beyond Crowland... only leaving a little plantation of alders standing around the abbey, as its own property.'66 Abbot Henry was not one to give up easily, however, and in 1193, on hearing that King Richard was being held in prison in Germany, travelled to Germany to plead his case with the king, arriving just fifteen days before the king's release. On his release, King Richard sent letters to England, directing that the abbot of Crowland 'should have seisin of his marshes, in conformity with the charter of his father and in such manner as he held the same when the king set out for Jerusalem.'67 The sheriff of Lincoln was instructed to put the king's orders into effect and the under-sheriff, Eustace de Ledenhall, 'caused solemn reseisin of their marsh to be made to the abbat [sic] and house of Crowland at the beginning of Lent; and the abbat [sic] held them peacefully and quietly all that year and the next.'[68]

Unfortunately, that was not the end of the case, and it was to drag on into the reign of King John, when in 1202 the abbot of St Nicholas at Angers, following pleas from the priory at Spalding, offering the king forty marks 'to have judicial record and reasonable judgement upon the matter.'[69] Geoffrey Fitz Peter, Earl of Essex, was ordered to deal with the matter by the king, and he sent instructions to 'Gerard de Camville the then sheriff of Lincoln and wrote to the following effect: – "Geoffrey, &c. to the sheriff of Lincoln, greeting. Know that the prior of Spalding has given us security by Simon de Kyme, that he will pay forty marks unto our lord the king, which he has promised to him for having seisin of the marsh between Crowland and Spalding; as to which a trial took place in the court of our lord the king, between him and the abbat [sic] of Crowland. Wherefore, by trusty summoners, you are to summon the said abbat [sic] to appear before us at Westminster on the Octave of Saint Martin, to hear record and reasonable judgement thereon and are there to have summoners and this writ.'"[70] The king's justices could not decide the case, despite days and days of hearing the arguments between the prior of Spalding and the abbot of Crowland. They resolved to send the matter to the king to be decided by him, and each monastery despatched their own envoy to plead their case before King John. The abbot of Crowland's envoy argued his case before the king who, 'on hearing this, expressed his willingness, both to let the warranty of King Richard hold good, and to receive the sum of one hundred marks that had been promised him by the abbat [sic] of Crowland.'[71] The matter was settled once and for all, with the king finding in the abbot's favour. One can imagine that, as the case had dragged on for eleven years, those who had been drawn into it, such as Gerard de Camville, would have been happy to finally see the end of it, whatever the result.

At some point in the 1190s Nicholaa and her sisters came to an agreement over the division of the de la Haye lands; J.H. Round suggests around 1197, 'at least two years before King Richard's death'.[72] The agreement left Nicholaa in control of the lands in England, while the family's Norman lands were divided between her sisters Gila and Isabel, and their respective spouses. While most Anglo-Norman families were forced into a division of their lands after the fall of Normandy in 1204, it seems that Nicholaa and her sisters came to their agreement during the reign of Richard I, since both Gila and Richard died before the fall of Normandy. Professor Daniel Power dates the division to between September 1189 and mid-April 1190, although it could conceivably have been as late as 1197, as Round suggests.[73] The agreement was witnessed by the king's chancellor, William Longchamp.[74] The earlier dates preclude the division of lands as being a ploy to avoid their confiscation by the crown following Nicholaa and Gerard's fall from grace, after they supported the king's brother John in his rebellion against Richard's justiciar, William Longchamp, in 1191; Gerard's lands were confiscated on Richard I's return to England in 1194 and he had to pay a rather large fine for their recovery.

The agreement between the sisters was concluded in the Norman exchequer court in the castle at Caen. Unfortunately, the only details of the pact that we have are from English court cases in the 1230s and 1250s, but they state that Nicholaa received all the lands in England, while Gila and Isabel divided the lands in Normandy. It appears that Gila received the castle and most of the barony of La Haye-du-Puits itself. However, it is not very clear what lands went to Isabel. This agreement reversed an earlier arrangement made by Richard the Lionheart just before his coronation, by which Nicholaa and Gerard de Camville received a share of two important manors in the Cotentin, Varreville and Pouppeville, the subjects of the *charte aux lacs d'amour* mentioned previously, and lands to which the de la Haye family had a very contested claim. Nicholaa and Gerard must have subsequently renounced their claim to these lands when they came to terms with Nicholaa's younger sisters. So Nicholaa did have a Norman estate for a short time. In a sequel to this agreement, Gerard de Camville exploited his family connections with the Hommets during the crisis in the Anglo-Norman aristocracy in 1204, when barons had to decide between holding land in Normandy and land in England; a man cannot serve two masters (France and England). He managed to take over the manor of Duddington Northamptonshire, which had been confiscated from the Hommets. Stories of his underhanded ruthlessness were remembered there long after.[75]

Where many families were forced into dividing their Anglo-Norman lands with the fall of Normandy in 1204, the de la Haye sisters had completed this almost a decade before. Rather than being a political move, based on what would be rather brilliant foresight, it seems more likely that it was done out of practicality and convenience. For maintaining and managing the lands. All three couples continued to have some lands in both England and Normandy. Richard II du Hommet and William de Rollos, or Roullours, both had extensive lands of their own in England. Or rather, Richard du Hommet would have, had he not predeceased his father. And until 1204 Gerard de Camville had a small estate at Camville-les-deux-Eglises in eastern Normandy, held of the earl of Leicester. Richard du Hommet's mother had been buried in Southwick Priory near Portsmouth, and his eldest son by Gila, William II du Hommet, probably hoped to recover the Hommet lands in England from King John during the war of 1213–14, only to see his hopes dashed, like many others, by John's failure to reconquer Normandy and Anjou. There is also evidence of messages being passed back and forth between the former English lands and William du Hommet in the years following the fall of Normandy.[76]

As previously mentioned, we know of the division of lands from a court case that was brought in the 1230s. The case also raises a question over the identity of one of the defendants, Nichola, who was the wife of Oliver d'Ayncourt. Bracton records the claim, dated 1231, by 'William Longespée and his wife, Idonea' against 'Oliver d'Ayncourt and his wife, Nichola' concerning 'the manor of Duddington', inherited from 'Idonea's grandmother, Nicholaa de la Haye, whose heir she was' which names 'Gerard de Camville and Nicholaa his wife, Richard du Hommet and Gila his wife and William de Rollos and Isabel his wife,' as the 'daughters and heirs of Richard de la Haye'.[77] The case does not explain the relationship between the second Nichola and Nicholaa de la Haye, presumably this second Nichola was closely related to the de la Haye family, but in what way, we do not know. We have few clues to her identity, nor to the generation in which she belonged. It is possible, I suppose, that she was a daughter or granddaughter, of Nicholaa de la Haye, or maybe a cousin or niece. Unfortunately, without further information, it is impossible to narrow down the possibilities in order to achieve a definitive answer. It is an intriguing conundrum.

Chapter Six

# 1191

Gerard de Camville was a talented administrator and was sheriff of Lincoln in 1189 and 1190 and again from 1199 to 1205. He was described by one chronicler as a 'factious man, prodigal of his allegiance'.[1] While another chronicler, William of Newburgh described him as 'a man rich and noble'.[2] The contradictory descriptions probably result from Gerard's own divided loyalties. Although he had sworn allegiance to King Richard on his accession, in 1191 Gerard paid homage to the king's brother John, then count of Mortain, for Lincoln Castle. It may be worth remembering here that Nicholaa's grandfather, Robert de la Haye had been seneschal to William the Conqueror's half-brother Robert, Count of Mortain. This meant that Gerard and Nicholaa were drawn into John's dispute with King Richard's chancellor, William Longchamp.

For what may have been the one and only time in his life, in 1191 John was on the right side, leading the opposition against the oppression of William Longchamp, whose heavy-handed administration of the country caused much dissent among the barons. Before King Richard's departure on crusade, the king had extracted a promise from John and their illegitimate half-brother Geoffrey, Archbishop of York, that neither would set foot in England for three years. Although it seems highly unlikely that Longchamp released John from his oath, the prince was back in England by 1191, possibly on the insistence of his mother, Eleanor of Aquitaine. Now freed from the captivity in which she had been held since her sons' rebellion of 1173–74, the queen mother was once again in a position of trust and power, watching over her favourite son's domains while he was away on crusade.

The catalyst for John's armed opposition to William Longchamp may well have been the king's recognition of his nephew, Arthur, Duke of Brittany still only a child of five years, as his heir, in peace negotiations with Tancred of Lecce in Sicily in 1190, in which he also agreed that

Arthur would marry one of Tancred's three daughters.[3] Richard was eager to continue on crusade and wanted a speedy resolution to the diversion that saw him rescuing his sister, Joanna, and settling the Sicilian succession crisis which had arisen on the death of Joanna's husband, William, King of Sicily. He may have only wanted to make Arthur a more attractive marriage prospect, dangling the possibility of his daughter becoming queen of England before Tancred. Richard's recognition of Arthur as his heir was a closely guarded secret; the only person in England who was meant to know was William Longchamp. However, it seems that Longchamp may have sounded out others to measure the level of support for Arthur. According to the chronicler William of Newburgh, he passed on the information to the king of Scots, at least, and possibly some of the Welsh princes.[4] In early 1191 the news was widely leaked, and John came to hear of it.

According to William of Newburgh, John had 'expected to become the successor to the kingdom, should the king, perchance, not survive his laborious and perilous undertaking.'[5] Indeed, Richard's advancement of his brother since his accession, in giving John lands in England and arranging his marriage to an English bride, all seemed to support this expectation. There was even evidence to suggest that, when the brothers had met in Normandy in 1190, Richard had named John his successor in Normandy, though not England.[6] Richard's actions in naming Arthur his heir, and Longchamp's support for this, threatened to undermine John's own claims and rights. In the late twelfth century, primogeniture was far from established in the rules of inheritance, and the son of a king (John) was often seen as having a greater right to a throne than the grandson (Arthur) of the same king, even if he was the son of the king's elder son. It did not hurt, either, that John was a grown man and would be able to take personal control, while Arthur was still a very young child and would be in need of regents.

Having heard the not-so-secret secret, John started building up his own powerbase. According to Richard of Devizes, John, 'when he knew for certain that his brother had turned his back on England, presently perambulated the kingdom in a more popular manner, nor did he forbid his followers calling him the king's heir.'[7] With tensions rising, a meeting was arranged between John and Longchamp, to be held at Winchester on 24 March 1191. According to Richard of Devizes, the meeting was intended to resolve issues concerning 'the custody of certain castles, and the money out of the Exchequer conceded to the earl by his brother.'[8] This last suggests John had not received all the money the king had promised him for his maintenance. The conference failed to resolve the issue and John set about building up his own support. According to Richard of Devizes 'certain nobles became busy'.[9] The chronicler reported that, as a result of the king's departure on crusade, the nobles were 'all stirred up in arms, castles closed, cities fortified and entrenchments thrown up.'[10] John sent out letters, in secret, eliciting the support of the nobles against the justiciar.

The king himself was concerned over events in England. In the spring, he had released Walter de Coutances, archbishop of Rouen, from his crusading vow and sent him back to England, with a letter:

> 'Richard king of the English to William his Chancellor, Geoffrey Fitz Peter, William Marshal, Hugh Bardolf and William Brewer, greeting. Since we bear a great love to the venerable father Walter archbishop of Rouen and have great trust in him, we send him to you for the safety and defence of our kingdom, releasing him from his pilgrimage with the consent of the pope; because we know him to be prudent, discreet and capable, and ever faithful to ourselves. Wherefore we command and firmly order you to act on his counsel in all matters concerning us, you and he taking each other's advice in all things for as long as he is in England and we are on our pilgrimage. And we order you to do what we told him to tell you about the archbishopric of Canterbury. Witness myself, 23 February 1191, at Messina.'[11]

The king must have had concerns about the efficacy of William Longchamp's rule, as he sent another letter, to William Marshal, Hugh Bardolf, Geoffrey Fitz Peter and William Brewer, in which he ordered 'If our chancellor does not act faithfully according to the advice of yourselves and others to whom we have committed the care of our kingdom, we order you to carry out your own dispositions in all the affairs of our kingdom, in castles and escheats, without any dispute.'[12] Walter de Coutances landed at Shoreham on 27 June, 1191. Tensions had already escalated, however.

In 1190, on returning from his investigation into the massacre of the Jews of York, Longchamp stopped at Lincoln. He accused Gerard de Camville of harbouring thieves and robbers who preyed on the merchants attending the fair at Stamford. Longchamp had demanded that Gerard de Camville, described as 'an enemy of the chancellor' by the Crowland Chronicle, relinquish his custody of Lincoln Castle and swear allegiance to him, personally, as justiciar.[13] Camville refused and instead 'had done homage to Earl John, the king's brother, for the castle of Lincoln, the custody whereof is known to belong to the inheritance of Nicholaa, the wife of the same Gerard, but under the king.'[14] In acting against Gerard de Camville, Longchamp had forced him into John's arms. On learning of Gerard's defiance, Longchamp sent overseas for foreign mercenaries and set out north with the troops he had under his command, attacking Wigmore along the way and forcing Roger de Mortimer, impeached for conspiracy against the king, to surrender his castles and abjure England for three years.[15] As Gerard de Camville joined John at Nottingham, Longchamp continued to Lincoln where he besieged the castle as 'Gerard was with the earl; and his wife Nicholaa proposing to herself nothing effeminate defended the castle like a man. The chancellor was wholly busied about Lincoln.'[16] The formidable Nicholaa refused to yield, holding out for forty days before Longchamp raised the siege, having heard that Tickhill and Nottingham had fallen to John.

Gerard's decision to leave Nicholaa in command of the castle, even though Longchamp was heading her way with an army, may have been to emphasise the standing of the de la Haye family in Lincolnshire, and its connections to the castle itself. The fact that Gerard left Nicholaa in charge, rather than a male deputy, is testament to his trust in her and her abilities. She had, after all, grown up with the castle as her birth right and would have been familiar with every part of its defences, its strengths and weaknesses. Although she would not have been able to fight, with sword and shield, she could direct the defence, placing soldiers where they were most needed, organising supplies of weapons and ammunition, and ensuring the stores of food and drink were suitably rationed.

Nicholaa was approaching forty when William Longchamp besieged the castle, no young, inexperienced girl, and she would have been used to command – and to her orders being obeyed. She was also a mother, of a daughter in her teens and at least two young boys, but it is unlikely that the children were in the castle; it is more likely they were being raised on her manor at Brattleby, just to the north of Lincoln. The castle itself may appear difficult to defend. The curtain wall was a third of a mile in length, but there was a steep drop on the south side. There were two main entrances, the East and West gates, and a number of postern gates. These had to be guarded closely. Similarly, the castle would also have been difficult to attack, and besiegers would have concentrated their energies on the main and postern gates. There is no record of Longchamp bringing up siege machinery, so it would have been a case of watching and waiting and hoping to starve out the castle occupants. Nicholaa held out for forty days, as demonstrated by the Pipe Roll of 1191, which showed that mercenaries were employed for that length of time on the siege of Lincoln Castle.[17] All the same, it must have been a relief for Nicholaa, when William Longchamp gave up the siege and marched his soldiers away.

According to Roger of Howden, the chancellor besieged Lincoln Castle, 'having expelled Gerard de Camville from the keepership and the office of sheriff of Lincoln; which former office the chancellor gave to William de Stuteville and made him sheriff as well.'[18] John, in turn moved north in support of Gerard, quickly taking the ill-prepared royal castles of Tickhill (in Yorkshire) and Nottingham and demanding that Gerard de Camville be reinstated, saying that he 'would visit him [the chancellor] with a rod of iron'.[19] John admonished Longchamp, saying 'it was not proper to take from the loyal men of the kingdom, well known and free, their charges and commit them to strangers and men unknown; that it was a mark of his folly that he had intrusted the king's castles to such, because they would expose them to adventurers; that if it should go with every barbarian with that facility, that even the castles should be ready at all times for their reception, that he would no longer bear in silence the destruction of his brother's kingdom and affairs.'[20]

In response, Longchamp summoned his chief supporters and claimed: 'Never trust me if this man speaks not to subjugate the kingdom to himself; what he presumes is exorbitant, even if he had a right to wear the crown by annual terms with his brother for [he] has not yet completed a full year in his government.'[21]

In the meantime, Walter de Coutances, Archbishop of Rouen but an Englishman by birth, had landed in England and hastened north to act as intermediary between the two warring factions.

Brattleby, the village from which Nicholaa held her barony. (*Author's collection*)

Barlings Abbey, founded by Nicholaa's uncle, Ralph de la Haye. (*Author's collection*)

Tree carving of Nicholaa de la Haye. (*Author's collection, used with the kind permission of Lincoln Castle*)

Plaque telling Nicholaa's story, Lincoln Castle. (*Author's collection, used with the kind permission of Lincoln Castle*)

Magna Carta Memorial, Runnymede. (*Courtesy of Jayne Smith*)

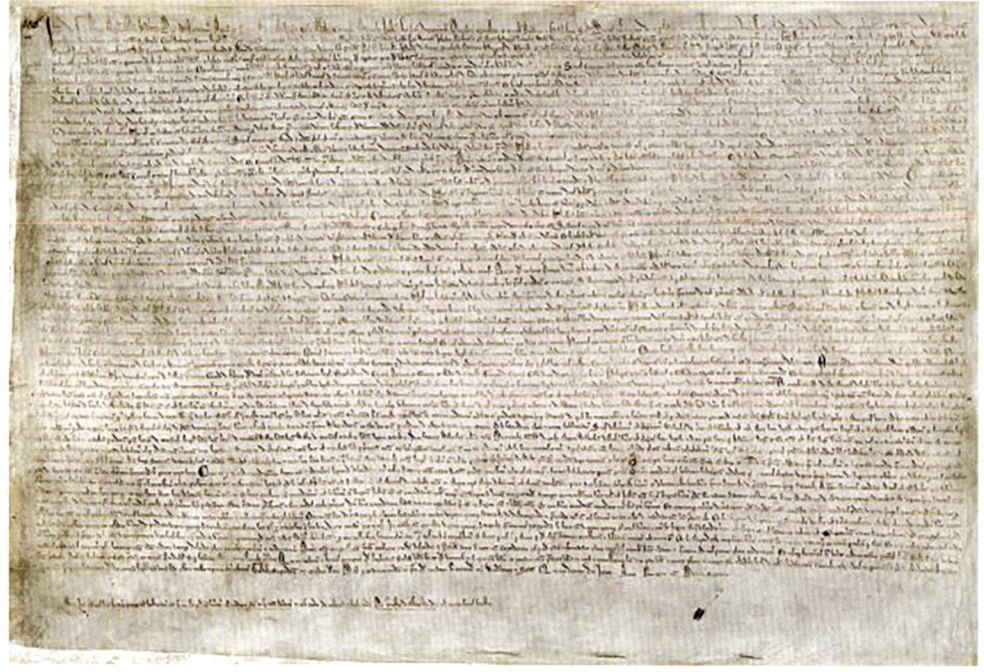

Magna Carta. (*Courtesy of the British Library Catalogue of Illuminated Manuscripts*)

King John, British Library. (*Courtesy of the British Library Catalogue of Illuminated Manuscripts*)

Nottingham Castle. (*Courtesy of Kristie Dean*)

Gatehouse of Tickhill Castle, Yorkshire. (*Author's collection*)

Seal of Nicholaa de la Haye, Lincoln Cathedral. (*Courtesy of Kristie Dean, used with the kind permission of Lincoln Cathedral*)

Gallery of Kings, Lincoln Cathedral, showing Henry II, Richard I, John and Henry III. (*Author's collection*)

Newark Castle. (*Author's collection*)

Newark Castle. The windows to the rooms in the gatehouse where King John died. (*Author's collection*)

Lincoln Cathedral. (*Author's collection*)

The Observatory Tower, Lincoln Castle. (*Author's collection*)

The West Gate viewed from inside the bailey, Lincoln Castle. (*Author's collection, used with the kind permission of Lincoln Castle*)

The Lucy Tower, Lincoln Castle. (*Author's collection, used with the kind permission of Lincoln Castle*)

The view looking towards Torksey, from where Marshal's army approached the city. (*Author's collection, used with the kind permission of Lincoln Castle*)

The Newport Arch, one of the gates through which Marshal's army would have entered the city. (*Author's collection*)

The East Gate of Lincoln Castle, where Faulkes de Breaute's men attacked the besiegers. (*Author's collection*)

View from the castle of the space between castle and cathedral, where most of the fighting took place. (*Author's collection, used with the kind permission of Lincoln Castle*)

1217 Battle of Lincoln from Matthew Paris. (*Courtesy of the British Library Catalogue of Illuminated Manuscripts*)

St Michael's Church, Swaton, where Nicholaa de la Haye is buried. (*Author's collection*)

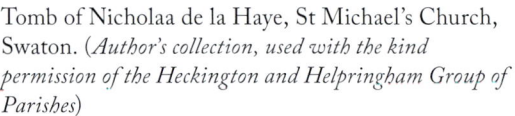

Tomb of Nicholaa de la Haye, St Michael's Church, Swaton. (*Author's collection, used with the kind permission of the Heckington and Helpringham Group of Parishes*)

At some point in the escalating tensions, as Roger of Howden reports, William Longchamp, as papal legate, also issued a sentence of excommunication on John's supporters, writing to Bishop Hugh of Lincoln that 'on the lands of those excommunicated, you are to permit the celebration of no Divine service, the baptism of children and penance excepted. The names of those who have been excommunicated by our lord the pope, and have been denounced as such by ourselves, of whose doings the evidence is so notorious that it cannot by any equivocation on their part be invalidated, are as follows.'[22] The list included John's leading supporters, as well as Walter de Coutances, archbishop of Rouen, and Gerard de Camville.

Walter de Coutances managed to get the two sides together at a conference in Winchester in July, though both John and Longchamp each brought a large number of troops with them, just in case. According to Devizes, John, fearing treachery due to Longchamp's 'craftiness, brought thither four thousand Welsh,' and had them 'placed in ambush close beside the conference'.[23] The chancellor, 'on the other hand, commanded that one-third of the soldiery, with all the arms of all England, should proceed to Winchester by the day appointed.'[24]

Despite the blatant mistrust on both sides, settlement was reached, with the aid of bishops trusted by both men, and of barons who 'swore that they would provide satisfaction between the earl and the chancellor concerning their quarrels and questions to the honour of both parties and the peace of the kingdom.'[25] Agreement, mostly favourable to John was reached whereby John would relinquish the castles he had taken, but then Longchamp would give Tickhill into the custody of Reginald de Wasseville and Nottingham to William de Wenn, both men of John's affinity who each agreed to give up a hostage to the chancellor. John also promised not to harbour outlaws in his lands. Longchamp also agreed to drop his support for Arthur as Richard's heir, to support John's claim and 'if the king should die...should promote him to the kingdom with all his power.'[26]

Especial mention was made of Gerard de Camville, who was reinstated to Lincoln Castle, and 'shall be reinstated in the office of sheriff of Lincoln, and on the same day a proper day shall be appointed for him to make his appearance in the court of our lord the king, there to abide his trial; and if in the judgement of the court of our lord the king proof can be given that he aught to lose that office as also the keepership of the castle of Lincoln, then he is to lose the same; but, if not, he is to keep it, unless in the meantime an agreement can be come to relative thereto on some other terms. And the lord John is not to support him against the decision of our lord the king, nor is he to harbour such outlaws or enemies to our lord the king, as shall be named to him, nor allow them to be harboured on his lands.'[27] So, Gerard and Nicholaa would be safe in their castle at Lincoln, at least for now. What may happen on the king's return was still to be determined. They also benefited from John's largesse; Gerard was appointed keeper of the honour of Wallingford.

In the meantime, Nicholaa and Gerard could get on with the business of maintaining Lincoln Castle. In 1190–91, the sum of £13 6s 8d was spent on the fortress in repairs and improvements but the exact buildings subject to the works are not specified.[28] The works may well have been conducted as a means of strengthening the castle, amid the growing unrest in the country, and with the escalating tensions between John and William Longchamp. The forty-day siege would have put these renovations to the test. Following the siege, the bailey of the castle was strengthened at a cost of £82 to the Exchequer in 1192–93, the work undertaken by Gilbert Hurell and Miles the mason.[29] It is possible that this sum of money represents a continuity of work upon the improvements that had been started in 1190–91 but may well have been as the result of some damage caused by the 1191 siege. It may be that the siege highlighted some weakness within the castle's defences, that now were rectified. There are no further entries in the Pipe Rolls for significant building works in the remainder of Richard's reign, except for a sum of £5 for repairs in 1198.[30] The nature of the strengthening of the bailey is not made clear in the Pipe Roll, although in 1199–1200 the constable spent £20 on the repair of the 'new tower' and gaol.[31] Unfortunately the Pipe Roll is not specific as to which building was viewed as the 'new tower', both the Lucy and Observatory towers and the West and East gates were at least fifty years old at the time. The Observatory Tower was the most recent of these, built towards the end of the Anarchy by the earl of Chester – it may have been nicknamed the 'new tower'. Another possibility is Cobb Hall, in the northeast corner of the bailey, which may have recently been completed as part of the strengthening works to the bailey in 1192–3. Although Cobb Hall may not be this early. It is possible it was built as part of the strengthening works carried out by the earl of Salisbury (costing £374) and Nicholaa de la Haye (£130) shortly after the battle of Lincoln Fair in 1217.[32]

William Longchamp would, however, remain in power; moreover, according to Richard of Devizes, King Richard had sent orders that his brother must obey Longchamp.[33] This uneasy peace was not to last the year, and the catalyst for further unrest arrived in the form of Geoffrey, the newly consecrated archbishop of York and John's half-brother. Still banned from England, Geoffrey had landed at Dover on 14 September 1191 and went to stay at St Martin's Priory, from where he was dragged bodily, having just celebrated Mass, after a five-day siege:

'The castellan's men grabbed him by the feet and arms, carried the struggling archbishop from the altar and handled him so roughly that his head hit the pavement of the church heavily. And when they came out of the church, they led him to a horse, which he did not wish to mount, but went on foot, carrying his cross in his hands at all times; and so he was brought through the muddy streets of the town to the castle where he was delivered to the constable.'[34]

Imprisoned for eight days before he was released, the archbishop's treatment, reminiscent of the treatment of Thomas Becket, though not as lethal, sent shockwaves through the English aristocracy. John took up his brother's cause and, exploiting public opinion, he presented himself as the champion of English liberties. Realising he had made a dreadful mistake, the chancellor sent representatives to speak with Geoffrey and assure him that the arrest had been in error, and he had played no part in it. The chancellor was not believed by his critics, nor by the archbishop himself. Longchamp had gone too far and, as a result, had given his detractors the ammunition they needed to bring about his downfall. Raising a coalition against the foreign justiciar, John wrote to the bishop of London, who was acting as go-between for John and Longchamp:

'John count of Mortain to Richard bishop of London, greetings. As you love the honour of God and the Church and the king and kingdom and me, be present at the bridge over the Loddon on 5 October, between Reading and Windsor, because, God willing, I will meet you there to confer about certain important and serious matters concerning the king and kingdom.'³⁵

The conference, to be held just outside Reading, was instigated by John and was ostensibly to reconcile chancellor and archbishop. Longchamp did not attend. The mutual distrust on both sides saw skirmishes between retainers, on the road to Windsor, and one of John's knights was killed. Longchamp refused to meet John, claiming the prince was intending to usurp the throne. He took refuge in the Tower of London. Within days John was being welcomed into London, recognised as heir presumptive and as all the nobles of the land were assembled in St Paul's church, 'the whole assembly…elected Earl John, the king's brother, chief justiciary of the whole kingdom, and ordaining that all the castles should be delivered to the custody of such as he should choose, they left only three of the weakest, and lying at a great distance from each other, to the now merely nominal chancellor.'³⁶

A conference was held in the Tower of London on 10 October, during which Longchamp resigned as justiciar and was replaced by Walter de Coutances. Coutances was no pushover, however, and John was denied full authority, having to work alongside the new justiciar. In the meantime, Richard had reached the Holy Land in the summer of 1191 and enjoyed some notable victories; he had captured Acre in July and defeated Saladin at the battle of Arsuf in September, writing home that he hoped 'to recover the city of Jerusalem and the Holy Sepulchre within twenty days after Christmas, and then return to our own dominions.'³⁷ However, Richard had also begun to alienate his allies, especially Philip II Augustus of France. Richard's marriage to Berengaria of Navarre, while en route to the Holy Land, had finally ended his long-standing betrothal to Philip's sister, Alix. Claiming that Alix had had an affair with his father, Richard paid Philip Augustus 10,000 marks in compensation; but the humiliation caused a rift that was not so easily repaired. The two kings continued to quarrel as they arrived in the Holy Land, taking opposing positions in political disputes and unable to agree on how to divide the spoils of war. Claiming he was too ill to continue the war, Philip II left the crusade in August 1191 and was home in France by Christmas. With his rival still in the Holy Land, Philip saw an opportunity to cause trouble for Richard; by nurturing a friendship with John, who he promised to recognise as ruler of the Angevin lands in France, in return for John marrying Alix, Richard's discarded fiancée. The fact John was already married to Isabella of Gloucester was seen as no hindrance, given the ambiguity of the marriage and the Archbishop of Canterbury's declaration of its invalidity shortly after the nuptials. Ever one to grasp an opportunity, John was preparing to leave for France when his mother arrived in England. It took several meetings between Eleanor of Aquitaine, John and the king's ministers to persuade the prince that his interests lay in England; the threat of losing all his English lands and castles finally convincing John that it was to his benefit to remain there.

Meanwhile, Richard's crusade had stalled. At Christmas 1191, he was camped within twenty miles of Jerusalem, but did not have the men or machines to take the Holy City and so withdrew to Ascalon. A second attempt to take Jerusalem, in the summer of 1192, was again called off due to lack of resources and renewed negotiations with Saladin resulted in a four-year truce, which meant Richard could return home to deal with his recalcitrant brother. However, Richard had made many enemies in the Holy Land and his route home was problematic. He needed to avoid territories over which Philip Augustus had influence; his ships were driven ashore by storms on the north-east coast of Italy and he was arrested as he headed north, having strayed into Austrian territory. Captured by his erstwhile ally, Duke Leopold of Austria, who was another powerful supporter he had offended in the Holy Land, Richard was handed over to Leopold's overlord, Henry VI, the Holy Roman Emperor.

News of Richard's capture and imprisonment in Germany saw the tables turned again. Philip II renewed his overtures to John, who grasped the opportunity with both hands and met with Philip in Paris; in January 1193 he sealed a treaty by which he relinquished the Norman Vexin to Philip and agreed to marry Alix. While Philip took Gisors, the capital of the Norman Vexin, and gathered an invasion fleet together, John returned to England to gather support for his enterprise. However, the king of Scots was not receptive to his overtures, unwilling to join a rebellion against a crusader king. Despite his predicament, Richard was dismissive of the threat John posed, saying, 'My brother John is not the man to seize any land by force, if anyone meets his attack with even the slightest resistance.'[38]

In the end, John could do little but hire some Welsh mercenaries, with whom he garrisoned the castles at Windsor and Wallingford. John tried to persuade the king's ministers that Richard was dead, but they were not deceived by the ruse. They besieged John's castles and prepared to defend England against Philip II's impending invasion. Seeing England prepared, the French king abandoned his plans. Loyalties were still conflicted, however, and in the north some magnates refused to join the siege against John's castle at Tickhill, Yorkshire, claiming to be his liegemen. Gerard and Nicholaa do not appear to have involved themselves in John's conspiracies, however, and remained quietly at Lincoln. It was a delicate balancing act for Richard's ministers. They had to keep John in check in order to protect King Richard's throne, but always had to keep in mind that, should anything happen to Richard, John was likely to be their next king. John was keenly aware of the quandary which faced the king's ministers and appears to have taken advantage of the situation whenever and wherever he could.

In April 1193 Hubert Walter returned from Germany, with the terms for Richard's release; the huge sum of 100,000 marks was demanded in ransom.[39] Military action against John was draining the treasury and in order to facilitate the collection of the vast ransom, peace needed to be established as John and Philip Augustus were still conspiring against Richard. Together Philip and John offered a bribe to Henry VI, Richard's captor, to keep the English king in prison, or hand him over to them; John's contribution was to be 5,000 marks.[40] However, Richard himself deflected this counteroffer by offering a further 50,000 marks for his release. As news of this latest twist reached Philip Augustus, he sent a message to John, saying 'Look to yourself, the Devil is loosed!'[41]

Despite Philip of France's dramatic exclamation, Richard was not yet free as the ransom was still to be raised and paid. Frustrated at being forced to relinquish a number of his castles, John turned once again to Philip, who gave him the castles of Arques, Drincourt and Evreux. Despite the two offering Emperor Henry further payments to keep Richard imprisoned, the king of England was freed on 4 February 1194. When Richard arrived back in England in March, John was given forty days to present himself before the king, or he would forfeit any future claim to the kingdom. Richard then rode south, he was crowned for a second time, at Winchester Cathedral, on 17 April, and crossed to Normandy four weeks later, where John and Philip Augustus had captured more castles and were in the process of besieging Verneuil.

As Richard's army camped overnight at Lisieux, John came to meet his brother face-to-face. John fell at the king's feet in supplication. Raising him up, Richard gave his younger brother the kiss of peace, and despite John being twenty-seven years old, he told his brother 'have no fear, John, you are a child and were left with bad guardians.'[42] Although Richard dismissed John's actions as those of a misguided youth, his reputation was badly scarred by his attempts to usurp his brother's throne; that he was trying to steal the lands of an imprisoned crusader king was unforgivable. In the call to crusade, the pope specifically promised that the property of crusaders would be preserved and protected while they responded to the church's call. John had broken this guarantee in a dramatic way; and had failed spectacularly. Where his failures in Ireland could be seen as youthful folly, and he was even praised for acting against the excesses of the unpopular justiciar William Longchamp, his betrayal of his crusading sibling exposed him as a disloyal, faithless brother. As William of Newburgh put it, John was 'heaping up endless curses on his own perfidious head.'[43]

Although Richard publicly forgave his brother, John's lands and castles were not returned to him; his supporters also fared badly. On 29 March 1194, King Richard was in Nottinghamshire, visiting the royal hunting lodge at Clipstone and Sherwood Forest. And on 31 March, he held the first day of his council at Nottingham, with his mother, Eleanor of Aquitaine, present, as well as Hubert Walter, Archbishop of Canterbury, and the king's own half-brother, Geoffrey, Archbishop of York. Many of the great nobles of England were present, including David, the brother of the king of Scots, William, the king's half-brother and Earl of Salisbury, and Hamelin de Warenne, Earl of Warenne and Surrey, the king's half-uncle. It was at this great council that Gerard de Camville's fate was decided, as 'on the same day, the king dispossessed Gerard de Camville of the castle and shrievalty of Lincoln, and Hugh Bardolph of the shrievalty of Yorkshire and the castle of York...and set up all the offices before-mentioned for sale.'[44]

Gerard's punishment for his support of John was still not over, however, as on 2 April 'by the advice and artifices of the chancellor, as it is said, Gerard de Camville was arraigned for harbouring some robbers, who had plundered the goods of certain merchants going to the fair of Stamford; and it was said that they had set out from his residence for the purpose of committing the robbery, and after committing it, had returned to him. They also accused him of treason, because he had refused to come at the summons of the king's justices, or take his trial as to the aforesaid harbouring of the robbers, or produce them before the king's justices; but made answer that he was a vassal of earl John, and would take his trial in his court. They also arraigned him for having taken up arms, and aiding earl John, and others of the king's enemies, in taking the castles of Tickhill and Nottingham.'[45] While the king could not act too severely against his brother, he was throwing the book at those who had supported him in his actions against William Longchamp in 1191. According to Roger of Howden, 'Gerard de Camville, however, denied all these charges which were so made by them against him; on which they gave pledges to follow their suit, and Gerard de Camville gave pledge to defend himself by one of his freeholders.'[46]

Unfortunately, Roger of Howden does not record the outcome of the proceedings, though given that Gerard de Camville was forced to pay a fine of 2,000 marks in order to recover the king's good will and his lands, we can assume that the trial did not end favourably. This sum had been paid off by 1197, all except £8, in payment of which Richard accepted two horses.[47] Gerard was fined an additional £100 to gain possessions of lands which had been declared forfeit when he had failed to send a knight to serve in Richard's army in Normandy.[48] In addition to Gerard's fine, Nicholaa herself was fined 300 marks to be allowed, to marry her daughter by William Fitz Erneis, Matilda, to whomever she wished except, of course, to an enemy of the king's. Nicholaa was still accounting for this debt until 1212 and had renegotiated the amount with King John in 1200; in 1201 she still owed £20, 40 marks and one palfrey (a horse).[49] Little is heard of Nicholaa and Gerard for the remainder of Richard's reign, it is likely they lived quietly on their estates, administering Nicholaa's barony of Brattleby and raising their family. The *Red Book of the Exchequer*, listing scutage payments for 1194/95, records Gerard de Camville as paying 'xxs., I militem' ('20s., 1 knight') for Oxfordshire and 'xvi*l*. de feodo Ricardi de Haia, xvi milites' ('£16 and 16 knights from the fee of Richard de la Haye') for Lincolnshire.[50] Gerard was assessed for the same scutage in Oxfordshire, 'xxs., I militem' ('20s., 1 knight'), in 1196/97.[51] In addition to Nicholaa's daughter, Matilda, we know that Gerard and Nicholaa had at least two children, sons named Richard and Thomas. Richard would become the heir to both his parents, while nothing is known of Thomas beyond his name, suggesting that he, perhaps, died young.

John's position as heir to the throne remained ambiguous. In 1190 Richard had named Arthur, but in 1191 the English council had recognised John. Nothing more was said on the matter, leaving John in a state of limbo. Perhaps, now reunited with his wife, Berengaria of Navarre, Richard hoped to produce a son and heir of his own? Richard's immediate concern, however, was the recovery of the lands in Normandy, lost to Philip Augustus – with the collaboration of John – during his imprisonment. John was sent to retake Evreux, a task apparently made easier by the fact the defenders did not know John had changed sides, and the garrison were slaughtered after allowing him entry. Although he enjoyed limited military success in the reconquest of Normandy, Richard recognised his brother's assistance and in 1195 'forgave his brother all the wrath and displeasure he felt towards him,' and restored some of his lands and titles.[52] John was once again Earl of Gloucester and Count of Mortain and was promised an income of £2,000 annually.[53] John's ambiguous position as Richard's possible heir was given a boost in 1196 when Richard failed to gain custody of the alternative claimant, Arthur Duke of Brittany. Despite an invasion of Brittany, Arthur slipped through Richard's grasp and was spirited away to the French court by the Breton nobles. Richard could hardly promise his throne to Arthur now that he was in the hands of his greatest rival, Philip II of France.

By 1197 it was becoming obvious that the king was not going to father a son of his own, and so John's standing, though never officially recognised as heir, was once again in the ascendancy. However, relations between Richard and John again cooled in 1198 when the king received a missive from Philip of France, claiming that John was once more plotting with him. Chroniclers are divided on whether King Philip was telling the truth, or merely attempting to sow discord. Richard, at least, found the claims credible and John was again deprived of his lands and titles. The brothers were still not reconciled when Richard began the siege of Châlus in 1199. On 26 March, while inspecting the progress made by his troops, protected only by helmet and shield, Richard was hit in the shoulder by a crossbow bolt fired from the ramparts. The wound turned gangrenous, and he died on 6 April 1199; his mother, Eleanor of Aquitaine, was at his bedside. Richard I was buried at Fontevrault Abbey, beside his father, Henry II. Roger of Howden claimed that, on his deathbed, Richard named John as his heir, 'he devised to his brother John the kingdom of England and all his other territories, and ordered fealty to be done to the aforesaid John by those who were present, and commanded that his castles should be delivered to him, and three-fourths of his treasures.'[54]

On hearing the news, John acted quickly and raced to Chinon to secure the Treasury. Although Arthur of Brittany had substantial support in Anjou, England, Normandy and Poitou immediately recognised John as king – as did his mother and her duchy of Aquitaine. John's succession was not without concerns, however, and the *Histoire de Guillaume le Maréchale* tells us of a keen debate between William Marshal, Earl of Pembroke, and Hubert Walter, Archbishop of Canterbury, when the news of Richard's death reached them in Rouen four days later. According to the *Histoire*, while the archbishop backed Arthur as having the greater right, William gave his full support to John, arguing against Arthur due to his close links with the king of France.[55] More with a nod to hindsight (the *Histoire* was written in the 1220s), than the skill of prophecy, the archbishop cautioned: 'This much I can tell you, you will never come to regret anything you did as much as what you're doing now.'[56]

John was invested as Duke of Normandy in Rouen before departing for England and his coronation; he was crowned in Westminster Abbey on 27 May 1199. The fifth and youngest son of Henry II and Eleanor of Aquitaine, John was never expected to become king. For the last ten years, the early deaths of three older brothers, and Richard's own inability to produce a son and heir had dangled the possibility tantalisingly in front of him. His own betrayals of his brother counted for nothing in the grand scheme of things and, in the end, John acceded to the throne with the support of his mother and the great magnates of Normandy and England. John's perfidy and self-interest, however, during the reign of his brother, had not gone unnoticed; his reputation as a 'mad-headed youth' who had become 'nature's enemy' not forgotten. Many must have looked forward to the new reign with mounting trepidation.

## Chapter Seven

# Lincoln Restored

King Richard's death in 1199, and John's accession to the throne, saw a dramatic change in circumstance for Nicholaa and Gerard. Not only were they restored to favour, but also to Lincoln Castle and Gerard was again appointed sheriff of Lincolnshire, a position he held for the next six years, and 'became a greater man than ever.'[1] John was in Normandy when he heard of his brother's death – or perhaps in Brittany. According to *the Life of St Hugh*, which tells the story of Hugh of Avalon, the saintly bishop of Lincoln, John was in Brittany with his nephew, Arthur.[2] Bishop Hugh was travelling to meet with King Richard at the time, and so may be well-placed to know John's whereabouts. If true, this would add credence to the accusations that John was yet again plotting against his brother, with Arthur and the king of France. Having received a messenger with the news of Richard's death, John headed for Chinon in Anjou to secure the Treasury; it was at Chinon that he was reunited with his mother, who had ridden there from Richard's deathbed. King Philip II and Arthur were not idle and, having heard of Richard's death, moved to advance Arthur's own claims to the Angevin lands. Philip took Evreux as Arthur progressed towards Le Mans; travelling with only a few attendants, John escaped the city just a few hours before his nephew's arrival. Arthur paid homage to Philip Augustus for Anjou, Maine and Touraine, now lost to John.

John headed north and was welcomed in Normandy, despite their fractious history during Richard's reign. He was invested as Duke of Normandy in Rouen Cathedral on 25 April, with Walter of Coutances 'placing a coronet worked with golden roses on the new duke's head.'[3] According to the *Histoire de Guillaume le Maréchale* (the *Histoire*) the Normans recognised John as their duke 'but the lords of Gascony and the Limousin, of Poitou, Anjou and Brittany did not – they had no wish to be ruled by him. Duke John, realising how opposed they were, made his way to those parts and made all manner of generous concessions to win them round, granting their every demand – and how he came to regret it! They respected him all the less! It won him neither their love nor their esteem, and they showed him no obedience but opposed him time and again.'[4]

In the meantime, having heard reports of increasing lawlessness in England, William Marshal and Hubert Walter were despatched there to keep the peace and to receive the oaths of loyalty from the barons and prelates. The time between the death of one king and coronation of the next was always an uneasy period; a new regime invariably brought uncertainty and, quite possibly, a change in fortunes for some. Marshal and Hubert Walter found that magnates had already started strengthening their fortifications and gathering their men. They extracted an oath of loyalty to John, from the barons and prelates of England. Many wanted to make their oaths conditional on the king accepting their rights but had to settle for a promise that John would at least give them a hearing.[5] John then led a punitive expedition into Anjou, to punish the disloyalty of Le Mans, as his mother did similar in other areas of the region; a demonstration of Angevin might. John and Eleanor then went their separate ways, with Eleanor heading south to secure her own Aquitaine, and John departing for England and his coronation at Westminster Abbey on 27 May, two days after he arrived in England:

'On Ascension Day 1199 John, under a canopy held by four barons, was led in procession into Westminster Abbey. On his knees before the high altar he swore, as his brother had ten years earlier, a triple coronation oath: to observe peace, honour and reverence towards god and the Church all the days of his life; to do good justice and equity to the people entrusted with his care; to keep good laws and destroy bad laws and evil customs that had been introduced into the land.'[6]

John was then stripped to his underclothes and anointed with holy oil on his head, chest and hands, before being dressed in royal robes, crowned, given the sceptre and virge (a rod of office) and seated on his throne. In order that John should keep the sacred oil on his head for the next seven days, John wore a coif which was held in place by straps tied under his chin.[7] According to Gervase of Canterbury, the ceremony was conducted 'in great glory'.[8] The ceremony was followed by Mass before John was led out of the abbey to his coronation banquet. According to the *Histoire*, 'liberal gifts were distributed there.'⁹ One cloud presented itself at John's coronation, and that was the ambassadors from Scotland, who informed him that King William the Lion would recognise John as king, if John returned the earldom of Northumbria. John offered to meet the king of Scots at Northampton ten days later to discuss the situation. However, King William failed to appear, but sent more ambassadors who issued John with an ultimatum: return Northumbria or William would take it by force. John, however, was keen to get back to Normandy, still under threat from Philip II, and so left William de Stuteville to deal with the defence of the north. On 20 June 1199 he sailed back to Normandy with 'a mighty English host'.¹⁰

John's strength in Normandy lay in the alliances forged by his brother, Richard, before his death. Thanks to Richard's help, John's nephew, Otto of Brunswick was now Holy Roman Emperor, and ready to support his uncle against France. In an assembly at Rouen, held in August 1199, fifteen French counts, led by Flanders and Boulogne, pledged to support John. It was in August, too, that John and Philip met face-to-face on the border between their lands. Philip complained that John had not paid him homage for the French lands held by the English king, he demanded the Vexin and that John relinquish Anjou, Maine and Touraine to Arthur. Anjou, Maine and Touraine were at the centre of the vast Angevin empire and relinquishing them was never an option. According to Gervase of Canterbury, John, supported by his mighty army and imposing collection of allies 'made up his mind to resist the French king like a man, and to fight manfully for the peace of his country.'¹¹

By September, John was winning the war. William des Roches, Arthur's seneschal in Anjou, offered to defect to John. He was bitter that Philip II had destroyed the Angevin fortress of Ballon after capturing it from John, rather than handing it to Arthur. This high-profile defection was followed by the submission of Arthur himself, and he and his mother met John at Le Mans. However, they received a warning that the king was planning to arrest and imprison them, and fled Le Mans in the dead of night, making their way to the French court. Whether the intelligence was true or not, John's past record of betrayal was obviously enough to sow distrust in the minds of Arthur and his mother and make the threat credible. Soon after, despite a truce with King Philip II, John's coalition collapsed; many of his French allies were preparing to go on crusade and news of his proposed betrayal of Arthur saw more deserting his side.

When the truce ended in January a more permanent peace was agreed, although now balanced heavily in Philip's favour. John was to cede to Philip the whole of the Vexin and the towns in south-east Normandy that Philip had taken in the wake of Richard's death. In return, Philip withdrew his support of Arthur, and also persuaded Arthur to withdraw his claims. In addition, Philip recognised John as heir to Anjou, Maine and Touraine while John promised to pay homage to Philip for those territories and Normandy, thus recognising King Philip as his overlord for his French lands. John also granted Philip 30,000 marks (£20,000); he would impose a tax of 3 shillings on each carucate of land in England to make the payment.[12] The peace would be sealed with a wedding, that of Philip's heir Louis with John's niece, Blanche of Castile. Blanche was the daughter of John's sister Eleanor and Alfonso VIII, queen and king of Castile. A five-month truce was agreed to give time for the bride to be fetched from Spain. Now in her late seventies, it was John's mother, Eleanor of Aquitaine, who made the perilous journey across the Pyrenees to select the bride (the choice was originally between Blanche and her sister, Urraca, and it was Eleanor who decided on Blanche) and bring her back to Normandy for the wedding.

Many were satisfied that the war was over, and peace achieved. The chronicler Ralph of Coggeshall praised John as 'a lover of peace, who intended to live a tranquil life free from wars, understanding how many enemies of the kingdom he faced, and what great misfortunes had befallen his father and brothers and all the kingdom from such wars.'[13] However, while the chroniclers, who were invariably monks, were happy at the prospect of peace, John's more martial subjects thought he had given in too quickly, and it is from this time that he earned the soubriquet 'Softsword'. Bertrand de Born said of John, 'No man may ever trust him, for his heart is soft and cowardly.'[14]

With the truce in place, John returned to England, intending to deal with William the Lion, whose threatened invasion of Northumbria had so far not materialised. John summoned the king of Scots to a meeting at York. William refused to appear, claiming the safe conduct provided by John was inadequate, and the matter remained unresolved. While in York, however, John was confronted by several Cistercian abbots who, traditionally exempt from taxation, refused to pay the new tax John had imposed to pay King Philip. Ralph of Coggeshall claimed that John 'wishes to oppress the order with the obligation of the tax.'[15] When the abbots refused to pay, John was incensed and ordered that his sheriffs 'should persecute them, show them no justice in their injuries and lawsuits and not help them in their disputes, but refer everything to the king.'[16] Intervention from the Archbishop of Canterbury did nothing to placate John, the archbishop 'reproached the king openly for his great harshness, pronouncing him a persecutor of the Holy Church who presumed to impose such great and so many injustices on these most worthy sons of the Church.'[17] The situation remained unresolved as John headed to Normandy once more, having refused a placatory offer of 1,000 marks from the archbishop for being 'so small', John 'crossed the sea, breathing threats and slanders against the disciples of Christ.'[18]

On 18 May 1200, Philip and John met at the border between the French and Angevin lands. The terms of the January treaty were ratified and four days later, the peace was sealed on the island of Le Goulet, in the middle of the River Seine. John did homage to Philip for his French possessions, Arthur did homage to John for Brittany. Louis and Blanche were married, at Port-Mort, on John's side of the river as France was at the time under interdict due to Philip's repudiation of his wife, Ingeborg of Denmark.[19] Once the treaty was sealed, John moved south with a large army, to subdue Anjou, Maine and Touraine, the territories that had resisted him for the past year. After a show of force, and taking 150 hostages, he moved further south, into Aquitaine, which had declared for him the previous year, but only after generous concessions had been made to the leading magnates. John now called two of them, the count of Angoulême and viscount of Limoges, to meet with him at the castle of a third, Hugh de Lusignan, Count of La Marche. Hugh and Audemar, Count of Angoulême had been locked in a bitter rivalry for many years, but had recently agreed to put it aside in favour of a marriage between Hugh and Count Audemar's daughter and heir, Isabelle.

John had divorced Isabella of Gloucester, his wife of ten years, shortly after ascending the throne. He had ensured that Isabella was not crowned with him in 1199 and a year later persuaded the bishops of Normandy to declare the marriage void; this was done with little difficulty, given the dubious legality of the marriage, the archbishop of Canterbury's objections when John married Isabella, and the lack of papal dispensation. It was also an advantage to John to be rid of an English wife; as king he was now a greater marriage prospect on the international stage and a marriage to a European princess would bring allies and prestige. John was hoping to marry the daughter of the king of Portugal, and in January 1200 he welcomed the Portuguese ambassadors to his court. This idea, however, seems to have fizzled out and by the summer of 1200 John's marriage plans lay elsewhere – in Angoulême.

The stories of John marrying Isabelle invariably describe a lecherous King John being enchanted by the beauty of twelve-year-old Isabelle. However, John's marriage to Isabelle was a smart political move; it prevented the union of the county of Angoulême with the Lusignan lands, which would have essentially created a powerful political bloc across the middle of Aquitaine. Moreover, it secured the loyalty of Count Audemar, to the English crown, whilst his daughter was queen. Unfortunately, it also served to alienate the powerful Lusignan family and drove Count Hugh into the arms of Philip II of France. As the *Histoire* wisely states, the marriage was 'pleasing to some and not to others'.[20] The wedding was celebrated on 24 August at Angoulême and by October the newlyweds were back in England; they were both crowned in Westminster Abbey on 8 October 1200.

The wedding was a pleasant interlude for John, but he was soon back to business. By November he was in Lincoln, meeting with William, King of Scots. As the local castellan and sheriff of the county, Gerard de Camville, and probably Nicholaa, were present during the visit. On the day after the first interview between the two kings, 'John, king of England, fearlessly and contrary to the advice of many of his followers, entered the cathedral church of Lincoln, and offered on the altar of Saint John the Baptist, in the new buildings there, a chalice of gold.'[21] On the same day, the two kings met 'outside the city of Lincoln upon a lofty hill, and there in sight of all the people, William, king of the Scots, did homage to John, king of England, as of his own right, and swore fealty to him, upon the cross of Hubert, Archbishop of Canterbury, for life and limb, and his worldly honour against all men and for preserving the peace toward him and his realm.'[22] The impressive witness list included many English earls, the brother of the king of Scots, Scottish earls, a Welsh prince, and 'Gerard de Camville and many others of the barons of

England and Normandy'.[23] The matter of Northumbria, however, went unresolved despite a lengthy discussion after William raised the subject. John decided it was a discussion for another time and proposed a truce until Pentecost (May 1201).

The mood would have been very sombre in Lincoln once the ceremonies were over, as on 16 November, it had lost its bishop, Hugh of Avalon, the future Saint Hugh. The bishop had died in London, but his body was escorted to Lincoln for burial 'where had gathered three archbishops and almost all the nobles of England,' for the meeting between the kings.[24] Lincoln Cathedral had been severely damaged by earthquake in 1185 and Bishop Hugh was supervising its rebuilding on a grander scale when he died. As the bishop's funeral procession approached the city, 'the people rushed out in a crowd to the procession of their pastor. The kings themselves, the archbishops and all the clergy and princes reverently attended. John, putting aside royal pomp, with the archbishops, heads bowed, humbly put the coffin on their shoulders and carried the holy burden for some time, ignoring the mud of the streets for the funeral of such a man.'[25]

For Nicholaa and Gerard, the visit of the kings of England and Scotland, with the funeral of Bishop Hugh immediately after, would have been a test of their organisational skills. As castellan of the royal castle, and as the sheriff of the county, Gerard would have been at the centre of the planning for the royal visit, organising security, accommodation and ensuring that each attending had the precedence in proceedings to which he was entitled. They may also have had to house some of the guests within the castle, and arrange for accommodation at other residences, such as the Bishop's Palace, just to the south of the cathedral. Some may also have stayed at St Mary's Guildhall, at the base of Steep Hill, where Henry II is known to have stayed on his visits to the city in 1175, 1179, 1181 and 1183.[26] There is evidence of a Great Hall within the grounds of Lincoln Castle, which may have been used on this occasion to host a feast in celebration and honour of the two kings meeting.[27] It may also have provided the opportunity for the family to celebrate the nuptials of Nicholaa and Gerard's son, Richard de Camville. Nicholaa's daughter by her first husband, Matilda Fitz Erneis, had probably been married in the late 1190s to William de Gisnei, and now lived in Kent. We know nothing of one son, Thomas, who may have died young. There are a number of Thomas de la Hayes who appear in the historical record, but none of them appear to have family or territorial links to Nicholaa and Lincolnshire. There may also have been another child, an unnamed daughter, as Rob de Meisy paid a fine to marry the (unnamed) 'daughter of Nicholaa and Gerard de Canmille' who was in the custody of William de Bretville in Norfolk, the fine is dated to 1200.[28] There is no other clue, however, to this child's identity.

Nicholaa and Gerard's son and heir, Richard de Camville, probably aged around fifteen or sixteen, did marry sometime in the year 1200. Richard was married to Eustachia, the daughter and heir of Gilbert Basset and his wife, Ageline de Courtenay, after Gerard offered £1,000 for her wardship. Basset, along with his brothers, Alan and Thomas, was in Lincoln for the meeting of the two kings. This would have been the perfect opportunity to celebrate the wedding, if it hadn't already taken place earlier in the year. It was the second marriage for Eustachia, who had been married to Thomas de Verdon in Oxfordshire in 1194 or 1195. Thomas had died in Ireland in 1199. There was some dispute over Eustachia's dower lands, when Eustachia claimed property as dower from Nicholas de Verdun in 1202. The dispute was settled on 20 Aug 1204, including payment for life of rents received from 'Henry de Verdon of the service he owes for the tenement he holds of the said Nicholas in Buckenhale, co. Stafford.'[29] The couple was to have one daughter, Idonea, or Idoine, who was the heiress of both Gerard and Nicholaa and who was married to William II Longespée, son and heir of William Longespée, third Earl of Salisbury and illegitimate son of King Henry II, and his wife Ela, Countess of Salisbury in her own right. The *Testa de Nevill* records for 1219 include an entry which states 'the Earl of Salisbury has in his custody the estate at Coleham, with the daughter and heir of Richard de Camville, who is in the king's gift, valued at 40*l.* a year.'[30] Although it must have been a happy occasion at the time, the marriage would have implications for Nicholaa later on, with Longespée challenging Nicholaa for control of parts of Idonea's inheritance.

Following the conference of kings, business in Lincoln continued as before, with Gerard controlling the castle, supervising repairs and administering the county as its sheriff. His son, Richard, also played his part, learning the ropes in anticipation of the time he would take over the duties from his father. Richard de Camville appears in the pleas at

Lincoln in the fourth year of the reign of King John, the Lincolnshire Eyre of 1202, where 'Sefrid, son of Reginald Cote, was arrested because it was said of him that he tallaged ships which came through the marsh, and he was replevied by Richard Bacun, John, Jordan's son, and Reginald Cote. And after his replevin he shaved his crown and made him a tonsure like a clerk's. But this was not his condition when he was delivered to his pledges, as is testified by Richard of Camville who delivered him [to his pledges] and by others. Afterwards his pledges came and confessed that while he was in their plevin he had his crown shaved, and they put themselves in mercy.'[31]

At the castle, other than the repairs noted to the 'new tower' in 1199–1200 there is little evidence to suggest that John invested significantly in new buildings at Lincoln, nor that Gerard had too much to do to maintain the existing buildings. Improvements and repairs to the gaol are recorded during several years in his tenure, such as in 1201–02 when over £5 was spent in repairs to the gaol and improvements are recorded at a cost of 20s. on two occasions in 1211–12 and 1213–14.[32] The *Red Book of the Exchequer* records Gerard holding one half of one knights' fee 'in Blakelande' in Wiltshire in 1210/1212.[33] The *Red Book* also records Gerard's scutage payments between 1201 and 1212 as being assessed at '16 soldiers, with his wife, of the barony of Richard de la Haye'.[34] It is interesting that, though she isn't mentioned by name, Nicholaa is included in the reference, as Gerard held the barony by right of his marriage. In the same records, he owed one knights' fee in Oxfordshire in scutage, probably from the same manor that he was assessed the same amount in 1194/95 and in 1196/97.[35] A writ of King John of 1212, recorded in the *Testa de Nevill* mentions 'Ricardi de Haia...predecessor domine Nicolæ uxoris Gerardi' ('Richard de la Haye...predecessor of Dame Nicholaa, wife of Gerard de Camville').[36] The same 1212 *Testa de Nevill* lists a number of Gerard de Camville's holdings in Lincolnshire. He is listed as being the lord of Scothern and Riseholme, for the service of two knights' fees, with Robert Bardolf holding the land from him for the same service. He is also the lord of Faldingworth and two other manors, for two further knights' fees, which land is held from him by Simon de Kyme. One knights' fee was owed for his manor at Engleby, which was held by William, son of Joscelin d'Engleby. The Engleby family were recorded as holding the same land from Richard de la Haye in 1166. Another family who traditionally held land from the de la Hayes was the Bardolfs and the *Testa de Nevill* records Gerard as owing one and a quarter knights' fees for Figlincham 'whence Dun (or Doun) Bardolf, who died was his feudal tenant.'[37] This Doun Bardolf had been married to Beatrice de Warenne, heir to the barony of Wormegay, before his death. He was succeeded by his son by Beatrice, William Bardolf. Beatrice would go on to marry Hubert de Burgh, King John's justiciar.[38] Gerard also held land at Brattleby and Cammeringham, 'where he lived as lord,' owing one knights' fee.[39] The abbess of Barlings Abbey also held 'in pure alms' two carucates and one bovate of land in Barlings 'from the gift of Richard de la Haye who was predecessor to the lady Nicholaa, wife of the aforementioned Gerard'.[40]

While at Lincoln, John's dispute with the Cistercian order was also resolved; the abbots were granted an audience where they fell at the king's feet and begged his forgiveness. Much to their surprise, John was inclined to be charitable, cancelled the oppressive edicts and promised his protection in the future. John even went so far as to promise to build a new Cistercian monastery in England, where he hoped he would eventually be buried. From Lincoln on 26 November John sent out an order to his sheriffs 'to protect, maintain and defend these men and all their possessions, just as if they were our own royal goods, and do them no injury or harm, nor permit them to suffer any harm or injury within your bailiwick.'[41] The initial crises of his reign all resolved, John and Isabelle celebrated Christmas at Guildford knowing his succession had been secured. Ominously, unbeknownst to the king, the dark clouds arising from his humiliation of Hugh de Lusignan were already gathering over Poitou.

In the early months of 1201, Hugh started causing trouble, attacking John's castles in Aquitaine. Eleanor of Aquitaine, in retirement at Fontevrault Abbey, wrote to John of the deteriorating situation within her domains. In retaliation, John ordered his officials to seize Hugh de Lusignan's county of La Marche, and the territories of Hugh's brother, Raoul (or Ralph), Count of Eu, despite the fact he had remained loyal to John and was in England in the king's service at the time of the unrest. War was averted by the intercession of King Philip II of France, who met John on the Norman-French border to resolve the issue. John promised to restore the Lusignan lands and to give them justice. John's idea of justice, however, was to charge the Lusignans with treachery and challenge them to a judicial duel, rather than taking them to court, with the best fighters from his dominions to act as his champions. The Lusignans refused the challenge and appealed to King Philip once again. And so started a year of toing and froing between John and Philip, with John refusing to meet the summons of the king of France. When John failed to appear in Paris by 28 April 1202, he was declared a contumacious vassal and his lands forfeit:

> 'At length the French court assembled and judged that the king of England should be deprived of all lands which he and his predecessors had held from the French king, because they had done scarcely any service owed for a long time, and had refused to obey their lord. King Philip, therefore, gladly accepted and approved of the judgement of his court; he gathered his army and immediately attacked the castle of Boutavant, which had been built by King Richard in Normandy, and razed it to the ground. Then he seized all the land of Hugh de Gournay and all the nearby castles. He took the county and castle of Aumâle, the county of Eu and the whole of that land as far as Arques and met with no resistance.'[42]

At this point, King Philip brought his trump card into play: Arthur of Brittany. Now sixteen years old, the French king knighted Arthur, invested him with Anjou, Maine, Touraine and Aquitaine, and betrothed him to his infant daughter, Mary.[43] A Plantagenet prince, Arthur was the posthumous son of John's brother Geoffrey, fourth son of Henry II of England and Eleanor of Aquitaine. Arthur's mother was the great heiress Constance of Brittany, and it was through her that Geoffrey had held the title duke of Brittany, which passed down to Arthur. Geoffrey had died in a tournament in August 1186 and Arthur was born several months later. Used as a foil against his uncle John, at one point Arthur had been recognised by King Richard as his heir. However, when Richard died in 1199, it was John who took the English throne. Ever eager to meddle in English affairs, Philip II of France sought to use Arthur as a weapon against John. He gave the young duke a small force and sent him south into Aquitaine to advance his claims as the rightful heir to the Angevin Empire. He was besieging his grandmother, Eleanor of Aquitaine, at Mirebeau, just north of Poitiers, when John came to his mother's aid; 'had he delayed she would have soon been captured, for the besieging force was great.'[44]

Taking Arthur's forces by surprise, John managed to achieve a substantial victory, capturing Arthur and Hugh and Geoffrey de Lusignan in the process. The young duke was imprisoned, first at Falaise and then at Rouen, where he was secretly murdered at Easter 1204, either on John's orders or at the king's own hand, though the former is most likely. Arthur's mysterious death certainly did nothing to help John's long-term reputation, nor his situation in France. However, the English chroniclers of the time appear to be more understanding. The Barnwell chronicler saw the obscurity of Arthur's grave as just reward for his pride. In 1216, Roger of Wendover recited the comments he believed to have come from Pope Innocent III:

'The chronicles tell us of the murder of innocent persons by many emperors and princes, the Kings of France as well as others, but we do not read that the murderers were ever condemned to death. Arthur was no innocent victim. He was captured at Mirebeau, a traitor to his lord and uncle to whom he had sworn homage and allegiance, and he could rightly be condemned without judgement to die even the most shameful of deaths.'[45]

It was perhaps only when John's later crimes started adding up, that Arthur's demise was added to the list. However, at the time, Arthur's death was considered, for the most part, justified.

By the summer of 1203 King Philip was again on the offensive, besieging Château Gaillard, the castle that had been the pride of Richard the Lionheart, in August. After failing to break the siege with both land and water-borne troops, John sailed for England on 5 December, leaving the magnificent castle to its fate. According to Ralph of Coggeshall:

'The constable of Chester was in the castle with many famous knights and sergeants, who for a long time strenuously held the castle against the force of the whole army of the French king. But when they urgently needed food supplies they could resist the enemy no longer. King John, indeed, was unwilling to send troops to the besieged because he always feared the treachery of his men, and in the winter in the month of December he crossed to England leaving all the Normans in great worry and fear.'[46]

Back on English soil John 'truly oppressed England with many demands for money, hoping to raise a great army and exterminate the forces of King Philip.'[47] Château Gaillard fell on 6 March 1204. During Lent, John sent a delegation to Philip to negotiate for peace, including William Marshal and the Archbishop of Canterbury. Philip, however, probably suspecting – or knowing – that Arthur was dead, made the young duke of Brittany's release a condition of any peace settlement: 'For if Arthur was now discovered to be dead, Philip hoped to marry his sister and thus to gain all her continental possessions. King Philip was unwilling to make peace because he was confident that he would soon possess all the lands of the English king.'[48] With John still childless, Arthur's sister was the king of England's heir. Arthur's older sister, Eleanor of Brittany, was in John's custody, but if Philip could marry Arthur's younger sister, Alix of Thouars, there was a chance he could have it all.

The fall of Château Gaillard had a devastating effect on morale and was the start of a domino-effect of Norman towns opening their gates to Philip, with Rouen capitulating on 24 June 1204. Eleanor of Aquitaine's death on 1 April 1204 had a similar effect on Poitou, with many Poitevin towns and lords now transferring their homage to Philip; the French king entered Poitiers in triumph in August 1204. To add to John's woes, his brother-in-law Alfonso VIII, King of Castile, invaded Gascony claiming Henry II had promised it as the dowry of his wife, John's sister Eleanor, on her mother's death.[49] By the end of 1204 John's continental possessions amounted to the ports of the west coast of France, from Bayonne to La Rochelle, and the fortresses of Chinon and Loches.[50] Matters were not improved in 1205 when John attempted to mount an expedition to the continent and recover his losses; he was thwarted by the English barons, whose reluctance to follow him led to the campaign being abandoned. Loches and Chinon surrendered to the French, leaving only the main Gascon towns holding out. Some success was achieved in that the Channel Islands were recovered, and Niort in Poitou. In 1206, John landed at La Rochelle, recovered Saintonge and consolidated his hold on his wife Isabelle's county of Angoulême, her father having died in 1202. He also managed to drive the last remaining Castilians from Gascony. On hearing that John was sailing with an army, Philip had moved north to defend Normandy, but now headed south, forcing John to abandon his advance on Anjou. A two-year truce was agreed in October, but the great continental possessions of the Angevin kings were now, effectively, lost forever, with John retaining only Gascony and south-western Poitou out of an empire that had once controlled half of France.[51]

The loss of Normandy and his vast continental empire meant that John could concentrate his energies on England, in a way that no king had done since the time of the Norman Conquest of 1066. The next five years saw John raising revenue from taxes and keeping a heavy hand on the administration of the country. His efforts to recover debts and aggressive form of government would see him alienating many of his barons and push the country, inexorably, towards the political crisis that would culminate in Magna Carta. In 1207 he levied a thirteenth, a tax at the rate of 1 shilling raising £57,425, more than twice the usual annual revenue. In the same year he moved against the earl of Leicester, depriving him of his lands for non-payment of debt. In 1208 the lands of William de Braose, once high in royal favour, were confiscated, ostensibly for non-payment of debts. In 1210 a tallage on the Jews raised 66,000 marks; the tallage became increasingly unpopular even outside the Jewish community, as John put pressure on those who were indebted to the Jews to pay back what they owed, so that he could be paid. Annual royal revenues rose dramatically after 1209, so that by 1212 it is estimated that John had 200,000 marks in coin stored in his treasuries at Bristol, Corfe and elsewhere.[52]

The first crisis following the loss of Normandy was John's dispute with the pope, Innocent III. As with most rulers of the era, John wanted to have control of church appointments, especially of senior bishops and archbishops. In England, especially, the king's authority over the church was strong. In 1205 John had arranged the election of Peter des Roches as bishop of Winchester. Following the death of Hubert Walter, Archbishop of Canterbury, the pope annulled the election of John de Gray, bishop of Norwich and John's candidate as his replacement, as being uncanonical. In his stead, in July 1205, the monks at Canterbury elected the pope's candidate, Stephen Langton, as their new archbishop. The pope had sanctioned the election and written to John for his approval. John, however, refused to give his consent. Langton's years in Paris making him unacceptable to the king. Nevertheless, Langton was consecrated archbishop in Rome in June 1207 and on 15 July, John expelled the monks from Canterbury. This act saw an exodus to the Continent of many senior church leaders:

'The bishop of London, the bishop of Ely, the bishop of Hereford, the bishop of Chester, the archbishop of York, who was the king's own brother, and numerous others, rich as well as poor, left England unable to bear the king's tyranny. There was not one man in the land who could oppose his will...Only the bishop of Winchester remained in the king's favour.'[53]

Relations with the pope and the church deteriorated further and on 24 March 1208 England was placed under interdict, the church's greatest weapon:

'...divine services were suspended throughout England. Great sorrow and anxiety spread throughout the country. Neither Good Friday nor Easter Sunday could be celebrated, but an unheard-of silence was imposed on all the clergy and monks by laymen. The bodies of the dead, whether of the ordinary folk or the religious, could not be buried in consecrated cemeteries, but only in vile and profane places.'[54]

John ordered the seizure of all clerical property in retribution and ordered the arrests of priests' and clerks' mistresses – though they were soon allowed to buy their freedom. John was worried that the election, against his wishes, of Langton would set a precedent for future clerical appointments, a stumbling block that would not be overcome in negotiations with the pope; neither would John's refusal to admit liability and pay compensation. As a consequence, in November 1209, Innocent III excommunicated the king of England. All the bishops of England save Peter des Roches, who stayed in England, and John de Gray, who was despatched to Ireland to act as justiciar, left for exile, leaving seven bishoprics and seventeen abbacies vacant.[55] Although negotiations between John and the papacy continued for a while, they were half-hearted and had broken off altogether by 1211, John being less concerned with his excommunication against the revenues he was receiving from the church lands now under his control.

In Lincoln, Gerard de Camville had been John's sheriff there since the king's accession. In 1205, when John was waiting for the arrival of his barons for a great council at Northampton, the king asked Reginald of Cornhill, custodian of the vacant sees of Canterbury and Winchester, to send him a copy of *Romanicum Historiae Anglie*, a history of England, and he also wrote to Gerard de Camville. He requested that the sheriff of Lincolnshire send him fifteen tuns of wine, 'with which no doubt he intended to regale his barons while he read them stirring extracts from the book about their ancestors' valiant deeds in Normandy.'[56] Later in the same year, Gerard de Camville was removed from the office of sheriff 'for inefficiency', according to Irene Gladwin.[57] He was eventually replaced by Thomas Moulton, who offered King John 500 marks and a yearly increment of 300 marks to farm Lincolnshire for seven years.[58] Gerard and Nicholaa retained custody of Lincoln Castle, however, and Gerard was still an active officer of the county. From 1208 to 1209 Gerard served as itinerant justice for Lincolnshire and Cambridgeshire and in 1208, during the interdict imposed by the pope, Gerard supervised the collection of the revenues for the diocese of Lincoln.[59]

While Gerard de Camville held the constableship of Lincoln Castle by the right of his wife, Nicholaa de la Haye, there are instances in the historical record whereby other men were identified in charters as constables and seneschals of the castle. Roger de Campville was named as constable in around 1210 and William de Newton signed as constable between 1215 and 21; around 1250 it would be William de Engleby, despite the constableship being in the hands of the earl of Salisbury at that point.[60] As a Reginald de Newton and Joselin de Engleby both appear among the knights of Richard de la Haye in his *Carta* of 1166, it can be safely assumed that these men, and others, were tenants of the de la Hayes and acted as deputies at the castle on behalf of the hereditary constables.

Outside Lincoln, the situation in England was getting worse. Relations with the other countries in the British Isles were also deteriorating as the reign progressed. In 1209 John, having heard of marriage negotiations between Scotland and France, marched on Scotland. William the Lion, King of Scots was ill and in order to avoid war, was forced to agree to the humiliating Treaty of Norham, in which he promised to pay John 15,000 marks to ensure the king of England's good will. He also agreed to hand over thirteen hostages and his two eldest daughters, for John to arrange their marriages. To be fair to John, he did indeed extend his good will to Scotland when King William was challenged by a rival to his throne, Guthred Macwilliam, in 1211. John knighted King William's son, Alexander, in London before sending him north with a band of soldiers from Brabançon and with them, Alexander 'captured Guthred, called MacWilliam, the leader of the rebels, and hanged him.'[61]

Campaigns in Wales in 1208, and again in 1211, and in Ireland in 1209–10 saw some successes for John but alienated more barons. Ralph of Coggeshall summed up the successes and failures of John's reign at this point; 'And many said that Merlin's prophecy had come about saying. "The sixth shall pull down the walls of Ireland" and "his beginning shall succumb to his own unstable nature." William I, William II, Henry I, Henry II, afterwards Richard. The sixth is John who acquired Ireland and in all other things was vain and useless.'[62] It seems King Stephen's reign is conveniently forgotten in order to make the prophecy work. John's pursuit and eventual destruction of William de Braose, first in Wales and then in Ireland, demonstrated the extent of John's animosity towards his enemies and their families. What was to stop him going against any one of his barons in the same relentless manner? He successfully invaded Gwynedd in 1211, forcing its prince, his son-in-law, Llywelyn ap Iorwerth, to surrender the whole of Gwynedd east of Conwy and to promise that all his lands would revert to King John, should he die without issue by his wife Joan, John's illegitimate daughter.[63] In Ireland, John's whirlwind nine-week campaign in 1210 saw Walter and Hugh de Lacy driven out of Meath and Ulster, the introduction of English laws and currency and an extension of English control. John had little interest in the native Irish lords and kings, and he left Ireland on less-than-friendly terms with the most prominent of Ireland's kings, Cathal Croibhdhearg and Aodh Ō Nēill. Ō Nēill's refusal to hand over hostages led to the Inisfallen annalist's assessment that 'The king of England came to Ireland and accomplished little.'[64] However, on the whole, he left Ireland under greater control of the English government and its justiciar, John de Gray, continued to make some gains, despite being unable to subjugate Aodh Ō Nēill.

John's successes in Scotland, Wales and Ireland were without precedent, as the Barnwell chronicler noted, there was 'no one in Ireland, Scotland and Wales who did not obey his nod – something which, as is well-known, none of his predecessors had achieved.'[65] However, John's successes so close to home gave him an optimism that was to lead to the greatest crisis of his reign and, eventually, to Magna Carta. In 1212, John turned his sights to the Continent, and he set about rebuilding the coalition that had dissolved in 1200, supported by Rainauld, Count of Boulogne and German

Emperor Otto IV. In July, plans were well in hand and a combined land and naval force was mustering at Portsmouth when they had to be diverted to Chester to deal with another Welsh revolt, united behind Llywelyn ap Iorwerth. In retaliation for the revolt, on 14 August, John hanged twenty-eight Welsh hostages at Nottingham. Although he would have considered the lives of the hostages forfeit, given they were held to guarantee the good behaviour of the Welsh, it is considered one of the cruellest acts of his reign, and one for which he has been judged harshly.

Whilst at Nottingham, John learned of a plot against his life and the two magnates held responsible, Robert Fitzwalter and Eustace de Vescy, fled to France and Scotland, respectively. Eustace de Vescy is said to have had a personal grudge against John as he had tried to seduce de Vescy's wife. The story goes that 'the baron had cunningly managed to smuggle a prostitute into the king's bedchamber instead. The next day John boasted to de Vesci how good the night had been. But the baron immediately confessed to the deception. He had to flee for his life.'[66] De Vescy was married to an illegitimate sister of the king of Scots and so fled north to Scotland. Another conspirator, Geoffrey of Norwich, an official of the Exchequer, was apprehended and died in prison. According to the Barnwell Chronicler, this was the catalyst of John's increasing paranoia; from this point on, he trusted no one and had an armed bodyguard accompany him everywhere he went:

> 'The King John's heart was troubled, since it was being said, without authority, that rumours had been heard that the barons who had gathered together were conspiring against him, and that in many ears there were tales of letters absolving the barons from John's allegiance. It was said that another king should be elected in his place and that John should be expelled from the kingdom...the king began to have misgivings and would go nowhere without either being armed or accompanied by a great force of armed men. Having taken captive some who seemed to be too intimate with the rebels, he quickly seized the castles of the earls and barons, so that there was unrest for some time.'[67]

John took hostages and castles from those barons he suspected of disloyalty, being especially thorough in the north. Prophecies, notably by

Peter of Wakefield, were predicting John's downfall, preaching 'that King John's reign would not last beyond the next Ascension Day, because it had been revealed to him that King John would reign for fourteen years, and that those things which had begun during those fourteen years would reach a happy conclusion.'[68] According to the Barnwell annalist, Peter's prophecies were added to and distorted in their retelling, and 'Every day false words of the common people were added to his falsehoods.'[69]

Peter was arrested and imprisoned; he and his son were hanged on 27 May 1213, four days after Ascension Day and the anniversary of John's accession. In a bid to increase his popularity across the social spectrum, and especially in the north, John chose this time to tackle the abuses of sheriffs and forest officials. He ordered forest officials to only exact the same amounts as they had under his father and repealed new exactions that had been imposed in the ports. Moreover, he reopened negotiations with Innocent III in November 1212. In a demonstration of his willingness to compromise, John 'exacted from all the prelates of the Church a confirmation of all that he had taken from them…so that in this way they would greatly modify their claims concerning what he had taken away.'[70]

By 1213 John was planning a new Continental expedition and negotiating with Toulouse and Aragon to open a southern front against King Philip of France. His plans were forestalled, however, when Philip himself announced in April that he was planning to invade England, apparently with encouragement from the pope. John's position was precarious, to say the least, the loyalty of his barons only maintained by a combination of bribery and intimidation. In response to Philip's announcement, the army was gathered with John at Dover, with his fleet just off shore. As a consequence, according to the Barnwell annalist, the majority of John's barons were present to witness John's surrender of the kingdom to Rome, on 15 May 1213, promising to pay 1,000 marks a year to Rome and swearing 'liege homage and fealty to Pope Innocent III and to his successors'.[71] Although this was a humiliation for John, his hold on his country and people was precarious and he had little choice but to submit to the church; it has been seen as 'a master stroke of diplomacy'.[72]

Chapter Eight

# The Magna Carta Crisis

England was now a papal fief, but John was still excommunicate and on 1 July he sent a delegation to Stephen Langton on the continent, headed by the archbishop of Dublin and the bishop of Norwich, urging the archbishop of Canterbury and his fellow exiles to return to England as quickly as possible. On 20 July, he met the former exiles at Winchester; they led the king to the doors of Winchester Cathedral where, in front of a host of nobles, clergy and commoners, he was absolved. The king swore an oath that he 'would henceforth love and defend the Church and renew the good laws of his ancestors.'[1] The interdict on England would finally be lifted on 2 July 1214, six years, three months and sixteen days after it was imposed.[2] Despite the fact compensation payments would take another year to settle, John's submission to the pope meant that Innocent was now a staunch defender of the king. However, it also meant that John's enemies, including Robert Fitzwalter and Eustace de Vescy, were now able to return from exile, alongside the abbots and clerics.

King Philip's fleet was destroyed by John's half-brother, William Longespée, Earl of Salisbury, on 30 May 1213 at Damme and in June John ordered his army to sail for Poitou. However, the magnates refused, with the northern barons – 'the northerners' – led by Eustace de Vescy, claiming that their conditions of tenure did not require them to serve in Poitou. Stephen Langton, now restored to his see at Canterbury, thwarted John's attempts to punish the rebels and when the king did finally sail for Poitou in 1214, several barons were absent, including Robert Fitzwalter, Eustace de Vescy and Geoffrey de Mandeville, the soon-to-be husband of John's first wife, Isabella of Gloucester. A two-pronged attack saw John landing at La Rochelle, while Longespée landed in Flanders, joining Otto of Germany, Rainauld of Boulogne and Count Ferrand of Flanders. The idea was to force Philip to divide his forces.

John sought a reconciliation with the Lusignans, agreeing to grant them Saintes and Oléron and to marry his daughter Joan to Hugh X de Lusignan, the son of Hugh IX de Lusignan, who had been betrothed to John's wife, Isabelle d'Angoulême. A similar peace offering, of the earldom of Richmond, to Pierre, Duke of Brittany, was less well received and the duke remained aloof. John's campaign was successful at first, with him entering Angers unopposed before he laid siege to Roche-au-Moine. However, he was forced to retreat on 2 July, with the approach of the army of Prince Louis of France and the refusal of the Poitevins to fight by his side. Although he was able to keep his own army intact, John's fate was sealed on 27 July when Longespée and the allies faced Philip at the battle of Bouvines and were decisively defeated. John's nephew, Otto IV managed to escape, but William Longespée was captured and taken to Paris, along with the counts of Flanders and Boulogne.

With the threat in the north neutralised, Philip was now able to join his army to that of his son, Prince Louis, and challenge John in the south. John had no choice but to seek peace and a five-year truce was agreed on 13 October, with Ralph of Coggeshall reporting rumours that it had cost John 60,000 marks.[3] At home, John's policy of reform of the sheriffs and forest officials in 1212–13 had resulted in a significant reduction in royal revenue, and the military campaign drained John's treasury. He was no longer a wealthy king. In October 1214 John returned to England, his defeat by the French at the battle of Bouvines had ended the king's hopes of regaining the lost empire. After his return home, baronial opposition to John now gathered pace. The refusal to pay scutage of 3 marks on the knights' fee demonstrating a coordinated effort by the magnates, rather than the individual disobedience that had been seen earlier in the reign. The barons' objections to John were almost beyond number. He had failed to face the French and had lost not only his family's continental possessions, but also those of his barons. Few had forgotten his treachery against his brother in trying to take the throne whilst Richard was on crusade.

Added to these catastrophes was the character and personality of John himself. By nature, John was paranoid, secretive and distrustful and his cruelty was widely known. He was accused of killing his nephew and rival claimant to the English throne; he had hanged twenty-eight Welsh hostages (sons of rebel chieftains); and he had hounded William de Braose and his family all the way to Ireland and back. De Braose's wife and son died in one of John's prisons, starved to death, whether by John's order or not is immaterial – he was responsible. *The History of William Marshal*, a biography of the great knight and statesman, claimed that John treated his prisoners harshly and with such indignity that it was a disgrace to all involved.[4] His barons even complained that he forced himself on their wives and daughters. With such military losses, accusations and seemingly acute character flaws stacked against him, it is no wonder England's king faced opposition by many of the most powerful in his realm.

In January 1215, in the midst of the rising political crisis in England, Gerard de Camville died, leaving Nicholaa a widow for the second time. Gerard died before 15 January 1215, when his son Richard secured possession of Gerard's property at Middleton Stoney.[5] Nicholaa was probably now in her late-fifties or early-sixties and was past child-bearing age. This gave her more freedom to decide her own future, as she was, to put it bluntly, a less attractive marriage prospect. Although she still held Lincoln Castle as part of her inheritance and, rather than handing the duties of castellan on to her son, Richard, who must have been in his mid-twenties by now, but had already established himself in the west Midlands, administering his inheritance from his father and the estates of his wife, Eustachia Basset. Nicholaa took on the duties herself. She secured her inheritance as a *femme sole*, meaning she had independent economic and legal status. She could now conduct business herself and run her own estates.[6] Her loyalty to John probably helped her to retain her lands and position, with Nicholaa rendering account for her bailiwick and appearing regularly in the records of the chancery and exchequer and following government orders. Although she received just three royal letters in 1215, between January 1216 and John's death in October of the same year, when Lincoln was at the heart of the struggle against the rebels, Nicholaa was the recipient of, or concern of, no less than twenty-eight royal letters, close and patent.[7] And she was now in command of Lincoln Castle, at a time when tensions were rising throughout the country.

John's acceptance of Nicholaa as constable of Lincoln Castle is demonstrated that same year, when a writ in the Close Rolls ordered Phillip Marc to provide Nicholaa de la Haye with six 'balistae ad strumum' and two 'balistae ad turnum' to fortify the castle. The former balistae, or crossbows, would have been provided with a stirrup in order to tension them for firing while the latter would have been worked by a winch.[8]

In January 1215 John arranged to meet with his challengers at the Temple in London, to hear their demands, and it was agreed that they would reconvene at Northampton on 26 April to hear the king's response. The disaffected barons demanded reform and the confirmation of the coronation charter of King Henry I, in which the king promised; 'Know that by the mercy of God and by the common counsel of the barons of England I have been crowned king of this realm. And because the kingdom has been oppressed by unjust exactions, being moved by reverence towards God and by the love I bear you all, I make free the Church of God…I abolish all the evil customs by which the kingdom of England has been unjustly oppressed.'[9] Although many of the clauses of this charter, also referred to as the Charter of Liberties, were now outdated, several still resonated with the barons, including that a baron's widow would not be married without her consent, that an heiress would not be married without the consent of her relatives and that, on the death of a baron, his heir would only pay a relief that was 'just and lawful'.[10] Whilst John was ruminating on these demands, both sides were preparing for war. John borrowed from the Templars to pay his mercenaries and on 4 March he took the cross. This latter move was seen as being highly cynical and no one seems to have believed that John would actually go on crusade. His purpose for doing so was political: a crusader's lands and properties were protected by the church and this action firmly identified the king's opponents as the 'bad guys'.

John failed to appear at Northampton. He did, however, send messages to the rebels. According to the Barnwell annalist the king 'tried to win them back through many emissaries, and there was much discussion amongst them, the archbishop, bishops and other barons acting as intermediaries, the king himself staying at Oxford.'[11] On 5 May the rebels formally renounced their fealty. John retained the support of some magnates, such as William Marshal and William de Warenne, but the majority were now standing against him. As was London, which opened its gates to the rebels on 17 May, despite John's granting the city the right to elect its mayor only eight days before. In the Welsh Marches the Braose family had allied with Llywelyn ap Iorwerth and had taken Shrewsbury. The rebels were ready to fight. After occupying London, they made one final attempt to prevent war, presenting the king with a list of their demands.

John had no choice but to make concessions and on 10 June agreed to further discussions of the rebels' terms. Following these negotiations, a long, detailed document was produced, dealing with particular grievances of the time and with injustices in general. It touched on the whole system of royal government. And it was granted to 'all free men of the realm and their heirs forever'.[12] Of its sixty-three clauses (see Appendix A) some terms were asking for immediate remedies, such as the removal of corrupt administrators and the sending home of foreign mercenaries. The clause stating that fighting outside of the kingdom could not be imposed by the king was a reaction to John's recent attempts to force his English barons to help him recover his Continental domains. Others had long-term aims. The document sought to guarantee the privileges of the church and the City of London. Restrictions were placed on the powers of regional officials, such as sheriffs, to prevent abuses. The royal court was fixed at Westminster, for justice to be obtainable by all, and royal judges were to visit each county regularly. Taxes could no longer be levied without the consent of the church and the barons.

Further clauses included the fixing of inheritance charges and protection from exploitation for underage heirs; the king was to take only what was reasonable from an estate (although 'reasonable' remained undefined). From henceforth a widow was to be free to choose whether or not to remarry and her marriage portion (dowry) would be made available to her immediately on her husband's death. Another clause sought to prevent the seizure of land from Jews and the king's debtors. Magna Carta even went so far as to regulate weights and measures. It also reduced the size of the king's forests and limited the powers of forest justices. Although most of the sixty-three clauses of Magna Carta are now defunct, three still remain as major tenets of British law, including 'to no one will we sell; to no one will we deny or delay right or justice.' That no person would be imprisoned, outlawed or deprived of his lands except by judgement of his peers and the law of the land has remained the cornerstone of the English legal system ever since.

Magna Carta was sealed at Runnymede, Berkshire, on 15 June 1215. John ordered that the charter be circulated around the towns and villages, throughout the realm. As a peace agreement between the king and his rebellious barons, however, it failed miserably. By July John was appealing to the pope for help. Pope Innocent III's response arrived in England in September. The treaty was declared null and void. According to Innocent, Magna Carta was:

> '...not only shameful and base but also illegal and unjust. We refuse to overlook such shameless presumption which dishonours the Apostolic See, injures the king's right, shames the English nation, and endangers the crusade. Since the whole crusade would be undermined if concessions of this sort were extorted from a great prince who had taken the cross, we, on behalf of Almighty God, Father, Son and Holy Ghost, and by the authority of Saints Peter and Paul His apostles, utterly reject and condemn this settlement. Under threat of excommunication we order that the king should not dare to observe and the barons and their associates should not insist on it being observed. The charter with all its undertakings and guarantees we declare to be null and void of all validity for ever.'[13]

The letter was accompanied by more papal letters, excommunicating the leading rebels, including nine barons and the Londoners. However, by the time the letters arrived in England, the dispute had already erupted into the Barons' War. John laid siege to Rochester Castle with his mercenaries and the castle surrendered on 30 November, after seven weeks. Deciding they could no longer deal with John's perfidy, the rebel barons had invited the King of France, Philip II, to claim the throne. Philip's son and heir, the future Louis VIII, accepted the offer. He was married to Blanche of Castile, the daughter of John's older sister, Eleanor (Queen Leonor of Castile), so he could, theoretically, claim the throne for his wife. It was enough to give him legitimate justification to take his chance on England. Louis sent an advanced guard to aid the rebels, which arrived in December 1215. Louis himself would arrive in the spring of 1216. He landed on the south coast and marched for London, where he was proclaimed King of England on 2 June 1216. In the meantime, while waiting for the French to arrive in force, the rebels and their allies were not inactive. Following a judgement in his favour from the Twenty-Five barons appointed to oversee the enforcement of Magna Carta, Alexander II, King of Scots, was awarded Northumberland, Cumberland and Westmorland and received the homage of the Northerners. In Wales, eleven Welsh princes united under Llywelyn ap Iorwerth, establishing him as *de facto* prince of Wales and in three weeks they captured seven castles, including Cardigan and Carmarthen.

In December 1215 John headed north and chased the Yorkshire rebels all the way to Scotland, where he captured Berwick on 13 January 1216. He then raided the Scottish Lowlands and set fire to Berwick before turning back south and heading for East Anglia in March 1216. The duties and responsibilities that John gave to Nicholaa demonstrate the king's continuing confidence in her abilities. Having been entrusted with a large amount of money, in April 1216, John wrote to her from Windsor, with an order for its release: 'The king to Nicholaa de la Haye etc. We command that you cause to be released forthwith to Ralph Ridell, our Sheriff of Lincoln, the money which we sent to be held by him and which you have in your keeping, as the said sheriff should hand over that money to our trusty Philip Marc to do our pleasure, as we have so ordered him.'[14] However, apparently Nicholaa had not acted on this order as promptly as John would have liked, and he sent a reminder to Lincoln when he was at Odiham on 16 April, with some more specifics about the money: 'Money to be paid. The king to Nicholaa de la Haye etc. We command that you send without delay to Philip Marc the sixty-two pounds which Ralph Ridell, our sheriff of Lincoln, has sent to you to enable our orders to be carried out.'[15] The king was obviously keen to gather as much money together as he could and have the money transfer go ahead as quickly as possible, as he also wrote to his sheriff at Lincoln:

> 'The king to Ralph Ridell, Sheriff of Lincoln, etc. We command that you send without delay to Philip Marc at Nottingham all the money which you have in your possession from the fines made with us when we were in your territory, any from fines made afterwards or from other acquisitions, and also from all other revenues of your county, to enable our orders to be carried out.'[16]

Nicholaa de la Haye is often featured in John's daily business and on 4 February he wrote to her and the sheriff of Lincoln with an order to hand over the lands of someone named de Kyme – probably Simon. Simon de Kyme was a rebel, who was trying to raise the ransom for his son Philip. He himself would be captured by Royalist forces in 1217 at the Battle of Lincoln, thus adding his own ransom to his rising debts to the crown:

'Nicholaa de la Haye is commanded that she cause Geoffrey de Neville, Chamberlain of the lord king, to have possession of the land that was [...] de Kyme's in her Bailiwick, which the lord king has granted to him. At Guisborough, the fourth day of February. The same is commanded of the sheriff of Lincoln. Witness the same in the same place.'[17]

In the same month, another order was made which touched Nicholaa on a more personal level. William Longespée, Earl of Salisbury, was given the right of marriage of Nicholaa's granddaughter by her son Richard, Idonea. Longespée intended to marry Idonea to his son, William II Longespée. Both children were very young at this point, with Idonea being, possibly, no older than eight, the youngest age that a betrothal was sanctioned by the church, though she could not be married until the age of twelve. John ordered:

'The Sheriffs of Oxford and of Berkshire are commanded that they cause William, Earl of Salisbury, to have the right of marriage of the daughter of Richard de Camville, born of Eustacia, who was the daughter of Gilbert Basset and wife of the said Richard, for William his first-born son by his wife Ela, Countess of Salisbury, with all the inheritance belonging to the said Richard's daughter from her mother in their Bailiwicks. Witness myself, at Reigate, the twenty-second day of April.'[18]

This order may be the source of Nicholaa's later wranglings with Salisbury, given that it appears to pass all of Idonea's inheritance from her mother into the custody of Longespée. Perhaps Longespée took this order to mean all of Idonea's inheritance, regardless of the fact Nicholaa was still very much alive at this time. Such an order also suggests that Richard de Camville may already have been deceased, despite most mentions of him have him dying in the first quarter of 1217. Alternatively, the order does not mention Richard's inheritance from his father, which would suggest that Richard was still alive, but no longer had custody of his daughter. Evidence certainly exists to suggest that Richard lived to at least 1218. The more likely explanation, therefore, is that Richard had joined the rebels. Richard de Camville certainly appears to have had a far less cordial relationship with King John than had his father, Gerard. In December 1215 his castle of Middleton was committed to the keeping of Engelard de Cigogné, one of the king's most reviled, if also most trusted, servants, and in the following May a royal order was issued for its destruction. In addition, his daughter and heir, Idonea, was in royal custody at Corfe Castle; her wardship was then sold to William Longespée, along with the lands she had inherited from her mother, Eustachia. Richard's lands would not have been included in the grant as they would have been forfeit to the crown. Given that the child had already lost her mother, this may have been a sensible arrangement and allowed her to be raised alongside her future husband.

The order was written on 22 February 1216 and on 23 February, John arrived in Lincoln, to make an inspection of the castle defences, having crossed the River Trent at Kinnard Ferry (now Owston Ferry). The crossing went well, and the King and his mounted escort made good speed from Kinnard ahead of the main column. He and his senior men were perhaps to be wined and dined by Nicholaa de la Haye at the castle that night. And maybe John informed Nicholaa of the arrangements regarding her granddaughter, though I suspect that Nicholaa had been involved in the decision from early on. The rebel, Simon de Kyme, again features in John's orders, or, more particularly, Kyme's hunting birds: 'The bearers of the lord King's letters patent travelling for the two goshawks which were Simon de Kyme's have letters of conduct in their coming to the lord King with those goshawks. Witness the King, at Lincoln, the twenty-third day of February, in the seventeenth year of the lord King's reign.'[19]

Having dealt with family matters, John's campaigning continued apace. While John appears to have held the initiative with his military successes, and he was able to win some rebels over to his side, the leaders remained firmly against him. His failure to take London and prevent the landing of Prince Louis on the Isle of Thanet on 14 May 1216, was a major setback. John spent the summer campaigning in the west of England as Louis advanced through Kent and took Canterbury before moving onto Winchester. The French prince was hailed as King of England in London in June of 1216. He then proceeded to extend his influence throughout the country. John seems to have been undecided as to how to act; he sent his oldest son Henry to safety at Devizes Castle in Wiltshire. Dover Castle, under the command of Hubert de Burgh, held out against the French and rebel forces, as did Windsor and Lincoln.

By autumn 1216, John was at his lowest point as the earls of Arundel, Warenne and Salisbury (John's own brother) submitted to Louis. Alexander II of Scotland met the French prince at Canterbury and paid him homage for the lands he held from the English crown. Two-thirds of his magnates had abandoned John, as had one-third of his household knights.[21]

Strategically placed in the centre of the country, Lincoln was a target for the rebel barons and their French allies. The northern barons and a party of French troops, led by Gilbert de Gant and the king of Scots, attacked Lincoln taking the city and laying siege to the castle. A tax was laid on the whole of Lindsey and in August, Gant received reinforcements from the north.[22] However, the northern barons 'were defeated in their attempts to take Lincoln. A certain lady called Nicholaa, who was the custodian's wife, freed herself from this siege with a money payment.'[23] Essentially, the castle held out and Nicholaa purchased a truce from the northern barons, who lifted the siege, but remained in control of the city. On 4 September, John wrote a letter in support of Nicholaa and her efforts to bring the rebels back into the king's peace:

'...the King to all those who may look upon these letters, greetings. Know that we have taken into our grace and favour all those of the county of Lincoln who wish to return to our fealty and our service by the hand of our well-beloved Nicholaa de la Haye and our trusty Robert de Gaugy [constable of Newark]; and, indeed, we gratefully welcome the fine which those who shall return to our fealty and our service have made with the said Nicholaa and Robert for having our peace. And in testimony hereof we have hereto made for them these our letters patent. Witness myself, at Oxford, the fourth day of September, in the eighteenth year of our reign.'[24]

John was not so magnanimous, however, with those who had not returned to his fealty. A forced march from Rockingham saw John arriving back in Lincoln on 22 September 1216, sending the rebellious army fleeing north.[25] The king chased the rebels as they retreated into the marshy Isle of Axholme in North Lincolnshire. Their Scottish allies retreated north on the eastern bank of the River Trent, thus evading the king's forces, who were concentrated on the western bank. John advanced beyond Lincoln, devastating the Isle 'with fire and sword'.

Matthew Paris depicts John as full of vengeful anger – and possibly frustration. Burning his way through Oundle and the manors of the Abbey of Peterborough, 'John, Savary de Mauleon "and their nefarious accomplices perpetrated unheard of wickedness". According to Paris, John ordered Savary to torch Crowland Abbey and its village while the King watched on. Savary did not carry out the order directly; instead he accepted from the fearful monks a sum of money as protection against destruction and brought this to the King. Such protection offerings, especially from monasteries, was a normal feature of the war, but John was enraged and hurled violent invective at his captain. He then picked up a torch and personally set alight the harvest fields, Paris depicting an apocalyptic figure of the King running through the flames and black smoke like a deranged demon. There may well have been method in John's madness, for Gilbert de Gant and his men had the fear of God put into them: leaving Lincoln in a hurry, they "fled before his face, dreading his presence as if it were lightning".[26]

King John was staying at Scotter, just north of Gainsborough, on 26 September, from where he issued an order benefiting Ralph de la Haye, Nicholaa's cousin. The King sent an order to Philip de Ulcote 'that you cause Ralph de Haye to have full seisin of all the land which was John the Sheriff's, who is with our enemies, since we have granted it to him to be in his custody for so long as it may please us. Witness myself, at Scotter, the twenty-sixth day of September.'[27] By 28 September, King John was back in Lincoln, and he stayed there for at least two nights. As it was Michaelmas, the general court leet was held and the bailiffs appointed.[28]

It may have been at this visit, or at the king's earlier visit to Lincoln in February, that the dramatic scenes related in the Hundred Rolls, commissioned by Edward I, were played out. Nicholaa is said to have met the king at the eastern gate of the castle. A widow for the last year, she offered the keys of the castle to the king:

'And once it happened that after the war King John came to Lincoln and the said Lady Nicholaa went out of the eastern gate of the castle carrying the keys of the castle in her hand and met the king and offered the keys to him as her lord and said she was a woman of great age and was unable to bear such fatigue any longer and he besought her saying, "My beloved Nicholaa, I will that you keep the castle as hitherto until I shall order otherwise." And she retained it as long as King John lived and after his decease she still kept it under King Henry, father of the king that now is'[29]

When Nicholaa spoke of her 'great age' she was not exaggerating. She was probably approaching sixty years of age at the time, a good age for anyone in those days, but John still had great confidence in her. Whether Nicholaa ever intended to resign Lincoln Castle at this point is open to debate. It is just as likely that the event was orchestrated as a public demonstration of John's continuing trust in Nicholaa's ability to hold and command the royal stronghold. During the visit, the business of government proceeded apace, with John sending out orders throughout the realm. One such order was sent to Nicholaa herself, regarding redistribution of land that had belonged to the Gant family, a prominent Lincolnshire family who were now among the rebels:

'The King to Nicholaa de Haye, greetings. Know that we have granted to our trusty and well-beloved Philip de Albini the manor of Teueneby with all its appurtenances, the which was Maurice de Gant's, who is our enemy. We have also restored to the said Philip as his right the manor of Engleby with all its appurtenances. We therefore command that you cause the said Philip to have full seisin of the aforesaid lands forthwith. Witness myself, at Lincoln, the twenty-eighth day of September.'[30]

It was as John was campaigning in the south of Lindsey (Lincolnshire) that 'grim misfortune struck him, for it was in those parts that the grievous sickness of which he died took hold, gripping him so dreadfully that he was incapable of moving.'[31] Making his way south, just two weeks after leaving Lincoln, the king's baggage train was lost as he crossed the Wash estuary and within a few more days John was desperately ill. John was at Lynn when, on the evening of 9 October, he suffered an attack of dysentery. His health deteriorated as he made his way west until he reached Newark on 16 October, from where 'he could go no further and that was that.'[32] He died there on the night of 18–19 October 1216 and was buried at Worcester Cathedral, 'not because he had asked to be buried there but because that place at that time seemed a safe one where his supporters could gather to deliberate on what was to be done next.'[33]

In the hours before his death John appointed Nicholaa de la Haye as sheriff of Lincolnshire, alongside Philip Marc, sheriff of Nottingham:

> 'The King to the archbishops, bishops, earls, barons, knights, freeholders and others of the county of Lincoln etc...Know that we have granted to our trusty and well-beloved, the lady Nicholaa de Haye and Philip Marc, the county of Lincoln with all its appurtenances, to be in their custody for so long as it may please us. We therefore command that you do heed and obey the said Nicholaa and Philip in all things as the bailiffs of the said county. And in testimony etc... Witness myself, at Newark, the eighteenth day of October, in the eighteenth year of our reign.'[34]

Nicholaa's son Richard was now a grown man, by this time, and able to inherit the position his father had held, but appears to have taken the side of the rebels, or may have been already ailing, given that he died in March the next year. Either way, he was not in a position to replace his mother as castellan or sheriff.[35] Philip Marc, who was also sheriff of Nottingham, seems to have disappeared from the Lincolnshire records shortly after. He was later replaced by Geoffrey de Serland, who was appointed as deputy 'under our beloved lady Nicholaa de la Haye'.[36] It was a very unusual move in a male-dominated world, and unprecedented. It was an acknowledgement of Nicholaa's own abilities, and of the esteem in which she was held by the king. It may also have been a testament to the desperate situation that John found himself in, that there were so few people he could trust to take on the role. Nicholaa was the first ever woman to be appointed sheriff in any English county. There was an incidence in Norfolk, with Margaret de Caisneto, who passed on the shrievalty to her husband through a hereditary claim from her father. However, she never held the position, nor exercised the duty in her own right.[37] Nicholaa's appointment did set a precedent that would later allow Ela of Salisbury, the wife of William Longespée, to take on the same duty for Wiltshire, on two separate occasions, in the reign of Henry III.

As his end drew close the king, according to the *Histoire*, summoned those closest to him and said:

'My death is upon me, sirs: there's no escape. I can endure this pain no more. In God's name, ask the Marshal to forgive me for all the harm and wrongs and troubles and woes I've caused him, for which I sorely repent. He has always served me faithfully and never wronged me no matter what I've done or said to him. By God who made the world, sirs, crave his pardon. And because I trust in his loyalty above all others, I pray you, let him be my son's protector, his guide and guardian in all matters: without his help and his help alone, he'll never govern these lands of mine.'[38]

The king's last hours were not peaceful and some would have been happy to see that he suffered so at the end, considering the pain he had caused others. The *Histoire* was more forgiving than some chroniclers would be, describing John's last moments with sympathy:

'And then pitiless Death, intent on inflicting all possible pain, began a final assault, rendering him powerless, robbing him of all strength and sense, reducing him to a sorry state indeed. I've heard a number of people say that he was truly repentant; but harsh, cruel, ruthless Death took him in Her grip and wrung him till he died. So the king was dead; there was no remedy.'[39]

John was lamented by few, especially among the clergy, who firmly believed he was going to Hell. A rhyme of the time repeated what many thought of John; 'With John's foul deeds, England's whole realm is stinking, as doth Hell too, wherein he is now sinking.'[40] Ralph of Coggeshall was more generous, stating:

'John was indeed a great prince but scarcely a happy one and, like Marius, he experienced the ups and downs of fortune. He was munificent and liberal to outsiders but a plunderer to his own people, trusting strangers rather than his subjects, wherefore he was eventually deserted by his own men and, in the end, little mourned.'[41]

John's fortuitous – sorry, unfortunate – death at Newark in October 1216 turned the tide against Louis and the rebels. The highly respected knight and statesman, William Marshal, Earl of Pembroke, was appointed regent for John's nine-year-old son, Henry III. Marshal's staunch loyalty was renowned throughout Europe; he was the embodiment of the chivalric code. Many barons who had previously sided with Louis saw the opportunity to come back from the brink, and rally around the young king.

Although John faced the fallout of Magna Carta, many of the injustices targeted by the barons can be seen in the reigns of his predecessors. Heavy taxes, arbitrary fines and the exploitation of wardships were long established royal revenue earners. However, where Henry II and Richard I had a whole empire to exploit, for the majority of his reign, John's need for money had to be met by England alone. Even John's disagreement with the church parallels the reign of Henry II and his clashes with Thomas Becket. As we have seen, John opposed the election of Stephen Langton as archbishop of Canterbury and refused to allow his consecration. Pope Innocent III placed England under interdict and excommunicated John himself; in 1213 King Philip II of France was even invited, by the papacy, to depose him.

It is hard to overstate the enduring significance of Magna Carta. Although it was initially a document conceived by rebel barons, the regents of Henry III exploited Magna Carta as a Royalist device to recover their loyalty. One of the first moves of William Marshal as regent was to reissue Magna Carta, in November 1216. However, since it was first issued Magna Carta has been used as a curb to all regal excesses and in 1265 it was invoked to create the first parliament. By the late 1200s Magna Carta was regarded as a fundamental statement of English liberties. Although a failure in the short term, in the long term, Magna Carta established defined limitations to royal rights, laying down that standard to be observed by the crown and its agents. The drawing up and issuing of Magna Carta in June 1215 was only the start of its journey and while its influence and impact on the country in general, and the barons who forced it on John in particular, is widely known, the charter's effect on the lives of the women who were associated with its creation, or affected by its clauses and implementation, has been largely ignored.

It did not, however, dissipate the war clouds that had gathered over England in 1215, nor would Magna Carta's reissue in 1216 prevent the confrontations that were to come, between the rebel army and their French allies, and the English Royalist army, now ably commanded by the capable but aging William Marshal.

## Chapter Nine

# 1217

The new king was now John's nine-year-old son, Henry III, with the famous and redoubtable William Marshal, Earl of Pembroke, acting as reluctant regent. Despite being charged by John to look after his son, Marshal initially refused to be the new king's guardian, saying he had 'no longer the strength needed for such a charge. I am too old, you must give this responsibility to another.'[1] Ten days after King John breathed his last, the loyal barons were gathered at Gloucester to witness the coronation of Henry III. Alongside the bishops of Winchester and Worcester and William Marshal was the papal legate, Guala, and a host of nobles, abbots and prelates. They had assembled on the day before to 'arrange for the coronation of Henry, the eldest son of King John.'[2] It was decided that, although Ranulf, Earl of Chester, had not yet arrived, the young king should be crowned immediately. Prince Louis was in England and had been proclaimed king in London, though no date for a coronation had been fixed, as the French prince was excommunicate and the pope had warned the English clergy of dire consequences, should any agree to crown him.[3] It was also decided that William Marshal should be the one to knight the king; as someone said to the assembled nobles 'not one of you rivals his greatness.'[4]

On the following day, the 28 October, 'The child was dressed in royal robes made to his size: he looked a fine little knight. The great men who were present carried him into the monastery.'[5] The legate, in company with the bishops and nobles conducted the king in solemn procession to the conventual church to be crowned; and there, 'standing before the great altar, in the presence of the clergy and people, he swore on the holy gospels and other relics of the saints that he would observe honour, peace and reverence towards God and the holy church and its ordained ministers all the days of his life; he also swore that he would show strict justice to the people entrusted to his care, and would abolish all bad laws and customs, if there were any in the kingdom, and would observe those that were good, and cause them to be observed by all.'⁶ In the absence of the archbishops of Canterbury and York, it was the papal legate, Guala, according to Roger of Wendover, who sang the Mass and 'crowned him King Henry III, assisted by the bishops who were assembled there.'⁷ The makeshift crown was a circlet of gold provided by the young king's mother, Isabelle d'Angoulême. Jocelin, bishop of Bath, undertook the administration of the coronation oath.⁸

In the council meetings following the coronation, and following the arrival of the earl of Chester, Marshal was eventually persuaded to accept the guardianship of the king and the kingdom on the insistence of the papal legate, Guala. Immediately after the coronation, William Marshal, Earl of Pembroke and the new king's regent, 'sent letters to all the sheriffs and castellans of England, enjoining them each and all to obey the newly crowned king, and promising them possessions and many presents besides, on condition of their faithfully adhering to the said king; and thus all the nobles and castellans who had served his father adhered more firmly to him, because they all thought the sin of the father ought not to be charged to the son.'⁹ The war was not over, however, and the royalists prepared to defend their lands. At Lincoln, Nicholaa was still in firm control of her castle, despite the fact the city was in rebel hands, as, after John's death, Gilbert de Gant, who had been created earl of Lincoln by Prince Louis after presenting the prince with Lincoln's ceremonial sword, had returned to the city and once again laid siege to the castle.¹⁰ According to Irene Gladwin, when John had driven the rebels from the city in September, 'those burgesses whose allegiance to the Crown seemed to be wavering had had their sons taken as hostages and their fathers had been forced to pay swingeing fines to obtain their release.'¹¹ With the king's death, the rebels returned in force. And though John had appointed Philip Marc, sheriff of Nottinghamshire, to assist Nicholaa in the county, he was too preoccupied with his own castles to give any aid to Nicholaa. According to Gladwin, 'Lincoln Castle was in a state of unbroken siege from October 1216 until the following May.'¹² This state of siege would intensify in March of the following year, when the French reinforcements arrived.

Following the coronation, king and court moved to Bristol. Magna Carta was reissued and some of the rebel barons returned to the fold, not wanting to make war on a child-king. Louis, who was besieging Dover when he received news of King John's death, informed its defender, Hubert de Burgh, the king's justiciar, of the king's death and entreated him to relinquish the castle. De Burgh responded that the king had sons and daughters to succeed him and after a discussion with his knights within the castle, informed Louis that they refused to surrender. Louis and his allies 'determined to reduce the smaller castles throughout the country, that, after the lesser fortresses were in their power, they might attack the larger ones; they then raised the siege and returned to the city of London.'[13]

Louis then laid siege to the castle at Hertford, where the defenders were in low spirits after the town was surrendered to Louis. Louis's ally – and English rebel – Robert FitzWalter asked that he be given the town. The prince consulted his French knights 'who told him that the English were not worthy of holding charge of such places as they were traitors to their own sovereign.'[14] Diplomatically, Louis told FitzWalter to be patient and that everyone would be rewarded once England was subdued. The king's men negotiated a twenty-day truce with Louis, in exchange for the castles of Hertford and Berkhamsted. A further twenty-day truce was negotiated at the expense of the castles at Orford and Norwich, but according to the *Histoire*, Louis 'didn't even keep the truce as he promised.'[15] Although Louis still had some powerful allies and did not seem keen to give up on his dream to rule England, support began to fall away from the French prince, and he returned to France to gather reinforcements. Marshal resolved 'to crush the pretensions of Louis' and blockaded the prince at Winchelsea.[15] As Louis appeared cornered, with Marshal surrounding him on land and a naval blockade preventing the prince from putting to sea, a French fleet, under the command of Hugh Tacon, arrived to break the blockade. Louis and his knights rode to Rye and from there to Dover, from where he took ship for France, to gather reinforcements.

The young king spent Christmas at Bristol, in the company of Guala, the papal legate, and William Marshal. According to Wendover, it was a time of soul searching for the English barony, as to which ruler they should support, 'for they were treated so contemptuously by the French that many of them rejected their assistance.'[16] Louis had disregarded his oaths to his English allies, and their complaints, and retained in his own hands 'the lands, possessions and castles of the said barons, which he had subdued with their help, and had placed foreign knights and people in charge of them.'[17] In the meantime, Louis had appealed to Rome in an attempt to get the sentence of excommunication, pronounced by Guala, lifted. He was informed that unless he left England, the sentence would be confirmed. A truce was then arranged between Louis and Henry III, to last until Easter. Louis broke the truce by crossing the English Channel during Lent. This gave some the excuse they had been looking for, and the earls of Salisbury, Arundel and Warenne, as well as William Marshal's eldest son – also called William – abandoned the prince's cause and returned to the king's fealty.[18]

In early 1217 he returned to continue the fight. Louis' forces, under the Comte de Perche, marched north intending to relieve Mountsorel Castle, which was being besieged by the earl of Chester. Chester had withdrawn as the French arrived and Perche's forces diverted to Lincoln, to reinforce Gilbert de Gant, who had been conducting a long siege without success. Henry III's regents wrote to Philip Marc, sheriff of Nottingham, on 12 February of hostages sent by Nicholaa's deputy:

> 'The king to Philip Marc, sheriff of Nottingham, greetings. We command that, when our trusty and well-beloved Geoffrey de Serland shall have sent to you at Nottingham Robert fitz Peter de Pons, Martin fitz Thomas de Paris and the other two hostages who are the children of the said Peter and Thomas, you should receive them; having received them you should forthwith release Thomas de Paris and Richard, first born son of Peter de Pons, whom you have in your custody. And in testimony hereof etc. we send there to you. Witness the earl [William Marshal] at Gloucester the twelfth day of February in the first year of our reign.'[19]

In the New Year, Geoffrey de Serland had been despatched to Lincoln to act as Nicholaa's deputy, both as sheriff and constable, replacing Philip Marc as Nicholaa's deputy sheriff. William Marshal was also concerned with protecting the property of Nicholaa and her family whilst she was trapped in Lincoln castle, including her son Richard, who must have returned to the king's peace by this time, and on the same day sent out a letter saying:

'The king to all those who may look upon these letters, greetings. Know that we have taken into our protection and defence our trusty and well-beloved lady Nicholaa de la Haye and her son Richard de Camville, and all their lands, affairs and possessions. We therefore command and firmly enjoin that you support, protect and defend the said Nicholaa and Richard, and all that is theirs, neither causing nor permitting to be caused against them any trouble, harm or harassment. If any forfeiture has been made against them or their people, that should be forthwith compensated to them; you should also permit the aforesaid Nicholaa and Richard to have the benefit of the use of their woods as they please. And in testimony, whereof etc...Witness the said earl, at Gloucester, the twelfth day of February.'[20]

Now in her sixties, Nicholaa de la Haye took charge of the defences, with the help of her deputy, Sir Geoffrey de Serland. Serland, was 'a local man who had no military forces at his command,' and so, according to Gladwin, Faulkes de Bréauté was commanded to go to Nicholaa's assistance, if at all possible.[21] She and her garrison now faced an army constituting English rebels and French forces provided by Prince Louis; an entire French battalion was quartered in the city.[22] Once in position 'the barons then made fierce assaults upon the castle, whilst the besieged returned their showers of stones and missiles with stones and deadly weapons with great courage.'[23] By March, the forces opposing Nicholaa were hoping that the isolation that she now found herself in – surrounded as she was, by French and rebel forces – might tempt or frighten Nicholaa into surrender. Despite assurances that no one would be hurt, Nicholaa refused to yield and she kept the guard 'very loyally,' settling in for another long siege.[24] Despite the French army outside her walls, she may have been quietly confident; this was, after all, her third siege and no one had ever managed to breach the castle walls. Lincoln Castle is a rather large fortress, with a curtain wall stretching over a third of a mile. It sits opposite the impressive cathedral and is perched on the top of a bluff – the hill going down to the town is not named Steep Hill for nothing!

The castle sits in the north-west corner of the city of Lincoln, with three sides of its curtain wall within the city's limits. Because of its unusual tradition of having numerous interests, both royal and comital, in the castle, it had two mottes, rather than one. There was also a steep drop to the south. It would not be an easy castle to attack, and almost impossible to encircle. The assaulting forces would have had to concentrate their men on the castle's main gates, one to the east and one to the west, and the small number of postern gates in the walls, one of which was in the Lucy Tower and gave access into the town by climbing down the cliff to the south. The aim of any attackers would not have been to reduce the castle by breaching its walls, rather to starve the inhabitants of supplies, or bombard the walls or tunnel under the ramparts in order to make the castle indefensible and force a negotiated surrender from a stronger bargaining position.[25]

The presence of a well within the castle walls, and Nicholaa's own courage and determination had, so far, held the besiegers at bay. She also had the use of six light balistae – crossbows – and a number of lighter crossbows, that had been provided by Philip Marc, the previous year, on King John's orders.[26] However, this siege was to last longer than the others. From March through to May, Louis' forces battered the walls of Lincoln Castle. The French prince had provided impressive siege engines, leaving them at Perche's disposal, fully expecting to hear of Lincoln's capitulation within weeks, if not days. However, he did not count on the tenacity of Nicholaa and her deputy, Sir Geoffrey de Serland, who rallied their troops and resisted the combined Anglo-French forces of the Comte de Perche, as they awaited reinforcements. Nicholaa just had to hold out long enough for William Marshal to come to her aid. Nicholaa also had to take care not expose herself to danger; she was too valuable to the loyalist cause to risk capture by the enemy.

For almost three months – from March to mid-May – siege machinery bombarded the south and east walls of the castle. When the small force proved insufficient to force a surrender, the French had to send for reinforcements. This meant that half of Louis' entire army was now outside the gates of Lincoln Castle. This would provide William Marshal with an opportunity; one decisive battle against Louis' forces at Lincoln could destroy the hopes of Louis and the rebel barons once and for all. Risking all on one battle was a gamble, but one that Marshal was determined to take. Spurred on by the chivalrous need to rescue a lady in distress William Marshal was determined to relieve Lincoln.

At Pentecost, 12 May, Marshal was at Northampton with the papal legate, Guala, William Marshal appealed to the knights with him:

'Heed my words, in God's name, for what I have to say is vital. Since we're about to take up arms in defence of our names, our land, our lives and the lives of those we love, our wives, our children, and to win the greatest honour, and to restore the peace of Holy Church which our enemies have shattered and violated, and to earn redemption and forgiveness for all our sins, be sure that none of you lacks courage this day! Part of our enemy's force has entered Lincoln, intent on besieging our castle, I know. But not all of them are there: Lord Louis, it seems, has gone elsewhere. His followers have made a grave mistake! And we'll be sorely wanting if we fail to take revenge now on those who've come from France to rob our people of their inheritance. They mean to ruin us entirely! So let's go to it with a will, mindful that if victory's ours we'll enhance our honour and preserve for ourselves and our descendants the freedom that our foes would outrageously steal. They'll not succeed – God wants us to defend our rights! And since they've divided their forces, we'll more easily defeat one part of their army than the whole! I'd say that's right and obvious – God wills it, and reason proves it! So it's only right that each of us should strive his utmost – how can we do otherwise? It's surely plain to all that we must cut a swathe with iron and steel! This is no time for idle threats – let's go straight to the attack! God in His grace has sent us the chance to avenge ourselves on those who've come to abuse and wrong us. No one should hold back: a man takes full revenge for the shame and wrong he's suffered when he overcomes his enemy!'[27]

While the young king Henry III waited at Nottingham, Marshal's forces prepared for war. Marshal mustered his men at Newark on 17 May; the Royalist army was made up of 406 knights, 307 crossbowmen and a large number of followers, including non-combatants. While at Newark, Marshal set out the order of battle, although not without some argument. The Norman contingent and Ranulf, Earl of Chester, both claimed the right to lead the vanguard. However, when Ranulf threatened to withdraw his men, it was decided to acquiesce to his demands. The papal legate, Guala, absolved the Royalist army of all their sins – of all the sins they had committed since their birth – and excommunicated the French forces, together with the city of Lincoln before riding to join the king at Nottingham. The regent led the relief of Lincoln himself, but was accompanied by the great and the good, including the warrior-bishop, Peter des Roches, Bishop of Winchester, Ranulf, Earl of Chester, William Longespée, Faulkes de Bréauté, John Marshal, Marshals' nephew, and William Marshal the Younger, the regent's son. Marshal was eager to relieve Lincoln before the besiegers could receive reinforcements.[28] On 19 May Marshal's forces marched along the River Trent from Newark and set up camp at Torksey, about eight miles to the north of Lincoln, with some troops possibly camped three miles away, at Stow according to Roger of Wendover; or, perhaps, at a site between the two villages.[29]

The next morning, the army arrayed for battle, with the earl of Chester leading the first squadron, William Marshal and his son commanding the second and the earl of Salisbury at the head of the third battalion, with Peter des Roches, the bishop of Winchester, in command of the fourth. At various points in the lead up to the battle, William Marshal is known to have made some stirring speeches, and while they cannot be taken as verbatim, having been written down some years after Marshal's death, they do give a sense of the terms and imagery used to rouse the men to battle. When battle was imminent, he made one more:

'Listen now, sirs! Glory and honour are at hand! Right here and now, you can win the country's freedom, truly: so damn any man who fails this day to challenge those who seize our lands and property! And may God see that right prevails! The enemy are here, right here in our hands. They're at our mercy, I promise you, come what may unless heart and courage fail us. And if we died in this mission, then God who sees and knows the good will set us in His paradise, in that I place my certain trust; and if we defeat them, without a lie, we'll have won lasting honour for all time, for ourselves and all our line! And I tell you, our enemies labour under another grievous burden: they're excommunicated! How much more that shackles them! What a dismal fate they have in store: they'll be going straight to Hell! They're waging war on God and Holy Church, and I swear God has placed them at our mercy. So come, make haste, let's fall on them – the time and the hour are upon us!'[30]

After all, it would have been 'dishonourable not to help so brave a lady'.[31]

As with all battles, the information gets confusing as fighting commences, timings get distorted, and facts mixed. No two sources give exactly the same information. It follows, therefore, that the story of a battle is a matter of putting the pieces together and making sense of various snippets of information – much as it would have been for the commanders on the day. William Marshal decided not to attack Lincoln from the south, which would have meant heading up the Fosse Way (the old Roman road) and forcing a crossing of the River Witham, before climbing the steep slope to the castle and cathedral. Instead, he chose to take a circuitous route, so he could come at the city from the northwest, the only direction which perhaps accorded him the opportunity to communicate with the castle's defenders without entering the city. It also meant he could attack close to the castle and cathedral, directly where the enemy troops were concentrated. Not being entirely sure of the loyalty of the citizens of Lincoln, the French had stationed their siege engines, and the majority of their forces, within the city.[32] In the dawn of 20 May, the English Royalist army marched south towards Lincoln. Marshal had hoped that, on reaching the plain in front of the city walls, the French would come out and meet him and a pitched battle would be fought outside of the city. Marshal was resting everything – the very future of England – on the outcome of that one battle. The *Histoire* says that leaders of the besieging army rode out to reconnoitre Marshal's forces and, seeing the impressive army arrayed against them, chose to draw their men back inside the city walls, convinced Marshal's forces were not strong enough to conduct an all-out assault on the city. Roger of Wendover reports a nonchalance in the French army, that 'the barons who were in the city and the French felt such great confidence in their cause, that when their messengers told them of the approach of their adversaries, they only laughed at them, and continued to hurl missiles from their mangonels, to destroy the walls of the castle.'[33]

The French refusal to meet the royalist forces in open battle gave William Marshal the opportunity for one more rousing speech to his own forces:

'See, my friends: those who were so keen to attack have cracked already – they're cowering behind the walls! God is fulfilling His promise: He's bestowing great glory upon us this day. Here's one victory already: the French, always first to enter a tourney, are hiding from us! God is at our side! They're handing us honour and demeaning themselves, surrendering the fields out here to us! And the city will be ours too, I promise you! Fight bravely now: it's God's will! Let all who've proved their worth in the past commit themselves to their very best, and have no cause to repent of this day.'[34]

Although Louis was in charge of the French forces in England, those in Lincoln were led by Thomas, Comte de Perche, himself a grandson of Henry II's daughter Matilda, and therefore a cousin of King Henry III. He was also a cousin of William Marshal himself. The commanders of the English rebels in the city included Robert FitzWalter and Saer de Quincy, Earl of Winchester. They led over 600 knights and several thousand infantry. Lincoln is an unusual city. Its castle and cathedral sit at the top of a hill, with the rest of the city to the south, at the hill's base. In the thirteenth century it was enclosed in a rectangular wall, which had stood since Roman times, with five gates, and the castle abutting the wall at the north-west corner. William Marshal's nephew, John Marshal was sent to the castle, to ascertain the situation within the city, but as he approached, Nicholaa's deputy, Geoffrey de Serland, was making his way out to report to the English commanders that the fortress was still in Nicholaa's hands. It is not hard to imagine Nicholaa or her deputy climbing the tallest towers of the castle, to watch out for the approaching relief force.

Seeing the Marshal's banners appearing in the north must have been an amazing feeling. The castle itself had two main gates, one in the eastern wall and one in the west, with postern gates in the Lucy Tower to the south-east of the castle and possibly the recently-built Cobb Hall to the north-east corner. Wanting to reconnoitre further, Peter des Roches, accompanied by a single soldier, then made his way inside the castle, by one of the postern gates. The *Histoire de Guillaume le Maréchal* tells how Peter des Roches managed to sneak into Lincoln Castle by a secret entrance; he had been sent by William Marshal to reassure Nicholaa that relief was on its way.[35] Nicholaa was delighted to hear the news and it must have bolstered the morale of the men under her command; all they had to do was sit tight and wait. The *Histoire* tells that as des Roches entered the castle, 'he met Sir Geoffrey de Serland in a fearful state. They could see the walls being battered, devastated, a distressing sight indeed; the bishop saw the wreckage of the walls and houses and the plight of the townsfolk, bombarded now by catapults and trebuchets. Some of the defenders were warning the bishop, begging him in God's name to take cover, for the mangonels and catapults were smashing everything in sight. Into the keep he went, where he found the good lady of the castle – may God preserve her, body and soul – who was doing her utmost to defend it. The lady was overjoyed by his coming, and he comforted her greatly with the news he brought.'[36]

Having met with Nicholaa de la Haye in the Lucy Tower, it seems Roches then made his way into the town via the postern, to check the defences and try to find a way into the city. Des Roches' reconnaissance proved successful, and he reported to Marshal that there was an old gate within the north-west wall of the city, which connected the walls of the town with those of the castle. Although blockaded with rubble and mortar, it could be cleared. The bishop ordered that the gate be cleared, then returned to the army. The earl of Chester was sent to attack the North Gate as a diversion and Faulkes de Bréauté and his crossbowmen were sent to enter the town via the newly-cleared gate. However, they did not find the unopposed gate and met with fierce resistance where they did attempt to enter the town. Faulkes de Bréauté eventually got into the castle and the crossbowmen were set to the ramparts above the East Gate, so their bolts could fire down on the besiegers. They were positioned on the castle walls, looking into the town, and rained a deadly barrage of crossbow bolts into the Anglo-French army. It must have been a fine sight for Nicholaa and her garrison to watch their relief march into the castle and engage the enemy in battle. The siege engines were destroyed, and fierce hand-to-hand fighting ensued.

The *Histoire* is the only source that mentions Peter des Roches' exploits in entering castle and city prior to the battle. Which suggests that the bishop himself was the source of this news as it is related, and may have exaggerated his role somewhat. Certainly Roger of Wendover, who covers the battle in detail, makes no mention of des Roches sneaking into the city. On the other hand, Faulkes de Bréauté fell into disgrace in 1224 and so the *Histoire de Guillaume le Maréschale* plays down his role in the battle. However, his crossbowmen, placed on the roofs of the buildings within the castle, and the castle ramparts, managed to keep the French forces focussed on the castle, rather than Marshal's forces outside the city. De Bréauté's crossbowmen 'discharged their deadly weapons against the chargers of the barons, levelling horses and riders together to the earth, so that in the twinkling of an eye they made up a large force of foot-soldiers, knights and nobles.'[37] Faulkes de Bréauté did make a sortie out of the East Gate, to attack the besiegers, but was taken prisoner and had to be rescued by his own men; although at what stage of the battle this happened is uncertain. It took several hours, it seems, for Marshal's men to break through the gates in the city's northern wall, but when they did, the seventy-year-old William Marshal was so eager to lead the charge that he had to be reminded to don his helmet. Once safely helmeted, he led his men down West Gate – whether this was the gate discovered by Peter des Roches, or another is unclear. Marshal's men then turned right to approach the castle from the north, his men spilling into the space between castle and cathedral, where the main force of the besiegers were still firing missiles at the castle. The majority of the army then forced their entrance through the Newport Arch, and advanced upon the enemy along Bailgate. The English forces took the enemy so totally by surprise that according to the *Histoire*, one man, the enemy's 'most expert stonethrower', thought they were allies coming to assist the besiegers in their assault on the castle. He continued loading the siege machinery, only to have his head struck from his shoulders by one of Marshal's men.[38]

Almost simultaneously, it seems, the earl of Chester had broken through the North Gate and battle was joined on all sides. Vicious, close-quarter combat had erupted in the narrow streets, but the fiercest fighting was in front of the cathedral. In the midst of the melée, William Longespée took a blow from Robert of Roppesley, whose lance broke against the earl. The aged Marshal dealt such a blow to Roppesley that the knight 'dropped to the ground and scurried off to hide in an upper room, not daring to stay in the street below.'[39] The Comte de Perche made his stand in front of the cathedral, rallying his troops; and it was there he took a blow from Reginald de Croc which breached the eye slit of his helmet. Croc himself was badly wounded and died the same day. The French began retreating down the hill into the city, but Marshal seized the Comte's bridle in the hope of claiming the ransom. The Comte continued to fight, and the Marshal struck three successive blows to his helmet so fierce that man and horse fell to the ground. It was thought the Comte was merely stunned until someone tried to remove his helmet and it was discovered that the point of Croc's sword had pierced the count's eye and continued into his brain, killing him. With the death of their leader, the French and rebel barons lost heart and started pulling back.[40]

The French soldiers and English rebels fled downhill, to the south of the city; 'both sides fought long and hard till even the strongest were tiring: there was no respite or hope of help – nothing but the giving and taking of blows.'[41] Although they briefly rallied, making an uphill assault, the battle was lost and there was a bottleneck at the South Gate and the bridge across the Witham as the enemy army fled. The fleeing forces faced one more stroke of bad luck when one of the gates out of the city was blocked by a cow that 'had wandered through the gate and triggered the bar, closing the gate so that no one on horseback could get through: they were well and truly stuck.'[42] In their desperation to escape, they killed the cow, but that just made matters worse, it was now an even less manoeuvrable object. Many knights were captured there. Those who did manage to escape rode night and day to get away from their pursuers, but only 200 men reached London.

The rebel leaders, Saher de Quincey and Robert FitzWalter were both taken prisoner, as were many others. In total, about half of the enemy knights surrendered, amounting to 46 rebel barons and 300 knights. Only three knights had died in the battle, an unknown rebel, the Comte de Perche and the man who killed him, Reginald de Croc.[43] Marshal's army advanced down the hill into the town itself and the Anglo-French encampment. From the time Marshal's men had first attacked, the entire battle was over in six hours. The Battle of Lincoln, on 20 May 1217, raged through the streets, the fierce fighting followed by looting and sacrilege in the medieval city. Sacking the city and attacking citizens who had collaborated with the French was considered a just punishment by the royalist forces. The city, which had supported the rebels, was pillaged, churches included; the excommunication pronounced by Guala seen as permission that everything was fair game. The battle earned the name 'The Lincoln Fair', probably because of the amount of plunder gained by the victorious English army. However, it may also refer to the fact the battle yielded only a small number of casualties on both sides.

Lincoln suffered dreadfully from the subsequent sacking. The precentor, Geoffrey of Deeping, lost eleven thousand marks of silver.[44] A sad story is related by Roger of Wendover, that, after the battle, women took to the river with their children, in small boats, to escape the attentions of the victorious army. However, not knowing how to control the overloaded craft, many capsized and the women and children drowned.[45]

Immediately after the battle was won, William Marshal, Earl of Pembroke, rode to Nottingham to inform the king of the victory. The Second Battle of Lincoln (the first being in the time of the Anarchy, the war between King Stephen and Empress Matilda) was one of two decisive battles that ended French hopes of winning the English throne. It turned the tide of the war. On hearing of the defeat, Louis immediately lifted his siege of Dover Castle and withdrew to London. Support for Henry III grew, and the young king's forces were soon marching on London to blockade Louis within the capital city.

Louis' situation became desperate, his English allies bristled against the idea of the French prince giving English land as reward to his French commanders and were beginning to see the young Henry III as rightful king – after all, the son could not be blamed for the actions of the father. In August of the same year Louis' forces were soundly defeated at sea in the Battle of Sandwich, off the Kent coast. The sea battle prevented Louis from receiving much-needed reinforcements and 'on 12 September, terms were made, concerning the release of those who had been captured; concerning the evil customs which had been the cause of the war; and concerning the observance of the liberties which had been sought by the English nobles. A financial settlement was made for the expenses which Louis had incurred in the kingdom.'[46] Peace was signed at Kinston Upon Thames and Louis was paid 10,000 marks (£7,000) to go home.

Magna Carta was issued a third time, along with a new charter, the Charter of the Forest, issued for the first time (see Appendix C). A newer version of Magna Carta was issued in 1225, on Henry III attaining his majority, and it is this 1225 Magna Carta which made it onto the statute books.

The biggest loser in the immediate aftermath of the 1217 Battle of Lincoln, was the woman whose stalwart defence of the castle had precipitated the battle and given William Marshal his decisive victory. Instead of being showered with gratitude and the laurels of victory, just four days after the battle, William Longespée, Earl of Salisbury, took the sheriffdom of Lincolnshire and seized the castle.

## Chapter Ten

# The In-Laws

William Longespée, Earl of Salisbury, was an illegitimate son of King Henry II, his fortune and position in society had always been linked with the fortunes of his royal half-brothers, King Richard I and King John. And now he was uncle to the new king, Henry III. William Longespée was the son of Henry II by Ida de Tosney, wife of Roger Bigod, Earl of Norfolk, from a relationship she had with the king before her marriage. For many years, it was thought that Longespée was the son of a common harlot, called Ikenai, and a full brother of another of Henry's illegitimate sons, Geoffrey, Archbishop of York. There were also theories that his mother was Rosamund Clifford, famed in ballads as 'the Fair Rosamund'. However, it is now considered beyond doubt that his mother was, in fact, Ida de Tosney, with two crucial pieces of evidence supporting this. There is a charter in the cartulary of Bradenstoke Priory, made by William Longespée, in which he refers explicitly to his mother as 'Countess Ida, my mother'.[1] There is also a prisoner roll from after the Battle of Bouvines, in which a fellow captive, one of the sons of Ida and the earl of Norfolk, Ralph Bigod, is listed as 'Ralph Bigod, brother [half-brother] of the earl of Salisbury'.[2] Ralph was a younger son of Earl Roger and Ida and had been fighting under Longespée's command in the battle in which both were taken prisoner.

Ida was probably the daughter of Roger (III) de Tosney, a powerful Anglo-Norman lord, and his wife, also called Ida.[3] She was made a royal ward after her father's death and became mistress of King Henry II sometime afterwards. She gave the king one son, William Longespée, who was born around 1176, making him ten years younger than the king's youngest legitimate son, John. Ida was married to Roger Bigod, Earl of Norfolk sometime around Christmas 1181. Through his mother's Norfolk family, Longespée had four half-brothers, Hugh, William, Ralph and Roger and two half-sisters, Mary and Margery.[4] Despite the misunderstandings over his mother, the identity of William Longespée's father was never in doubt. He was Henry II's son and acknowledged by his father; he served two of his half-brothers, Richard I and King John. He adopted the coat of arms of his paternal grandfather, Geoffrey Plantagenet, Count of Anjou, of azure, six leoncels rampant or [gold], to emphasise his descent from the Angevin counts.[5] The moniker of Longespée (also Lungespée or Longsword) harkens back to his Norman forebear and namesake William Longsword, second Duke of Normandy (reigned 928–942), from whom he was descended through his father, the king. Little is known of Longespée's childhood, upbringing or education, though a letter of 1220 that Longespée sent to Hubert de Burgh reminds the justiciar that they were raised together, probably fostered in a noble household.[6] In 1188 he had been given the manor of Appleby in Lincolnshire by his father, but he did not come into prominence until the reign of his half-brother Richard I.

At the time of his marriage to Ela of Salisbury, from whom he received his earldom, Longespée was in his early-to-mid-twenties, while his bride was not yet ten years old, although she would not have been expected to consummate the marriage until she was fourteen or fifteen. Ela was born at Amesbury in Wiltshire, probably in 1187.[7] She was the only surviving child – and sole heir – of William Fitzpatrick, Earl of Salisbury, and his wife, Eleanor de Vitré, daughter of Robert III de Vitré, Baron of Vitré in Brittany. Ela's father was a descendant of Walter, an ally of William the Conqueror, who had been rewarded for his support at Hastings with great estates which eventually passed to Ela. Her grandfather, Patrick of Salisbury, had been created earl of either Wiltshire or Salisbury (there seems to be some confusion as to which) by Empress Matilda before 1147, but was styled Earl of Salisbury.[8] As earl, Patrick witnessed the 1153 peace treaty between King Stephen and Henry of Anjou, which would see Henry succeed Stephen as king. He served as sheriff of Wiltshire in 1160 and was leading the king's troops in Aquitaine when he was killed by the Lusignans in 1168. Earl Patrick had been escorting Eleanor of Aquitaine when their party was ambushed in an attempt to kidnap the queen of England. Patrick suffered a fatal spear wound during the ensuing skirmish and was buried in Poitiers. A younger member of the party, William Marshal, the future earl of Pembroke and regent, was wounded and taken prisoner during the encounter; Queen Eleanor would later negotiate his release. William Marshal was the son of Patrick's sister,

Sybil, making him a cousin of Ela. Patrick's son William, Ela's father, eventually succeeded to the earldom.

William, Earl of Salisbury, had carried the sceptre at Richard I's coronation, but when the king was taken prisoner in Germany, William supported his brother John, Count of Mortain, in his struggles against Richard's justiciar, William Longchamp. In 1194 he served as high sheriff of Somerset and Dorset and in 1195 served with King Richard in Normandy. In the same year, he was one of the four earls who supported the canopy of state at Richard's second coronation, and attended the great council, called by the king, at Nottingham. He died in 1196, leaving his only child, Ela, as his sole heir. Ela became Countess of Salisbury in her own right, and the most prized heiress in England. There is a story that little Ela, only nine years old at the time of her father's death, was kidnapped by her uncle, her father's brother, and hidden away in a castle in Normandy, so that he could gain control of the vast Salisbury inheritance. According to the mid-fourteenth-century *Book of Lacock*: 'when Ela was deprived of both her father and her mother she was secretly taken into Normandy by her relations and there brought up in close and secret custody.'[9]

Another version of the story has Ela taken to Normandy by her mother, in order to protect her from her grasping uncle; this suggestion 'would account for her daughter's confinement by an anxious and affectionate mother, that she might be placed out of reach of those who perhaps might have meditated worse than confinement.'[10] The story has obvious inconsistencies, but it may be that the countess thought her daughter would be safer being raised among her own family on the Continent, away from her brother-in-law who would have inherited the earldom had anything happened to Ela. She may also have preferred the security of her family in Normandy to the court of King Richard I, where Ela would be under the prying eyes of those who would seek an advantageous marriage with the little heiress.

As the tale goes, an English knight, named William Talbot toured the Norman castles in search of poor Ela singing ballads beneath castle windows in the hope that the little countess would hear him and join in with his singing. He is said to have wandered Normandy for two years, dressed as a pilgrim, in search of the little countess. When he found her, he exchanged his clothing with that of a troubadour in order to gain entry to the castle in which she was being held. He engineered her escape, took her back to England and presented Ela to King Richard, who promptly married her to his half-brother, William Longespée. It is a story that closely resembles that of the legendary Blondel, who was said to have toured the castles of Germany, singing ballads beneath windows in an attempt to find King Richard during his imprisonment. Whether a romantic legend or a true story, the distance of time makes it difficult to be certain, but there appears to be little basis in truth. William Talbot, however, was a faithful retainer of the Salisbury family and witnessed several of the earl's charters.[11]

Whether Ela was rescued, or never kidnapped in the first place, we do not know. However, what we do know is that, on her father's death, Ela's wardship passed into the hands of the king himself, Richard I, the Lionheart. The king saw Ela as the opportunity to reward his loyal, but illegitimate, brother, William Longespée (or Longsword), by offering him her hand in marriage. The Salisbury lands were a suitable reward for a king's son, especially one born out of wedlock, and would give him a power base in England. Ela and Longespée were married in the same year her father died, 1196, so if Ela had been spirited away to Normandy, she was soon recovered, and the story of William Talbot wandering Normandy for two years in search of her is an exaggeration, to say the least. It may also be that Ela was quickly married off to prevent any further kidnap attempts. The couple would not have lived as husband and wife until Ela was at least twelve years old, the church's legal age of marriage for a girl. Her husband was an experienced soldier and statesman and would be able to protect Ela, her lands and interests. William acquired the title Earl of Salisbury by right of his wife and took over the management of the vast Salisbury estates.

William (I) Longespée had an impressive career during the reigns of both of his half-brothers. He first served in Normandy with Richard between 1196 and 1198, attesting several charters for his brother at Château Gaillard, and taking part in the campaigns against King Philip II of France, gaining essential military experience. He took part in John's coronation on 27 May 1199 and was frequently with John thereafter. The half-brothers appear to have enjoyed a very cordial relationship; the court rolls record them gaming together and John granting Longespée numerous royal favours, from gifts of wine to an annual pension.[12] By

1201 Longespée, along with William Marshal and Geoffrey fitz Peter, Earl of Essex 'were seen by John at this stage in his reign as the main props to his rule, and lavish gifts followed.'[13]

Although Longespée's marriage to Ela of Salisbury gave him rank and prestige, it was not a wealthy earldom. The barony commanded fifty-six knights' fees and gave the earl custody of the royal fortress of Salisbury, but Longespée had no castle of his own. He was made sheriff of Wiltshire on three separate occasions, 1199–1202, 1203–07 and 1213–1226, but was never granted the position as a hereditary right by the king. As sheriff, it was Longespée's task to hunt down the famous outlaw Fulk Fitzwarin, whom he besieged in Stanley Abbey in 1202. Fitzwarin and his band of about thirty men were pardoned in 1203, Longespée was among those who secured the pardon from the king.[14] During his career, William was also entrusted with several important diplomatic missions. In 1202 he negotiated a treaty with Sancho VII of Navarre and in 1204 he and William Marshal escorted the Welsh prince Llywelyn to the king at Worcester. He was also sent to Scotland on a diplomatic mission to King William the Lion in 1205 and was with John at York in November 1206 when the two kings met. The earl was also instrumental in the election of his nephew, Otto, as German emperor, heading an embassy to the princes of Germany which resulted in Otto's coronation.

William Longespée's most prominent role during the reign of King John, however, was as a military leader. He was a commander of considerable ability. In August 1202 he had fought alongside William Marshal and William de Warenne, Earl of Surrey, hounding the retreating forces of King Philip II of France. The French king had withdrawn from the siege of Arques following news of John's victory over his nephew, Arthur, at Mirebeau. Longespée and his lightly armed fellow earls, however, narrowly escaped capture from a counterattack led by William des Barres. Following the fall of Normandy, Longespée was given command of Gascony in May 1204. In September of the same year, he was also given custody of Dover Castle and made warden of the Cinque Ports; he retained both offices until May 1206.[15] In 1208 Longespée was appointed warden of the Welsh Marches and in 1210 he joined King John on the Irish expedition which had been prompted by William de Braose fleeing to Ireland to escape John's persecution. In 1213 the earl, allied with the counts of Holland and Boulogne, led an expeditionary force to the aid of Count Ferrand of Flanders against King Philip II and on 30 May he achieved a significant naval victory when his forces destroyed the French fleet off the Flemish coast near Damme, burning many enemy ships and capturing others. The victory forced King Philip to abandon plans for an invasion of England.

In 1214 William Longespée commanded an army in northern France for the king, while John was campaigning in Poitou. He managed to recover most of the lands lost by the count of Flanders. In July of the same year, however, he commanded the right-wing of the allied army at the Battle of Bouvines, alongside Renaud de Dammartin, Count of Boulogne. William fought bravely but was captured, after being clubbed on the head by Philippe, the bishop of Beauvais. According to the *Histoire de Guillaume le Maréchal* the battle had been fought against the earl's advice, and if it were not for Longespée's own heroic actions, Emperor Otto would have been taken prisoner or, worse, killed.[16] The battle was a military disaster for the English forces in France and ended John's hopes of recovering his Continental possessions. William Longespée was held prisoner for almost a year. He was eventually ransomed and exchanged in March 1215, for John's prisoner, Robert, son of the count of Dreux, who had been captured at Nantes in 1214.

William Longespée was back in England by May 1215 and appointed to examine the state of royal castles, which would have included Lincoln. However, England was reaching crisis point by this time with the rebellion gathering pace. Although unable to prevent rebels from gaining control of London, he was effective against the rebels in Devon, forcing them to abandon Exeter. He was named among those barons who had advised John to grant Magna Carta, though whether he was actually present at Runnymede, when the charter was sealed, is unknown. He was granted lands from the royal demesne in August 1215 in compensation for the loss of Trowbridge, which had been returned to Henry de Bohun, one of the twenty-five barons appointed to the committee to oversee the enforcement of the terms of Magna Carta.[17] Also in 1215, following the fall of Rochester, on 30 November, Longespée was given the task of containing the rebels in London, while John led the rest of his forces north. Alongside Faulkes de Bréauté and Savaric de Mauléon, he led a punitive *chevauchée* through Essex, Hertfordshire, Middlesex, Cambridgeshire and Huntingdonshire. However, in the early weeks of 1216, when Walter

Buc's Brabançon mercenaries ravaged the Isle of Ely, it was Longespée who protected the women from their worst excesses.

Longespée was still supporting John when Louis, the French prince, landed on 21 May 1216; however, the prince's rapid advance through the southern counties led the earl of Salisbury to submit and ally with Louis after Winchester fell to the French, in June 1216. He remained in opposition to his half-brother for the rest of John's life.[18] Unfounded rumours, recorded by William the Breton, suggested that Longespée's desertion of John was caused by the king's seduction of Ela while the earl was a prisoner of war in France.[19] It seems more likely that, like so many others, he saw John's cause as lost and decided to cut his own losses. With Longespée's defection, and that of William de Warenne, Earl of Surrey, John's support was severely diminished and in retaliation, John ordered his brother's lands seized in August 1216. The king still had the adherence of William Marshal and Ranulf de Blundeville, Earl of Chester, with only the earls of Derby and Warwick offering additional support.[20]

Despite the death of King John in October 1216, Longespée remained with Louis and even called for Hubert de Burgh to surrender Dover to the French.[21] However, when Louis returned to France in March 1217, Longespée submitted to the king, swearing loyalty to his nine-year-old nephew, Henry III. He was also absolved of the sentence of excommunication which had been passed on all those who had defected to Louis. Along with Longespée, William Marshal's eldest son, William (II), and a hundred other men from Wiltshire and the south-west, returned to the king's peace. Longespée was now instrumental in driving the French from England and defeating the remaining rebel barons. He was part of William Marshal's army at the Battle of Lincoln Fair on 20 May 1217, when Lincoln Castle and its formidable castellan, Nicholaa de la Haye, were finally relieved following a three-month siege by the French under the Comte de Perche.

We know little of Ela's whereabouts during Longespée's various adventures, nor how she felt about her husband's defection from John to Louis. We know nothing of their married life, although it appears to have been a happy one. The couple had at least eight children together, if not more; four boys and four girls. Of their three youngest boys, Richard became a canon at the newly built Salisbury Cathedral, Stephen became seneschal of Gascony and justiciar of Ireland, and their youngest son, Nicholas, was elected bishop of Salisbury in 1291; he was consecrated at Canterbury by Archbishop John Pecham on 16 March 1292. Already in his sixties, Nicholas died on 18 May 1297.[22] Of Ela and William's four daughters, Petronilla died unmarried, possibly having become a nun. Isabella married William de Vescy, Lord of Alnwick, and had children before her death in 1244. Another daughter, named after her mother, married, firstly Thomas de Beaumont, Earl of Warwick and, secondly, Phillip Basset; sadly, she had no children by either husband. A fourth daughter, Ida, married Walter Fitzrobert; her second marriage was to William de Beauchamp, Baron Bedford, by whom she had six children.

In 1216, the oldest son, William II Longespée, fourth Earl of Salisbury, was granted marriage by King John to Idonea, granddaughter and sole heiress of the formidable Nicholaa de la Haye. Both children were very young when the grant was made, with Idonea being, possibly, no older than eight, the youngest age that a betrothal was sanctioned by the church, though she could not be married until the age of twelve. It was through this marriage that Longespée, the young groom's father, asserted his claims to the constableship of Lincoln Castle, and his rights to the shrievalty of Lincolnshire, just days after the Battle of Lincoln. Given the months of siege that Nicholaa had just endured, it would be surprising if Longespée had expected her to give in without a fight. Though, maybe he thought that she had no fight left in her. If he did, he was very wrong. William Longespée and Nicholaa de la Haye would spend several years in legal disputes over the inheritance of Nicholaa's Lincolnshire holdings. Nicholaa would only resign her possession of Lincoln Castle once he was dead, in fact, she resigned three months after his death in 1226. From that time on, William (II) would hold the position of hereditary constable at Lincoln by right of his wife, Idonea.

With his father's death, William (II) would take full control of Idonea's inheritance from both her parents. On 23 September 1226, the sheriff of Northamptonshire was ordered 'to place in respite, until the octaves of Michaelmas in the tenth year, the demand of £20 that he makes by summons of the Exchequer from William Longespée and Idonea, his wife, for Richard de Camville , for debts of the Jews, having accepted security that they, or someone else for them, will be there upon the Exchequer to satisfy the king for that debt.'[23] And on 24 May 1228, the king ordered the sheriff of Cambridgeshire 'to take into the king's hand all land with appurtenances in Hildersham which is of the inheritance of Idonea de Camville, wife of William Longespée, and which W. earl of Salisbury committed to Roger de Akeny to sustain him, and to keep it safely so that nothing is removed until the king orders otherwise.'[24]

In November 1230, with the death of her grandmother, Nicholaa, Idonea and William (II) Longespée were given 'full seisin without delay of all lands and fees which the same Nicolaa held of the king in chief and which fall to the same Idonea by hereditary right.'[25] William and Idonea would have four children, three sons and a daughter. Their eldest son, William (III) Longespée, married Maud Clifford, a granddaughter of Llywelyn ap Iorweth, known as Llywelyn Fawr or the Great; their daughter, Margaret would succeed Ela of Salisbury as Countess of Salisbury in her own right, and married Henry de Lacey, Earl of Lincoln.

William (II) Longespée went on crusade with Richard, Earl of Cornwall, in 1240–41 and later led the English contingent in the Seventh Crusade, led by Louis IX of France. His company formed part of the doomed vanguard, which was overwhelmed at Mansourah in Egypt on 8 February 1250. William's body was buried in Acre, but his effigy lies atop an empty tomb in Salisbury Cathedral. His mother Ela is said to have experienced a vision of her son's last moments at the time of his death. Idonea outlived her husband, dying on either 1 January 1251 or 21 September 1252.[26] On 9 January 1251, at Westminster, the king committed to Idonea's son, William Longespée, who was also the king's valet, 'two thirds of the manor of Winterbourne Earls, which manor is extended at £18 13½d., to hold for as long as it pleases the king, rendering two thirds of the aforesaid extent to the king annually for it at the Exchequer, namely a moiety at the Exchequer of Easter and the other moiety at the Exchequer of Michaelmas. Order to H. of Wingham and his co-escheator in Wiltshire to cause William to have full seisin of the aforesaid two thirds, saving the advowson of the same manor to the king and saving to Idonea, who was the wife of William Longespée, father of the aforesaid William, the third part of the same manor for her dower.'[27] This would suggest that Idonea died in 1252, as there would be no need to preserve her dower if she had died eight days earlier.

As a couple, William Longespée and Ela were great patrons of the church, laying the fourth and fifth foundation stones for the new

Salisbury Cathedral in 1220. William de Warenne, Earl of Surrey and a cousin to Ela, also laid a foundation stone.[28] In the first half of the 1220s, Longespée played an influential role in the minority government of Henry III and also served in Gascony to secure the last remaining Continental possessions of the English king. In 1225 he was shipwrecked off the coast of Brittany and a rumour spread that he was dead. While he spent months recovering at the island monastery of Ré in France Hubert de Burgh, first Earl of Kent and widower of Isabella of Gloucester, proposed a marriage between Ela and his nephew, Reimund. Ela, however, would not even consider it, insisting that she knew William was alive and that, even if he were dead, she would never presume to marry below her status. It has been suggested that she used clause 8 of Magna Carta to support her rejection of the offer: 'No widow is to be distrained to marry while she wishes to live without a husband.'[29]

However, as it turned out, William Longespée was still alive and he eventually returned to England and his wife, landing in Cornwall and then making his way to Salisbury. From Salisbury he went to Marlborough to complain to the king that Reimund had tried to marry Ela whilst he was still alive. According to the *Annals and antiquities of Lacock Abbey* Reimund was present at Longespée's audience with the king, confessed his wrongdoing and offered to make reparations, thus restoring peace.[30] Unfortunately, Longespée never seems to have recovered fully from his injuries and died at the royal castle at Salisbury shortly after his return home, on 7 March 1226, amid rumours of being poisoned by Hubert de Burgh or his nephew.[31] He was buried in a splendid tomb in Salisbury Cathedral. Although the title earl of Salisbury still belonged to his wife, his son, William (II) Longespée was sometimes called Earl of Salisbury, but never legally bore the title as he died before his mother.

Ela did not marry again. On her husband's death, she was forced to relinquish her custody of the royal castle at Salisbury, although she did eventually buy it back. More significantly, she was allowed to take over her husband's role as sheriff of Wiltshire, which he had held three times in his career and continuously from 1213 until his death in 1226. Ela herself served twice as sheriff of Wiltshire from 1227 until 1228 and again from 1231 to 1237. Nicholaa de la Haye's appointment as sheriff of Lincolnshire ten years earlier, in 1216, may have aided Ela in attaining the post, serving as a precedent.[32] The countess also appeared in person at the

Exchequer to render accounts, demonstrating her personal involvement in the management of her household and estates.[33]

In 1225, William Longespée had been given the wardship of his nephew, the heir to the earldom of Norfolk, Roger Bigod. When young Roger was married to Isabella, sister of Alexander II, King of Scots, that same year, however, his wardship was transferred to the Scottish king as he was still underage. Two years later, still early in Ela's widowhood, debts concerning Bigod's wardship and her status as the countess of Salisbury were taken into account:

'1227 29 Oct. Rochester. To the barons of the Exchequer. The king has granted to Ela, countess of Salisbury, formerly the wife of William Longespée, former earl of Salisbury, uncle of [the earl of] Salisbury (sic.), that the 550 m. which the executors of the testament of the aforesaid earl of Salisbury ought to render to the king of the fine that Alexander, King of Scots, made with them for having custody of the land formerly of Earl Hugh Bigod, which was in the hand of the aforesaid earl of Salisbury, are to be allowed to the same countess of Salisbury in the debt of £1075 12s 3d which is exacted from her at the Exchequer for the debts that the aforesaid earl of Salisbury owed to the king. The king has also granted to the countess that she may render 100 m. of the residue of the same debt each year at two terms, namely 50 m. at Easter in the twelfth year and 50 m. at Michaelmas in the same year, and 100 m. thus from year to year at the same terms until the rest of the aforesaid debt is paid in full. The king has further granted to the countess that if death befalls her before the rest of the debt is paid to the king, the heirs of the aforesaid earl of Salisbury and the countess are to render the aforesaid debt each year at the same terms, namely 100 m., until the debt is paid to the king.

Order to cause this to be done and enrolled thus.'[34]

It is a testament to Ela's own considerable abilities, in the management of her money and estates, that the crown dealt directly with her in relation to the debts of her husband. When Roger Bigod was in the earl's wardship, the revenues from his estates passed directly to William. However, when his wardship was handed over to his brother-in-law, King Alexander, accounting had to be taken of the revenues of Roger's lands and Ela had to renegotiate the debt her husband had incurred in purchasing the Bigod wardship.

Ela was also known as a great patron of religious houses; she and her husband had co-founded Salisbury Cathedral and Ela herself founded two Augustinian abbeys. She managed to lay the foundation stones of both, at Hinton and Lacock, sixteen miles apart, on the same day in 1232. The abbey at Hinton, Somerset, was endowed for monks, in memory of her husband, after the original house, founded by Longespée at Hathorp, proved to be unsuitable. The foundation of Lacock Priory had been three years in the planning; in 1229 Ela's charter, granting the manor and church of Lacock to the abbess and nuns of the newly-founded priory of Lacock, was confirmed by her son, William (II) Longespée and witnessed by many of the leading nobles of the kingdom, including, among others William (II) Marshal, Earl of Pembroke, Hubert de Burgh, Earl of Kent and justiciar and William de Warenne, Earl of Surrey.[35] On April 3 of the same year an indented agreement was made between Ela and John, rector of the church at Lacock, whereby John gave his assent to the building of Lacock priory and Ela, in return, promised that she and her heirs would preserve the indemnity of the church. The agreement was witnessed by many of the leading officers of Salisbury Cathedral, including the bishop of Salisbury, Robert de Bingham.[36]

Lacock Priory was established in 1232 as a house for Augustinian canonesses at the village of Lacock in Wiltshire. Ela herself entered the priory in 1237 and became its first abbess when it was upgraded to an abbey in 1239. As abbess, Ela was able to secure many rights and privileges for the abbey and its village, including a charter from Henry III, granting the right to hold a fair for St Thomas of Canterbury, a grant to hold a market on Tuesdays, permission for the nuns to host a fair on the vigil and feast of Saints Peter and Paul, including the six days following, and a charter permitting Lacock's abbess to take a cart through the forest of Melksham to collect dead wood for firewood.[37] All these grants, and the establishment of a village with reeve, ploughmen, shepherds, fishermen and others, ensured that the abbey was self-sufficient and prosperous.

As abbess of Lacock, Ela obtained a copy of the 1225 issue of Magna Carta, which had been given to her husband for him to distribute around Wiltshire. Despite her seclusion, she did retain contact with her family and with her lands. Held in the National Archives at Kew one grant is made by her son, William (II) Longespée to Ela as 'abbess of Lacock, of all the lands which had belonged to her daughter Ela, countess of Warwick, his sister, held in marriage in Chitterne [Wiltshire], which she has quitclaimed to him, as well as the homage and service of Robert de Holta, clerk, for the tenement which he holds of him in the same vill.'[38] The grant is witnessed by William of York, Bishop of Salisbury and Richard Longespée, Ela's son, and others. The grant must have been made sometime after 1256, when William of York became bishop of Salisbury, but before 1259, when Ela resigned as abbess after twenty years in that position.

Ela remained at Lacock Abbey after she retired as abbess and, having eventually outlived both her eldest son and grandson, died there on 24 August 1261. On her death Ela was succeeded as countess of Salisbury by her great-granddaughter, Margaret, who was the daughter of William (III) Longespée. Margaret was married to Henry de Lacey, third earl of Lincoln and grandson of John de Lacy and Margaret de Quincey. Margaret was the mother of Alice de Lacey, fourth Countess of Lincoln and the unfortunate, unloved wife of Thomas, Earl of Lancaster, who was killed in rebellion against Edward II, at the Battle of Boroughbridge in 1322.

Ela, third Countess of Salisbury, was described in the *Register of St Osmund* as 'a woman indeed worthy of praise because she was filled with the fear of the Lord.'[39] Ela was not buried alongside her husband in Salisbury Cathedral, but was given a funeral fit for a countess and laid to rest within the abbey church of Lacock that she had founded and ruled – and had called her home for the last twenty-four years of her life. Her tombstone demonstrates the high esteem in which she was held and records the words: 'Below lie buried the bones of the venerable Ela, who gave this sacred house as a home for the nuns. She also had lived here as holy abbess and Countess of Salisbury, full of good works.'[40] A generous patron of the church and influential in her political connections as sheriff and countess, Ela is described by Linda Elizabeth Mitchell as having been 'one of the two towering female figures of the mid-thirteenth century'.[41]

## Chapter Eleven

# Retirement – Eventually

The 1217 Battle of Lincoln had turned the tide of the war with the barons. After a further defeat at sea in August of the same year, the Battle of Sandwich, which meant reinforcements would not be coming, the French were forced to seek peace and returned home. The battle had been a magnificent victory for the seventy-year-old regent, William Marshal, Earl of Pembroke, and is a testament to his claim to the title 'The Greatest Knight'. He staked the fate of the country on this one battle and pulled off a decisive victory, saving his king and country. Magna Carta was soon reissued and Henry III's regents set about healing the country. Nicholaa de la Haye also earned praise for her actions, though the French chronicler Anonymous de Béthune, probably bitter at the defeat meted out at Lincoln, described her as 'a very cunning, bad-hearted and vigorous old woman'.[1]

Nicholaa had been constable of Lincoln Castle throughout the First Barons' War. The castle had been under almost constant siege from the moment of King John's death to its relief by William Marshal – seven months in total. The last two months had been particularly harrowing, with the castle under constant bombardment from French siege weapons. Nicholaa had been involved in organising the castle's defences, rationing supplies and rallying the troops. As sheriff of Lincolnshire, Nicholaa had taken firm control of the county's affairs, issuing letters of protection to such as the deans and canons of Lincoln cathedral and supervising the transfer of hostages.[2] As sheriff, Nicholaa was also responsible for the confiscation of rebels' lands and property during the civil war, some of which added to her personal wealth. She received temporary grants of the vill of Torksey and the custody of William of Huntingfield's lands that lay in her bailiwick. In addition, Nicholaa was awarded William of Huntingfield's castle at Frampton and, eventually, all his lands in the county of Lincoln.[3]

Critics of King John might use Nicholaa's actions over these lands as an accusation of Nicholaa being just like the king, and perhaps an explanation of why Nicholaa supported John to the very end. They were alike. Nicholaa exploited the lands to her own financial gain, and to the detriment of the previous owners. However, she was not the only one to use land in this way, nor would she be the last. In the 1218 Lincolnshire eyre, Huntingfield, a rebel and one of the twenty-five enforcers of Magna Carta, sued Nicholaa to the value of £273 8s. 6d. for the recovery of chattels she had taken from him after the peace was signed with Prince Louis in September 1217. Nicholaa contested the action, and a compromise was eventually reached, much to Nicholaa's benefit, whereby Nicholaa gave William thirty silver marks on the understanding that he remitted and quitclaimed to Nicholaa 'all the right and claim that he had against her'.[4] Surely for Nicholaa, who had fought and, perhaps, bled for the crown, this was a just reward for her years of loyal service? She certainly would have seen it that way.

As we have seen, Nicholaa spent the early months and spring of 1217 defending Lincoln Castle against the English rebels and their French allies, under the command of the earl of Winchester and Comte de Perche, respectively. They besieged the castle 'in which a noble woman, Nicholaa, manfully defended herself'.[5]

In spite of Nicholaa's impressive record, both as sheriff and constable, and in what is probably one of the most remarkable examples of ingratitude ever – and surely would have been worthy of King John himself – Nicholaa was relieved of her duties as sheriff of Lincolnshire just four days after the Battle of Lincoln. The position was handed to the king's uncle, William Longespée, Earl of Salisbury. Salisbury immediately took control of the city and seized the castle.[6] Perhaps the regency council thought they were helping Nicholaa? She had, after all, tried to resign the castle to King John in 1216 and she had recently endured a gruelling, relentless siege. She may also have since lost her son – or soon would. One can't help thinking that, maybe, they should have asked her first. Nicholaa's offer to relinquish the castle to John in 1216 was more likely orchestrated play-acting, in order to give John the platform from which he could display his absolute confidence in Nicholaa, a recently widowed woman. And if Nicholaa had intended to resign in 1216, she had offered up her resignation on her terms, not been forced into it by an ungrateful regency council. It may have made matters worse for Nicholaa that her beloved castle was being handed to Longespée, a man who had betrayed his brother and had, until recently, been aligned with the rebels.

Salisbury's seizure of Lincoln appears to have been the start of a family feud and was precipitated by Salisbury's purchase of the wardship of Nicholaa's granddaughter and heir, Idonea, earlier in the year. Idonea was married to Salisbury's son, William II Longespée. She had already received her inheritance from her mother, which was being administered by Salisbury. On her father's death, which probably happened sometime in 1217 or 1218, she would be able to inherit the Camville lands. The situation was made more complicated by the fact Nicholaa held the barony of Brattleby and Lincoln Castle in her own right, so Idonea would not be entitled to inherit the de la Haye lands until Nicholaa's death, although that did not appear to stop Salisbury from seizing the fortress.

Not one to give up easily Nicholaa travelled to court to remind the king's regents of her services, both to Henry III and to his father, King John, and request her rights be restored to her. In October 1217, after peace had been achieved and the French had gone home, before the regency council in London, Nicholaa insisted on the restoration of her hereditary rights to the castle.[7] Her plea was heard, and the earl of Salisbury was ordered to relinquish the castle and the shrievalty to Nicholaa. Though he reluctantly handed over the castle, the earl refused to relinquish control of the county as a whole, it was one of the richest counties in England, after all. In order to pacify Salisbury, a compromise was reached whereby the earl of Salisbury remained as sheriff of the County, while Nicholaa held the city of Lincoln itself, and the castle. So, on 4 December 1217, Nicholaa was ordered to hand over the county to Salisbury.[8] While in London, Nicholaa also had to make a special appeal to the council for the return of two of her manors in Somerset, seized by Hubert de Burgh, for reasons now lost.

The settlement does not appear to have sat well with Longespée. In February 1219, the king sent an order to 'H. bishop of Lincoln and his associates, itinerant justices in Lincolnshire, that, immediately after having viewed these letters, they are to take into the king's hand the city of Lincoln, unless they have previously done so. Immediately after they take it into the king's hand, they are to hand it over to Nicholaa de la Haye to keep. Witness the earl. By the same in the presence of the bishop of Winchester.'[9] In the same year, following the death of William Marshal, who may well have seen himself as Nicholaa's protector following her exploits in 1217, Longespée once again tried to gain control of Lincoln Castle, issuing 'a general letter in which he declared to one and all that he was taking all the shire's revenues into his own hands and would be personally answerable for them to the Exchequer "until such time as the Council of the King satisfies us in the matter of the lands and other things promised us".'[10]

News reached the government in London that the earl of Salisbury was attacking Lincoln Castle. Nicholaa made the long journey to the capital and appealed to the council in person, reminding them of her long and devoted service, of the great financial losses she and her husband had suffered in the service of the crown, and of the risk to her own life she had undertaken on its behalf. On 23 August, the council sent a letter patent to the earl of Salisbury, in which he was ordered 'to maintain, protect and defend the lands, goods and men of our trusty and well beloved Nicholaa de la Haye within his bailiwick, to cause her no molestation, injury or damage, nor to meddle in any way with her debts to the Crown or in any matter concerning her until he received orders to do so.'[11]

It may have been during her visit with the council that Nicholaa met with the king himself. Although still only a child of eleven in 1219, he regularly received visitors. In just the space of a few months in 1219–20, the young king received Earl Warenne, the countess of Eu (who was Earl Warenne's niece), Faulkes de Bréauté, the abbot-elect of Fountains Abbey and Nicholaa de la Haye.[12] It may well be that Nicholaa approached Henry in the hope that he would pressure his ministers to intervene on her behalf. If she did, the tactic appears to have worked. In addition to the order to the deputy sheriff of Lincolnshire to preserve Nicholaa's rights and properties, the council also sent physical aid. A force led by Hubert de Burgh, Peter des Roches and Faulkes de Bréauté was despatched to Nicholaa's aid, racing from Northampton to confront Salisbury's forces.

In order to guarantee Nicholaa's security, and her continued possession of the castle, Faulkes de Bréauté was assigned to 'the assistance and defence of Lincoln castle…for the conservation of the peace of the kingdom of England'.[13] De Bréauté, who was sheriff of the neighbouring shires of Cambridge and Northampton (among others), moved into the castle with his company of crossbowmen, leaving them to aid Nicholaa in her defence of the castle for the next nine months.[14] However, it seems that the earl of Salisbury was not one to give up easily and when de Bréauté was absent on other business, made another attempt on the castle, prompting Nicholaa to appeal to de Bréauté to return immediately. Faulkes de Bréauté hastened to her assistance, declaring 'God helping me, with the force at the Dame's command I will take good care that he shall not get in.'[15] De Bréauté was true to his word and beat off the earl, but not without suffering for his success; Salisbury plundered de Bréauté's estates in Devon in retaliation. And again, in January 1220, Faulkes de Bréauté had written to Hubert de Burgh after Nicholaa de la Haye had appeared before the king at Northampton, when the earl of Salisbury had again tried to gain access to the castle, this time offering up his son and nephew as hostages.[16] This appears to have been the final attempt by the earl to gain control of the castle, and for the next six years, Nicholaa remained in command, except for a brief period in 1223, when all royal castles were relinquished to the crown and redistributed. This was when the king first asserted his right to personal rule. All royal castles were ordered to be surrendered into the king's hands.[17] The patent rolls suggest that the castle was given into the hands of Stephen of Segrave, before being given into the custody of the bishop of Lincoln. However, while some constables were permanently relieved of their positions, Nicholaa was back in possession of Lincoln Castle on 23 June 1224, when Henry III instructed the bishop to return the castle to her.

Despite all these attempts to usurp her position at the castle, Nicholaa remained in command. And, after the damage caused by the 1217 Battle of Lincoln, she had her work cut out for her. The aftermath of the siege and battle had left the castle in a damaged state which must have been extensive, since more than ten years of rebuilding works were undertaken.[18] In 1217–18 Nicholaa de la Haye had received 40 marks for repairs to the castle and a further 60 marks for improvements, in addition to more modest sums for the general maintenance of the castle.[19] In the same year a further sum of 40 marks was paid by the Mayor and Provosts of Lincoln for repairs to the castle. Nicholaa also received an annual sum, to support the maintenance of the castle, which continued until she resigned the post in 1226. Some of the work was commissioned by the king himself. Nicholaa received the total sum of £130 for repairs in the period 1218 to 1220.[20] Although what work was carried out is unrecorded, it was undoubtedly to repair damage caused by the siege. Other entries in the Pipe Roll indicate that it was the sheriff who was responsible for the repair and maintenance of the gaol in this period. In 1224 the earl of Salisbury was to receive £374 15s. 0d. from the Exchequer for the money he had paid out by royal precept for the work on the castle and a further £85 for the expenses of soldiers and serving-men in the castle.[21] It is apparent from the Close Roll that this sum of money was a back payment for work in the period from 1216 to 1218, some of which would have been intended for Nicholaa. A record in the Fine Rolls of Henry III, of 17 May 1218, also refers to Nicholaa's time as sheriff, whereby she was to account for the scutage collected during that time. Or, rather, her steward was: 'To the sheriff of Lincolnshire. Robert Griffin has mainperned [confined] before the barons of the Exchequer for Nicholaa de la Haye, as her steward, that she will satisfy the king at the Exchequer for the scutage she received in Lincolnshire while the county was in her custody, both her own scutage and that of others. Order not to vex or permit Nicholaa or her people to be vexed for this reason, or to cause any distraint to be made against her or her people or to permit anyone to make any distraint against them.'[22]

The sums of money paid to Nicholaa, and Salisbury are generally described as repairs rather than new works to the castle but are not inconsiderable. Unfortunately, there is no specific reference as to what parts of the castle were subject to these repairs, although it can be assumed that much of the damage inflicted on the castle would have been as a result of the siege artillery that was used in 1217 and so would have been directed at repairing the curtain wall and buildings within the bailey. It is also possible that some of the repairs were to strengthen the castle's East Gate, which may have been weakened or undermined during the siege. From 1223–24 entries in the Pipe Roll relating to Lincoln Castle were costs for improvements, rather than repairs. In the first year 36s. 10d. was paid for improvement to the houses in the castle, while new irons were purchased to better secure the prisoners in the gaol at a cost of 14s. 6d.[23] In the year 1224–25 a sum of £20 was spent in repairs and improvements to the gate of Lincoln Castle facing the church of St Mary, the tower of 'Luce' and the building of a barbican.[24] The reference to the construction of a barbican could refer to that which was located in front of the east gate although it could be read in the original text as a structure associated with the Lucy Tower. Archaeological evidence suggests that at least one of the chambers in the Lucy Tower was abandoned at this time. The East Gate was also rebuilt to include the latest military features to aid in the castle's defence.[25]

In 1225–26 the constable of Chester was ordered to let the constable of Lincoln Castle have 40 oaks for strengthening the castle, and the constable, or rather deputy constable, Osbert Giffard, was also to receive 60 marks for operations in the castle.[26] The work on the East Gate took almost four years to complete, so was probably unfinished when Nicholaa finally relinquished the constableship of the castle in June 1226. As far as can be established from the documentary evidence the works between 1224 and 1229, which would have been commissioned by Nicholaa even if she was not there to see it completed, encompassed the reconstruction of the East Gate and the erection of a barbican presumably that which stood in front of the East Gate, works to the houses in the bailey, strengthening works on the curtain walls and possibly the reroofing of the Lucy Tower, including the sealing up of the abandoned chamber.[27]

Nicholaa was one of the subjects in an entry in the Fine Rolls of Henry III also recorded for 14 December 1218, that 'the nuns of Stainton give the king 20s. for summoning Robert of Burgate, William Talbot and Nicholaa de la Haye before the itinerant justices in Lincolnshire for a debt of 160 loads of wheat. Order to the sheriff of Lincolnshire to take security for those 20s. to the king's use.'[28] *The Testa de Nevill* records a list of Nicholaa's landholdings in Lincoln in 1219, which includes, 'by the gift of the lord king, her land of Swaton valued at £20 a year'.[29] In the same year, the sheriff of Somerset was ordered to 'place in respite, until the octaves of the Close of Easter in the fourth year, the demand he makes from Nicolaa de la Haye for 500 m., by which she made fine with King John, father of the king, for having her lands and liberties in peace, and which the king's father pardoned her, so that it may be better known by the barons of the Exchequer and other of the king's faithful men if Nicolaa ought to answer for this fine or not. Witness H. etc. By the same.'[30]

In addition to the lands of William of Huntingfield being assigned to her in 1216, Nicholaa was also assigned, in joint custody with her son, Richard de Camville, the manors of Chertsey and Henxterugge, 'whereof they had been dispossessed by Hubert de Burgh, Justice of England'.[31] And in 1218–19, for her support in keeping the castle at

Lincoln, the lordship of Munden was assigned to her. The manor had been in the king's hands since the death of Gerard de Furnivall.[32] It must also be noted that Nicholaa provided considerable support to the loyalist cause, not just in her staunch defence of Lincoln Castle, but also in the influence that she exercised over her own tenants, only one of whom, Adam of Buckminster, joined the rebels. In addition, on 16 October 1225, the sheriff of Lincolnshire, was ordered 'to place in respite, until Easter in the tenth year, the demand he makes from Nicolaa de la Haye by summons of the Exchequer for the scutage of Poitou from the time of King John etc. and for the scutage assessed in the king's time for removing Louis, first-born son of the King of France, from England. By the justiciar.'[33]

A staunchly independent woman, Nicholaa issued charters in her own name, of which some twenty-five have survived. She made grants to various religious houses, including Lincoln Cathedral and Castle Acre Priory. The grants to Lincoln Cathedral included property in the bail of Lincoln, so the dean could extend his courtyard.[34] A further grant to the cathedral, sometime around 1225 was for 'all the space between the ancient entrance to the cathedral's cemetery and the late archdeacon of Bedford's houses, for the fabric of the church'.[35] Nicholaa also continued her family's tradition in supporting Castle Acre, the Cluniac priory in Norfolk which had been founded by the de Warennes. She was also a generous patron to Barlings Abbey, founded by her uncle, Ralph de la Haye. At Barlings, it was Nicholaa who enlarged the abbey's grounds by granting the park and meadows that lay within Barlings parish.[36] Nicholaa also made a grant of 100s to Combe Abbey in Warwickshire, to pray for Gerard de Camville's soul on the anniversary of his death.[37] Combe Abbey had been founded by Gerard's father, and was where Gerard de Camville had been laid to rest. Nicholaa also secured a royal grant for a weekly market at her manor of Swaton, a concession which would have greatly benefited both the local economy and Nicholaa's own finances. Fifteen of Nicholaa's charters record new grants made by Nicholaa, some of which were exchanges of property with lay people or religious houses. While ten charters were in confirmation of earlier grants, of lands and rights, made by Nicholaa's forebears, husband or tenants.[38] One such land grant was made in 1221 to Peter the Woodseller who, in return, gave Nicholaa £20 and a pound of wax annually.

A most able adversary for some of the greatest military minds of the time, and a loyal supporter of King John, she was unique among her peers. Although praised by the chroniclers, they seemed to find difficulty in describing a woman who acted in such a fashion; the Dunstable Annals refer to her as a 'noble woman', saying she acted 'manfully'.[39] It is impossible not to feel admiration for a woman who managed to hold her own in a man's world, who fought for her castle and her home at a time when women had so little say over their own lives – and at such an advanced age. Her bravery and tenacity saved Henry III's throne. Not surprisingly, Henry III referred to her as 'our beloved and faithful Nicholaa de la Haye'.[40]

Only a few examples of Nicholaa's seal have survived the centuries. One is attached to a charter held in the National Archives at Kew, and another is in the possession of Lincoln Cathedral, I saw it on display in their new exhibition gallery as I was researching the book. Though the legend on both seals is lost, and the seal in Lincoln Cathedral is only a partial one, we can see a woman standing with her right hand on her hip, holding a hawk in her left hand. It is a common motif on seals for women of Nicholaa's rank in the twelfth and thirteenth centuries.

By late 1226 Nicholaa had retired to her manor at Swaton in Lincolnshire. Having lived well into her seventies, Nicholaa died there on 20 November 1230 and was buried in St Michael's church. Her granddaughter Idonea succeeded to Nicholaa's lands in Lincolnshire. The Fine Rolls record William II Longespée, Earl of Salisbury, paying homage to the king 'for the lands that Nicholaa de la Haye held in dower in Charlton and Henstridge of the honour of Carmel, which fall to Idonea, wife of the same William, daughter and heiress of Richard de Camville, by hereditary right, and which William and Idonea ought to hold of the king in chief by the service of two knights. Order to the sheriff of Somerset to cause William and Idonea to have full seisin of the aforesaid lands with appurtenances without delay.'[41] And on the same day, a record was made of Nicholaa's holdings at the time of her death, amounting to: 'Nicholaa de la Haye held Swaton of the king in chief for one knight's fee. In Spanby, half a knight's fee. In Billingborough, one knight's fee. In Horbling and Dembleby, one knight's fee. In Newton, one knight's fee. In Pickworth, one knight's fee and three parts of a fee. In Houstorp', one knight's fee. In Kirkby Underwood, three parts of a fee.

In Ashby and Marston, one-and-a-half knights' fees. In Willoughby, one knight's fee. In Faldingworth, Scawby, Ingham, Bullington, and Kirkby, two knights' fees. In Riseholme, one knight's fee. In Fillingham, one knight's fee and the fourth part of a fee. In Ingleby, one knight's fee. In Faldingworth, the fourth part of a fee.[42]

The king also wrote of Idonea and her husband, on the same day, to the sheriff of Lincolnshire, with the instruction that he 'cause them to have full seisin without delay of all lands and fees which the same Nicholaa held of the king in chief and which fall to the same Idonea by hereditary right. By the king's letters under the privy seal and by letters of the justiciar.'[43] One manor was held back from Idonea's inheritance, that of Duddington in Northamptonshire and on 7 December 1230, an order was sent to the sheriff of Northamptonshire 'to take into the king's hand the manor of Duddington, which Nicolaa de la Haye held by bail of the king, and to keep it safely until the king orders otherwise. Witness J. bishop of Bath. By the king's letters under the privy seal.'[44]

Nicholaa's steadfast hold on Lincoln Castle against an Anglo-French force saved England and turned the tide in favour of the regents of Henry III. Nicholaa's actions are remarkable, not only because she was a woman but also in view of her advancing years. At an age when even men would expect to be allowed to sit by the fire and reminisce about their past exploits, Nicholaa stood firm, holding a key stronghold against an invading army.

Nicholaa de la Haye's bravery and tenacity saved Henry III's throne and has earned her a place in history as one intricately linked to the struggles of King John and the fight for the creation of Magna Carta. The fact she was appointed sheriff of Lincolnshire, on 18 October 1216 just hours before John's death, is testament not only to the high esteem in which John held her, but also to her singular abilities which made her well suited to the role.[45] Her actions thereafter, in the lead up and execution of the Second Battle of Lincoln, only served to justify John's trust in Nicholaa and her unique abilities. William Marshal's approval of her and belief in her abilities are demonstrated in the *Histoire de Guillaume le Maréchal*'s description of her as 'the good dame' and the prayer for Nicholaa 'whom God preserve both in body and in soul.'[46]

## Chapter Twelve

# The Legacy of Nicholaa de la Haye

Nicholaa de la Haye's story is unique in English history. No other woman successfully defended a castle on three separate occasions, nor commanded defences during such a prolonged siege, that lasted from October 1216 until May 1217. Nicholaa not only passed her barony and the castle of Lincoln onto her two husbands, but she was an active participant in the management of both, as demonstrated by her husband, Gerard's willingness to leave Nicholaa in charge when William Longchamp came knocking, in 1191. And King John's faith in her is clearly demonstrated by his refusal to allow her to retire in 1216. He needed Nicholaa to hold the strategically important castle, but he also needed his barons to see how much he trusted Nicholaa. And he needed them to see Nicholaa's demonstration of loyalty. It was a perfect propaganda moment.

Nicholaa and John needed each other and, I think, that is why they worked in such harmony. However, Nicholaa's legacy is not just entwined in the story of King John. It must also be seen in the example she set to others. It is because of her strength and tenacity that many girls born in Lincolnshire after 1217 were named Nicholaa, or Nicola. And it may well be because of the example that she set that her own descendant, Alice de Lacey, became such a formidable woman in Lincolnshire, herself.

The story of Alice de Lacey is like something straight from a novel, with rebellion, kidnappings and love all wrapped up in the life of this one countess. Alice was born at Denbigh Castle on 25 December 1281. She was the daughter of Henry de Lacey, fifth Earl of Lincoln and, through her mother Margaret, granddaughter of William (II) Longespée, Earl of Salisbury and his wife, Idonea de Camville. Through her descent from William (II) Longespée Margaret was countess of Salisbury in her own right; and through her descent from Idonea, she was also hereditary constable of Lincoln Castle and baroness of Brattleby. Through her mother, Alice was therefore descended from two of the greatest women of the thirteenth century, Nicholaa de la Haye, hereditary constable of Lincoln Castle, and Ela of Salisbury, Countess of Salisbury in her own right. And it is through Alice that the county and castle of Lincoln finally come together as one.

Alice was one of three children. With two brothers, Edmund and John, she was, of course, not expected to inherit her father's earldom. However, two family tragedies made Alice one of the richest heiresses in England. Young Edmund, it appears, drowned in a well at Denbigh Castle and John fell to his death from the ramparts of Pontefract Castle, leaving Alice as her parents' sole heir. In 1294 Alice's marriage was arranged by no less than the king – Edward I – who saw her as a suitable bride for his nephew Thomas, Earl of Lancaster and son of the king's brother Edmund Crouchback. Alice and Thomas were married on or before 28 October 1294; he was about sixteen years old and Alice was not yet thirteen. Edward I had shown his unscrupulous nature in the marriage settlement. He insisted that Thomas was given part of the Lacey inheritance on the marriage, with the rest to pass to Thomas on Henry de Lacey's death. The settlement further stipulated that the de Lacey lands would pass to Thomas of Lancaster in the event of Alice's dying without issue; thus excluding all collateral heirs to the earldoms of Salisbury and Lincoln.

Alice's mother Margaret, Countess of Salisbury in her own right, died in 1309 and by June 1310 her father had remarried; probably in the hope of securing an heir for his earldom. In the event, it was not to be, and the Earl of Lincoln died in 1311, with his estates passing through his daughter, to Thomas Earl of Lancaster and Leicester. With five earldoms to his name, Thomas now became one of the richest and most powerful men in the kingdom. Although he was initially a supporter of the new king, his cousin Edward II, he would soon turn against him and his favourites, making enemies along the way. Poor Alice got caught in the middle of one of Thomas's feuds.

In 1314 John de Warenne refused to join the king's campaign against Scotland, which would culminate in English defeat at the Battle of Bannockburn. John and his brother-in-law the earl of Arundel claimed that they had not been summoned in the correct way, and that the campaign had not been sanctioned by parliament. As the king had secured taxation for the expedition, this last argument was lame, to say the least. The truth was far more personal; tensions between the king and John were fraught due to John's attempts to seek an annulment of his marriage to Edward's niece, Joan. And John de Warenne blamed Thomas of Lancaster for blocking his attempts to divorce Joan. Despite his failure to take part in the Bannockburn campaign, John de Warenne steadfastly supported King Edward throughout the political crises of the ensuing years. In 1317, he was among a small number of noblemen summoned by Edward to a colloquium at Clarendon; although we do not know what was discussed, it is possible that the continuing problems in Scotland were raised, and the possibility of an attack on Lancaster.

Shortly afterwards, John de Warenne abducted Alice, Lancaster's wife: 'In this year, on Monday preceding the Ascension of our Lord, the Countess of Lancaster, the lawful wife of the noble man, Lord Thomas, Earl of Lancaster, was seized at Cranford, in Dorset, by a certain knight of the house and family of John, Earl Warenne, with many English retainers called together for the detestable deed, as it is said, with the royal assent. And she was conducted, with not a little pomp, to the said Earl Warenne, to his castle of Reigate. And while the lady was so conducted, behold during the journeying among the woods and fences, between Haulton and Farnaham, the leaders saw at a distance flags and banners, for the priests were going with the people, making processions in the usual manner about the fields (Rogation days). The conductors, therefore, of the countess, struck with sudden fear and terror, thinking that the Earl of Lancaster, or some people sent by him to obtain the said lady, and vindicate themselves against so great an injury, fled with all celerity, leaving the countess almost alone. But when the truth of the affair was discovered, they returned with threats and bluster. With them was a certain man of miserable stature, lame and hunchbacked, called Richard de S. Martin, exhibiting and declaring constantly his evil intentions towards the lady, so miserably led away. He, puffed up by great encouragement, demanded her as his wife, firmly declaring that he had known her carnally before she married the Earl of Lancaster. Also he stated that she publicly acknowledged it, and admitted it to be true... Therefore the said Richard, exalting himself above himself, dared to claim in the King's Court the earldom of Lincoln and Salisbury, in the name of his wife – jure uxoris – but in vain.'[1]

Alice was kidnapped in 1317 from her manor in Canford, Dorset, by John de Warenne's man, Sir Richard de St Martin, supposedly with the king's knowledge. Several reasons for the abduction have been put forward; one is, of course, that Alice and St Martin were having an affair while another is that the affair was between Alice and John de Warenne, Earl of Surrey, himself. John's reputation alone could give credence to that theory, given he was trying to divorce his wife in order to marry his mistress. Given the king's involvement, the kidnapping may have been an attempt to antagonise the earl of Lancaster; something John would have been happy to do, given Lancaster's recent obstruction of John's divorce attempts. Following her abduction, Alice was held at Reigate Castle, Surrey. Her kidnapping set off a private war between the two magnates, although Lancaster seems to have made little effort to actually rescue his wife and there is no record of how and when she was eventually released.

In the escalating feud, and unable to strike against the king directly, for fear of being charged with treason, Lancaster attacked John de Warenne's Yorkshire estates, which were close to his own castle at Pontefract. In October and November, he sent forces to seize the Warenne castles at Sandal and Conisbrough. Lancaster's men found the gates of Conisbrough closed to them. The castle was defended by only six men, including the town miller and three brothers, Thomas, Henry and William Greathead, who were men-at-arms.[2] The siege lasted less than two hours and the defenders appear to have relinquished the castle after apparently putting up a token resistance; the three brothers were fined for drawing blood.[3] The chapel in the castle's inner bailey may have been damaged in the brief altercation, as the following year, Lancaster sent orders to his castellan at Conisbrough, John de Lassell, to 'repailler la couverture de la chapele de Conynggesburgh'. ('repair the roof of Conisbrough's chapel').[4]

Edward tried to stop the fighting, sending messages to Lancaster:

'The King has lately heard that the earl has, with a multitude of armed men, besieged and captured divers castles of John de Warenne, Earl of Surrey, in the county of York, and that he still detains them; and has done many other things in those parts to the disturbance of the King's peace. Wherefore, the King orders him to desist entirely from these proceedings; and if he have done any such things to cause them to be amended in due form: and forbids him to go armed, or to assemble men-at-arms: or to do anything else to this disturbance of the King's peace. The King is prepared to do justice in his Court concerning the things that the earl has to prosecute against the Earl of Surrey and certain others.'[5]

Lancaster was relentless, even ejecting John's mistress, Maud de Nerford, from her property. In June 1318, Lancaster attacked John's Welsh lands at Yale and Bromfield; again, these lands were in close proximity to Lancaster's own property. John de Warenne wrote to the king, complaining of Lancaster's actions on his Welsh estates:

'The Earl Warenne to the King: The Earl offers reverence and all honour to his most noble and most honourable Prince and most dear lord and wishes the king to understand that news comes to him out of Wales, in haste, day and night, from his people of Bromfeud and Ial [Bromfield and Yale], that the Earl of Lancaster has… [in] his letters to them bid them attourn themselves to him, and that he wishes by all means to have such lands and he has menaced the Earl's said people to the effect that they shall attourn themselves to him in one manner or another, which fact the king may more fully see by the transcript of the letter which they have sent to the petitioner, which he sends to the king enclosed within this. It is great marvel that the Earl of Lancaster wishes to move in such manner upon the petitioner more than he has done, since good peace and agreement were lately made between the king and him, the Earl of Lancaster, on all points. In this agreement the petitioner intends that the business between the Earl and himself shall be brought to good end by means of the king's good lordship, and by his aid and counsel. Wherefore petitioner prays and demands of his highness that on these things he will, if it is his pleasure, take counsel and good advice and will send his letters to the Earl, ordering him to surcease from making or commending such threats against the peace, to the dishonour of the king and the grave loss of the petitioner; and that the king, if it please him, may send other letters to his justices of Wales and Chester and to the sheriffs of those parts, that if any people come in force to enter the petitioner's lands, that they, the officers mentioned, may take action, that the king's people in those same parts may be ready with all their power, well and openly to withstand, and to defend the petitioner's lands. May the king command these things to be done in the greatest haste possible....'[6]

In response to John's desperate letter, it was agreed in council that the earl should be ordered to proceed to Bromfield to protect his territories and ascertain what could be done. It was also decided that the earl of Lancaster should be ordered not to do anything which disturbed the peace. Given that Lancaster gained control of both Bromfield and Yale, it is obvious that he chose to ignore the king's commands. Shortly afterwards, the king and Lancaster temporarily resolved their differences, meeting somewhere between Loughborough and Leicester on 7 August, when they exchanged the kiss of peace in front of the court. Within two days of the meeting, 'Roger Damory and the rest, except Hugh le Despenser the Elder and the Earl Warenne, humbly presented themselves before the earl, [and] were received into his grace.'[7] John de Warenne, it seems, was abandoned by the king in the interests of peace, leaving Lancaster to pursue his personal feud with the earl. John was hunted down and imprisoned in Lancaster's castle at Pontefract. Beaten into submission, he was forced to come to terms with Lancaster, coming to an agreement in 1319 which meant giving up most of his Yorkshire estates and some of his lands in Wales and Norfolk, in exchange for land in Devon, Wiltshire and Somerset. Edward, perhaps feeling guilty on how John had been hung out to dry for the sake of national harmony, altered the grant so that Lancaster could only hold the lands during John's lifetime; they would revert to John's heirs on his death. John also acknowledged that he owed Lancaster a debt of £50,000, an astronomical sum, though none of it was ever collected.[8]

Alice and Thomas's marriage does not appear to have been a happy one, as demonstrated by the fact he made no attempt to recover her from John de Warenne. Instead, he used her kidnapping as a justification for pursuing his own ambitions against John de Warenne and his lands. There is some evidence that they were actually divorced in 1318, with Thomas retaining Alice's earldoms after enforcing the marriage contract. The divorce was supposedly on account of her adultery with the Earl of Surrey's squire, Sir Eubolo Lestrange (although this may be a confusion of facts from her abduction and her later marriage). It has also been claimed that Alice and her abductor, Richard de St Martin, were pre-contracted before her marriage to Thomas of Lancaster. However, although this is not impossible, it does seem unlikely, given Alice's tender age on the day of her wedding to Thomas.

Whether or not Alice and Thomas did divorce is still open to debate. If the divorce occurred, it certainly did not protect Alice from the reprisals meted out after her husband's failed rebellion and defeat at the Battle of Boroughbridge on 16 March 1322. While Thomas was executed Alice, along with her stepmother, Joan, dowager Countess of Lincoln, was imprisoned in York Castle. It must have been a truly terrifying time for the two women; with no protectors they were at the mercy of the king's favourites, Hugh le Despenser the Younger and his father, also called Hugh le Despenser. Both had a reputation for ruthlessness and acquisitiveness. They had amassed a vast fortune through the confiscation of lands, not always lawfully. Threatened with execution by burning Alice and Joan were forced to turn over the majority of their estates. Having paid an enormous ransom of £20,000 Alice was finally released, securing her titles, a small percentage of her estates and the right to remarry. Her stepmother, Joan, died in October 1322; we can only surmise as to whether or not her demise was as a consequence of her imprisonment, but it will not have improved her state of health.

Alice would eventually recover Lincoln Castle and the earldom of Lincoln, but many of her estates were given to her erstwhile abductor, John de Warenne, and only returned to her by Edward III, many years later. By November 1324, Alice had married again, this time to a minor baron from the Welsh Marches, Sir Ebule, or Eubolo, Lestrange of Shropshire. The marriage demonstrated that Alice had managed to come out of the disaster of her first husband's downfall with enough income and property to make her an attractive proposition as a wife. Although, it does seem possible that this marriage was a love-match. The marriage appears to have been a happier one, given that Lestrange moved over to Lincolnshire to look after his wife's interests, and that it was with Sir Eubolo that Alice chose to be buried, when the time came. Alice and Sir Eubolo were married for over ten years, although towards the latter part Lestrange was away campaigning in Scotland, where he died in September 1335. Alice was named as one of his executors and he was buried in Barlings Abbey, Lincolnshire, the Premonstratensian house founded by Ralph de la Haye in 1154, and to which Alice was herself a generous patron.

Following Sir Eubolo's death, Alice took a vow of chastity and looked determined to settle into a life of quiet retirement. However, her adventures were not quite at an end. In 1335, or early 1336, Alice was kidnapped for a second time; she was abducted from her castle at Bolingbroke and raped, by Sir Hugh de Freyne. Freyne was a Herefordshire knight and royal keeper of the town and castle of Cardigan. Although there appears some suggestion that Alice was in collusion with Sir Hugh, historians remain undecided. The theory is that her abduction was orchestrated as a way for her to escape her vow of chastity. It seems more likely that Alice acquiesced to a situation over which she had little control. Edward III was furious and ordered the imprisonment of the couple, but they were reconciled with the king in 1336 and allowed to marry officially. The marriage did much to improve Freyne's status and brought him a summons to Parliament in November 1336. However, such success was short-lived as he died at Perth in December 1336 or January 1337.

Shortly after her third husband's death, the bishop of Lincoln issued a demand that Alice keep her prior vow of chastity. And as there were no further marriages – or abductions – we can probably assume that she did. Alice died on the 2 October 1348 at the grand age of sixty-six. She was buried with her second husband at the Premonstratensian House of Barlings, in Lincolnshire. Having had no children from any of her three marriages, Alice's lands and titles, as according to her marriage settlement fifty-four years earlier, passed to the house of Lancaster and her husband's nephew, Henry of Grosmont, first Duke of Lancaster and father of Blanche of Lancaster, John of Gaunt's first wife.

It was Alice who promoted her family's foundation of Barlings Abbey as the mausoleum of the earls of Lincoln. She bolstered the monastery's economy by gifting it the manor of Swaton, with the advowson of St Michael's church in 1322. It was at St Michael's that Nicholaa de la Haye had been buried in 1230. And it seems likely that Alice had Nicholaa in mind when making the donation. At some point in the ten years following the donation, it seems that Nicholaa's rather splendid tomb was installed in St Michael's, probably commissioned by Alice. There was some doubt as to whether the tomb was Nicholaa's, as the clothing on the effigy is of a later fashion – more akin to the 1330s than the 1230s. As David Stocker explained to me, the fashion is right for Alice's time and has convinced me that the tomb is Nicholaa's but was installed a hundred years after her death.

Given the trials she had to endure, it is not hard to imagine Alice de Lacey looking for inspiration in Nicholaa's own story. She may have told herself, in her darkest moments, that if Nicholaa could endure months under bombardment in Lincoln Castle, and in her sixties, then Alice herself was just as strong and could endure also. In those desperate times, imprisoned at the mercy of Hugh le Despenser and under the threat of being burned at the stake, she must have wondered where her own William Marshal was.

Nicholaa's fame may not have survived the centuries as much as she surely deserved, but her exploits at the time elicited much admiration. A most able adversary for some of the greatest military minds of the time, and a loyal supporter of King John, Nicholaa de la Haye was unique among her peers. Although praised by the chroniclers, they seemed to find difficulty in describing a woman who acted in such a fashion; the Dunstable annalist referred to her as a 'noble woman', saying she acted 'manfully'. Not surprisingly, both King John and Henry III referred to her as 'our beloved and faithful Nicholaa de la Haye'. One cannot fail to feel admiration for a woman who managed to hold her own in a man's world, who fought for her castle and her home in a time when women had so little say over their own lives – and at such an advanced age. Her bravery and tenacity saved Henry III's throne.

And Lincoln itself has never forgotten its most remarkable daughter. The castle commemorates Nicholaa's exploits with a blue plaque and, until recent years, her image was carved on a tree stump that held pride of place in the centre of the bailey. Unfortunately, the wood is now rotting, but the thought was there. And in the 2017 knights' trail that the city put on to celebrate the 800th anniversary of the Battle of Lincoln, Nicholaa had her own statue, dressed in blue and taking pride of place in front of the East Gate of her castle, still guarding it. Her name lives on in the house names in local schools and in the building named after her at the University of Lincoln, though they have sadly dropped the 'h' and the extra 'a' and use the modern-day spelling of Nicholaa.

Nicholaa de la Haye, the woman who saved England.

At least she is remembered.

# Appendix A

# The 1215 Magna Carta

John, by the grace of God, King of England, lord of Ireland, duke of Normandy and Aquitaine, count of Anjou, to the archbishops, bishops, abbots, earls, barons, justiciars, foresters, sheriffs, stewards, servants and all his officials and faithful subjects, greeting. Know that we, from reverence for God and for the salvation of our soul and those of all our ancestors and heirs, for the honour of God and the exaltation of Holy Church and the reform of our realm, on the advice of our reverend fathers, Stephen, archbishop of Canterbury, primate of all England and cardinal of the Holy Roman Church, Henry, archbishop of Dublin, William of London, Peter of Winchester, Jocelin of Bath and Glastonbury, Hugh of Lincoln, Walter of Worcester, William of Coventry and Benedict of Rochester, bishops, Master Pandulf, subdeacon and member of the household of the lord pope, Brother Aimeric, master of the knighthood of the Temple in England, and the noble men, William Marshal, earl of Pembroke, William, earl of Salisbury, William, earl of Warenne, William, earl of Arundel, Alan of Galloway, constable of Scotland, Warin fitz Gerold, Peter fitz Herbert, Hubert de Burgh, seneschal of Poitou, Hugh de Neville, Matthew fitz Herbert, Thomas Basset, Alan Basset, Philip d'Aubigny, Robert of Ropsley, John Marshal, John fitz Hugh and others, our faithful subjects:

**Clause 1**
In the first place have granted to God and by this our present charter have confirmed, for us and our heirs in perpetuity, that the English church shall be free, and shall have its rights undiminished and its liberties unimpaired: and we wish it thus observed, which is evident from the fact that of our own free will before the quarrel between us and our barons began, we conceded and confirmed by our charter freedom of elections, which is thought to be of the greatest necessity and importance to the English church, and obtained confirmation of this from the lord pope

Innocent III, which we shall observe in good faith in perpetuity. We have also granted to all the free men of our realm for ourselves and our heirs for ever, all the liberties written below, to have and hold, them and their heirs from us and our heirs.

## Clause 2

If any of our earls or barons, or others holding of us in chief by knight service shall die, and at his death his heir be of full age and owe relief, he shall have his inheritance on payment of the ancient relief, namely the heir or heirs of an earl £100 for a whole earl's barony, the heir or heirs of a baron £100 for a whole barony, the heir or heirs of a knight 100*s*. at most for a whole knight's fee; and anyone who owes less shall give less according to the ancient usage of fiefs.

## Clause 3

If, however, the heir of any such person has been under age and in wardship, when he comes of age he shall have his inheritance without relief or fine.

## Clause 4

The guardian of the land of such an heir who is under age shall not take from the land more than the reasonable revenues, customary dues and services, and that without destruction and waste of men or goods. And if we entrust the wardship of the land of such a one to a sheriff, or to any other who is answerable to us for its revenues, and he destroys or wastes the land in his charge, we will take amends of him, and the land shall be entrusted to two lawful and prudent men of that fief who will be answerable to us for the revenues or to him to whom we have assigned them. And if we give or sell to anyone the wardship of any such land and he causes destruction or waste, he shall lose the wardship and it shall be transferred to two lawful and prudent men of the fief who shall be answerable to us as aforesaid.

## Clause 5

Moreover so long as the guardian has the wardship of the land, he shall maintain the houses, parks, preserves, fishponds, mills and the other things pertaining to the land from its revenues; and he shall restore to the heir when he comes of age all his land stocked with ploughs and wainage such as the agricultural season demands and the revenues of the estate can easily bear.

## Clause 6
Heirs shall be given in marriage without disparagement, yet so that before a marriage is contracted it shall be made known to the heir's next of kin.

## Clause 7
After her husband's death, a widow shall have her marriage portion and her inheritance at once and without any hindrance; nor shall she pay anything for her dower, her marriage portion, or her inheritance which she and her husband held on the day of her husband's death; and she may stay in her husband's house for 40 days after his death, within which period her dower shall be assigned to her.

## Clause 8
No widow shall be compelled to marry so long as she wishes to live without a husband, provided that she gives security that she will not marry without our consent if she holds of us, or without the consent of the lord of whom she holds, if she holds of another.

## Clause 9
Neither we nor our bailiffs will seize any land or rent in payment of a debt so long as the chattels of the debtor are sufficient to repay the debt; nor shall the sureties of the debtor be distrained so long as the debtor himself is capable of paying the debt; and if the principal debtor defaults in the payment of the debt, having nothing wherewith to pay it, the sureties shall be answerable for the debt; and if they wish, they may have the lands and revenues of the debtor until they have received satisfaction for the debt they paid on his behalf, unless the principal debtor shows that he has discharged his obligations to the sureties.

## Clause 10
If anyone who has borrowed from the Jews any amount, great or small, dies before the debt is repaid, it shall not carry interest unless the heir is under age, of whomsoever he holds; and if that debt falls into our hands, we will take nothing except the principal sum specified in the bond.

**Clause 11**
And if a man dies owing a debt to the Jews, his wife may have her dower and pay nothing of that debt; and if he leaves children under age, their needs shall be met in a manner in keeping with the holding of the deceased; and the debts shall be paid out of the residue, saving the service due to the lords. Debts owing to others than Jews shall be dealt with likewise.

**Clause 12**
No scutage or aid shall be levied in our realm except by the common counsel of our realm, unless it is for the ransom of our person, the knighting of our eldest son or the first marriage of our eldest daughter; and for these only a reasonable aid is to be levied. Aids from the city of London are to be treated likewise.

**Clause 13**
And the city of London is to have all its ancient liberties and free customs both by land and water. Furthermore, we will and grant that all other cities, boroughs, towns and ports shall have all their liberties and free customs.

**Clause 14**
And to obtain the common council of the realm for the assessment of an aid (except in the three cases aforesaid) or a scutage, we will have archbishops, bishops, abbots, earls and greater barons summoned individually by our letters, and we shall also have summoned generally through our sheriffs and bailiffs all those who hold of us in chief, for a fixed date, with at least forty days' notice, and at a fixed place; and in all letters of the summons we will state the reason for the summons. And when the summons has thus been made, the business shall go forward in the day arranged according to the council of those present, even if not all those summoned have come.

**Clause 15**
Henceforth we will not grant anyone that he may take an aid from his free men except to ransom his person, to make his eldest son a knight and to marry his eldest daughter once; and for these purposes only a reasonable aid is to be levied.

## Clause 16
No man shall be compelled to perform more service for a knight's fee or for any other free tenement that is due therefrom.

## Clause 17
Common pleas shall not follow our court but shall be held in some fixed place.

## Clause 18
Recognizances of novel disseisin, mort d'ancestor, and darrein presentment shall not be held elsewhere than in the court of the county in which they occur, and in this manner: we, or if we are out of the realm our chief justiciar, shall send two justices through each county chosen by the county, shall hold the said assizes in the county court on the day and in the place of meeting of the county court.

## Clause 19
And if the said assizes cannot be held on the day of the county court, so many knights and freeholders of those present in the county court on that day shall remain behind as will suffice to make judgements, according to the amount of business to be done.

## Clause 20
A free man shall not be amerced for a trivial offence, except in accordance with the degree of the offence; and for a serious offence he shall be amerced according to its gravity, saving his livelihood; and a merchant likewise saving his merchandise; in the same way a villein shall be amerced saving his wainage; if they fall into our mercy. And none of the aforesaid amercements shall be imposed except by testimony of reputable men of the neighbourhood.

## Clause 21
Earls and barons shall not be amerced except by their peers and only in accordance with the nature of the offence.

**Clause 22**
No clerk shall be amerced on his lay tenement except in the manner of the others aforesaid and without reference to the size of his ecclesiastical benefice.

**Clause 23**
No vill or man shall be forced to build bridges at river banks, except those who ought to do so by custom and law.

**Clause 24**
No sheriff, constable, coroners or others of our bailiffs may hold pleas of our Crown.

**Clause 25**
All shires, hundreds, wapentakes and ridings shall be at the ancient farm, without any increment, except our demesne manors.

**Clause 26**
If anyone holding a lay fief of us dies and our sheriff or bailiff shows our letters patent of summons for a debt which the deceased owed us, it shall be lawful for the sheriff or our bailiff to attach and list the chattels of the deceased found in lay fee to the value of that debt, by the view of lawful men, so that nothing is removed until the evident debt is paid to us, and the residue shall be relinquished to the executors to carry out the will of the deceased. And if he owes us nothing, all the chattels shall be accounted as the deceased's saving their reasonable shares to his wife and children.

**Clause 27**
If any free man dies intestate, his chattels are to be distributed by his nearest relations and friends, under supervision of the Church, saving to everyone the debts which the deceased owed him.

**Clause 28**
No constable or any other of our bailiffs shall take any man's corn or other chattels unless he pays cash for them at once or can delay payment with the agreement of the seller.

## Clause 29
No constable is to compel any knight to give money for castle guard, if he is willing to perform that guard in his own person or by another reliable man, if for some good reason he is unable to do it himself; and if we take or send him on military service, he shall be excused the guard in proportion to the period of his service.

## Clause 30
No sheriff or bailiff of ours or anyone else is to take horses or carts of any free man for carting without his agreement.

## Clause 31
Neither we nor our bailiffs shall take other men's timber for castles or other work of ours, without the agreement of the owner.

## Clause 32
We will not hold the lands of convicted felons for more than a year and a day, when the lands shall be returned to the lords of the fiefs.

## Clause 33
Henceforth all fish-weirs shall be completely removed from the Thames and the Medway and throughout all England, except on the sea coast.

## Clause 34
The writ called *praecipe* shall not, in future, be issued to anyone in respect of any holding whereby a free man may lose his court.

## Clause 35
Let there be one measure of wine throughout our kingdom and one measure of ale and one measure of corn, namely the London quarter, and one width of cloth whether dyed, russet or halberjet, namely two ells within the selvedges. Let it be the same with weights as with measures.

## Clause 36
Henceforth nothing shall be given or taken for the writ of inquisition of life or limb, but it shall be given freely and not refused.

#### Clause 37

If anyone holds of us by fee-farm, by socage or by burgage, and holds land of someone else by knight service, we will not, by virtue of that fee-farm or socage or burgage have wardship of his heir or of land of his that belongs to the fief of another; nor will we have custody of that fee-farm or socage or burgage unless such fee-farm owes knight service. We will not have custody of the heir or land of anyone who holds of another by knight service, by virtue of any petty sergeanty which he holds of us by the service of rendering to us knives or arrows or the like.

#### Clause 38

Henceforth no bailiff shall put anyone on trial by his own unsupported allegation, without bringing credible witnesses to the charge.

#### Clause 39

No free man shall be taken or imprisoned or disseised or outlawed or exiled or in any way ruined, nor will we go or send against him, except by the lawful judgement of his peers or by the law of the land.

#### Clause 40

To no one will we sell, to no one will we deny or delay right or justice.

#### Clause 41

All merchants are to be safe and secure in leaving and entering England, and in staying and travelling in England, both by land and by water, to buy and sell free from all maletotes by the ancient and rightful customs, except, in time of war, such as come from an enemy country. And if such are found in our land at the outbreak of war they shall be detained without damage to their persons or goods, until we or our chief justiciar know how the merchants of our land are treated in the enemy country; and if ours are safe there, the others shall be safe in our land.

#### Clause 42

Henceforth anyone, saving his allegiance due to us, may leave our realm and return safe and secure by land and water, save for a short period in time of war on account of the general interest of the realm and excepting those imprisoned and outlawed according to the law of the land, and natives of an enemy country, and merchants, who shall be treated as aforesaid.

## Clause 43
If anyone dies who holds of some escheat such as the honours of Wallingford, Nottingham, Boulogne or Lancaster, or of other escheats which are in our hands and are baronies, his heir shall not give any relief or do any service to us other than what he would have done to the baron if that barony had been in the baron's hands; and we shall hold it in the same manner as the baron held it.

## Clause 44
Henceforth men who live outside the forest shall not come before our justices of the forest upon a general summons unless they are impleaded or are sureties for any person or persons who are attached for forest offences.

## Clause 45
We will not appoint justices, constables, sheriffs or bailiffs who do not know the law of the land and are willing to keep it well.

## Clause 46
All barons who have founded abbeys of which they have charters of the kings of England, or ancient tenure, are to have custody of them when they are vacant, as they ought to have.

## Clause 47
All forests which have been afforested in our time shall be disafforested at once; and river banks which we have enclosed in our time shall be treated similarly.

## Clause 48
All evil customs of forests and warrens, foresters and warreners, sheriffs and their servants, river banks and their wardens are to be investigated at once in every county by twelve sworn knights of the same county who are to be chosen by worthy men of the county, and within forty days of the inquiry they are to be abolished by them beyond recall, provided that we, or our justiciar, if we are not in England, first know of it.

**Clause 49**
We will restore at once all hostages and charters delivered to us by Englishmen as securities for peace or faithful service.

**Clause 50**
We will dismiss completely from their offices the relations of Gerard d'Athée that henceforth they shall have no office in England, Engelard de Cigogné, Peter and Guy and Andrew de Chanceaux, Guy de Cigogné, Geoffrey de Martigny with his brothers, Philip Marc with his brothers and his nephew, Geoffrey, and all their followers.

**Clause 51**
Immediately after concluding peace. We will remove from the kingdom all alien knights, crossbowmen, sergeants and mercenary soldiers who have come with horses and arms to the hurt of the realm.

**Clause 52**
If anyone has been disseised or deprived by us without lawful judgement of his peers of lands, castles, liberties or his rights we will restore them to him at once; and if any disagreement arises on this, then let it be settled by the judgement of the Twenty-Five barons referred to below in the security clause. But for all those things for which anyone was disseised or deprived without lawful judgement of his peers by King Henry our father, or by King Richard our brother, which we hold in our hand or which are held by others under our warranty, we shall have respite for the usual crusader's term; excepting those cases in which a plea was begun or inquest made on our order before we took the cross; when, however, we return from our pilgrimage, or if perhaps we do not undertake it, we will at once do full justice in these matters.

**Clause 53**
We shall have the same respite, and in the same manner, in doing justice or disafforesting or retaining those forests which Henry our father or Richard our brother afforested, and concerning custody of lands which are of the fee of another, the which wardships we have hitherto by virtue of a fee held of us by knight's service, and concerning abbeys founded on fees other than our own, in which the lord of the fee claims to have a

right. And as soon as we return, or if we do not undertake our pilgrimage, we will at once do full justice to complainants in these matters.

### Clause 54
No one shall be taken or imprisoned upon the appeal of a woman for the death of anyone except her husband.

### Clause 55
All fines which were made with us unjustly and contrary to the law of the land, and all amercements imposed unjustly and contrary to the law of the land, shall be completely remitted or else they shall be settled by the judgement of the Twenty-Five barons mentioned below in the security clause, or by the judgement of the majority of the same, along with the aforesaid Stephen, archbishop of Canterbury, if he can be present, and others whom he wishes to summon with him for this purpose. And if he cannot be present the business shall nevertheless proceed without him, provided that if any one of more of the aforesaid Twenty-Five barons are in such a suit they shall stand down in this particular judgement, and shall be replaced by others chosen and sworn in by the rest of the same Twenty-Five, for this case only.

### Clause 56
If we have disseised or deprived Welshmen of lands, liberties, or other things without lawful judgement of their peers, in England or in Wales, they are to be returned to them at once; and if a dispute arises over this it shall be settled in the March by judgement of their peers; for tenements in England according to the law in England, for tenements in Wales according to the law in Wales, for tenements in the March according to the law of the March. The Welsh are to do the same to us and ours.

### Clause 57
For all those things, however, of which any Welshman had been disseised or deprived without lawful judgement of his peers by King Henry our father, or King Richard our brother, which we have in our possession or which others hold under our legal warranty, we shall have respite for the usual crusader's term; excepting those cases in which a plea was begun or inquest made on our order before we took the cross. However, when

we return, or if perhaps we do not go on our pilgrimage, we will at once give them full justice in accordance with the laws of the Welsh and the aforesaid regions.

**Clause 58**
We will restore at once the son of Llywelyn and all the hostages from Wales and the charters delivered to us as security for peace.

**Clause 59**
We will treat Alexander, king of Scots, concerning the return of his sisters and hostages and his liberties and rights in the same manner in which we will act towards our other barons of England, unless it ought to be otherwise because of the charters which we have from William his father, formerly king of Scots; and this shall be determined by the judgement of his peers in our court.

**Clause 60**
All these aforesaid customs and liberties which we have granted to be held in our realm as far as it pertains to us towards our men, shall be observed by all men of our realm, both clerk and lay, as far as it pertains to them, towards their own men.

**Clause 61**
Since, moreover, we have granted the aforesaid things for God, for the reform of our realm and the better settling of the quarrel which has arisen between us and our barons, wishing these things to be enjoyed fully and undisturbed in perpetuity, we give and grant them the following security: namely, that the barons shall choose any twenty-five barons of the realm they wish, who with all their might are to observe, maintain and cause to be observed the peace and liberties which we have granted and confirmed to them by this our present charter; so that if we and our justiciar or our bailiffs or any of our servants offend against anyone in any way, or transgress any of the articles of peace or security, and the offence is indicated to four of the aforesaid twenty-five barons, those four barons shall come to us or our justiciar, if we are out of the kingdom, and shall bring it to our notice and ask that we have it redressed without delay. And if we or our justiciar, should we be out of the kingdom, do not redress

the offence within forty days from the time it was brought to the notice of us or our justiciar, should we be out of the kingdom, the aforesaid four barons shall refer the case to the rest of the twenty-five barons and those twenty-five barons with the commune of all the land shall distrain and distress us in every way they can, namely by seizing castles, lands and possessions, and in such other ways as they can, saving our person and those of our queen and our children, until, in their judgement, amends have been made; and when it has been redressed they are to obey us as they did before. Anyone in the land who wishes may take an oath to obey the orders of the said twenty-five barons in the execution of the aforesaid matters, and to join with them in distressing us to the best of his ability, and we publicly and freely permit anyone who wishes to take the oath, and we will never forbid anyone to take it. Moreover we shall compel and order all those in the land who of themselves and of their own free will are unwilling to take an oath to the twenty-five barons to distrain and distress us with them, to take the oath aforesaid. And if any of the twenty-five barons dies or leaves the country or is otherwise prevented from discharging these aforesaid duties, the rest of the aforesaid barons shall on their own decision choose another in his place, who shall take the oath in the same way as the others. In all matters the execution of which is committed to these twenty-five barons, if it should happen that the twenty-five are present and disagree among themselves or anything, or if any of them who has been summoned will not or cannot come, whatever the majority of those present shall provide or order is to be taken as fixed and settled as if the whole twenty-five had agreed to it; and the aforesaid twenty-five are to swear that they will faithfully observe all the aforesaid and will do all they can to secure its observance. And we will procure nothing from anyone, either personally or through another, by which any of these concessions and liberties shall be revoked or diminished; and if only such thing is procured, it shall be null and void, and we will never use it either ourselves or through another.

### Clause 62

And we have completely remitted and pardoned to all any ill will, grudge and rancour that have arisen between us and our subjects, clerk and lay, from the time of the quarrel. Moreover we have fully forgiven and completely condoned to all, clerk and lay, as far as pertains to us, all offences occasioned by the said quarrel from Easter in the sixteenth year of our reign to the conclusion of peace. And moreover we have caused letters patent of the Lord Stephen, archbishop of Canterbury, the Lord Henry, archbishop of Dublin, the aforesaid bishops and Master Pandulf to be made for them on this security and the aforesaid concessions.

**Clause 63**

Wherefore we wish and firmly command that the English church shall be free, and the men in our realm shall have and hold all the aforesaid liberties, rights and concessions well and peacefully, freely and quietly, fully and completely for them and their heirs in all things and places forever, as is aforesaid. Moreover an oath has been sworn, both on our part and on the part of the barons that all these things aforesaid shall be observed in good faith and without evil intent. Witness the abovementioned and many others. Given under our hand in the meadow which is called Runnymede between Windsor and Staines on the fifteenth day of June in the seventeenth year of our reign.

# Appendix B

# Enforcers of Magna Carta – The Twenty-Five

A committee of twenty-five barons, all in the forefront of the opposition to King John, were appointed to oversee the enforcement of the terms of Magna Carta, as directed by clause 61 of the charter, the security clause, which authorised the barons to:

'...choose any twenty-five barons of the realm they wish...so that if we transgress any of the articles...then those twenty-five with the commune of all the land shall distress and distrain us in every way they can, namely by seizing our lands, castles and possessions.'[1]

**In no particular order, the Twenty-Five were:**

Richard de Clare, Earl of Hertford
Gilbert de Clare
Geoffrey de Say
Geoffrey de Mandeville, Earl of Essex and Gloucester
Robert Fitzwalter
Roger (II) Bigod, Earl of Norfolk
Hugh Bigod
Robert de Vere, Earl of Oxford
Richard de Montfichet
William of Huntingfield
William de Lanvallei, Lord of Walken in Hertfordshire
Henry de Bohun, Earl of Hereford
William Mallet, Lord of Shepton Mallet
William Marshal the younger
Saher de Quincy, Earl of Winchester
William d'Aubigné, Lord of Belvoir
John de Lacy, Lord of Pontefract, later Earl of Lincoln

John fitz Robert, Lord of Warkworth
Robert de Ros, Lord of Wark-on-Tweed
William de Forz, Count of Aumale
Eustace de Vescy
William de Mowbray
Richard de Percy
Roger de Montbegon, Lord of Hornby
Serlo the Mercer, Mayor of London

# Appendix C

# The Charter of the Forest 1217

Henry, by the grace of God, king of England, lord of Ireland, duke of Normandy, Aquitaine, and count of Anjou, to the archbishops, bishops, abbots, priors, earls, barons, justiciars, foresters, sheriffs, governors, officers, and all his bailiffs and faithful subjects. Greeting.

Know that we, for the honour of God and for the salvation of our own soul and the souls of our ancestors and successors, for the exaltation of Holy Church and the reform of our realm, have granted and by this present charter have confirmed for us and our heirs for ever, by the counsel of our venerable father, the lord Guala, cardinal priest of St Martin and legate of the apostolic see, of the lord Walter archbishop of York, William bishop of London and the other bishops of England and of William Marshal earl of Pembroke, guardian of us and of our kingdom, and of others our faithful earls and barons of England, these underwritten liberties to be held in our kingdom of England for ever.

### Clause 1
In the first place, all the forests made by our grandfather king Henry [II], shall be viewed by good and lawful men, and if he made any other than his own proper woods into forests to the damage of him whose wood it was, it shall forthwith be disafforested. And if he made his own proper woods forest, it shall remain forest, saving the common right of pasturage, and of other things in the same forest, to those who were formerly accustomed to have them.

### Clause 2
Men who live outside the forest, from henceforth shall not come before our justiciars of the forest, upon a common summons, unless they are impleaded there or are sureties for any other persons who were attached for something concerning the forest.

**Clause 3**
Also all woods which were afforested by King Richard our uncle, or by King John our father, until our own first Coronation, shall forthwith be disafforested, unless they shall be our demesne.

**Clause 4**
Archbishops, bishops, abbots, priors, earls, barons, knights and freeholders who have woods within forests shall have them the same as they held them at the time of the first coronation of our grandfather king Henry [Sunday 19 December 1154], so that they shall be discharged forever of all purprestures [trespass and the erection of illegal dwellings], wastes [wasteland], and assarts [land cleared for cultivation] made in their woods after that time until the beginning of the second year of our coronation. And those who in future shall without our licence make wastes, purprestures or assarts within them, shall answer for such wastes, purprestures or assarts.

**Clause 5**
Our regarders shall go through the forests to make a view as it was used to be made at the time of the first coronation of our grandfather, king Henry, and not otherwise.

**Clause 6**
The inquisition or view for declawing dogs [cutting off the claws of a dog to hinder its chasing of deer] living within the forest, for the future shall be when the view ought to be made, namely, the third year in three years; and then it shall be done by the view and testimony of lawful men, and not otherwise. And he whose dogs shall be found then still clawed shall give three shillings for mercy, and for the future no one's ox shall be taken for failure to declaw. Such declawing also shall be done by the assize commonly used; which is, that three claws shall be cut off outside the ball of the fore-foot. Nor shall dogs be declawed from henceforth, excepting in places where it hath been customary to expedite them from the time of the first coronation of king Henry our grandfather.

**Clause 7**
No forester nor beadle shall for the future make any scotale [keeping of an ale-house within a forest by an officer of the forest], nor collect sheaves

of corn or oats, or any grain, or lambs, nor shall make any gathering but the view and oath of twelve regarders; and when they shall make their view: as many foresters shall be appointed to keep the forests, as they shall think reasonably sufficient for the purpose.

### Clause 8
No swainmote [court held by the foresters as judges, with freemen of the forest as jury] for the future shall be held in our kingdom, excepting thrice a year; namely, in the beginning of fifteen days before the feast of Saint Michael when the agistators meet for the agisting of our (royal) demesne woods; and about the feast of Saint Martin, when our agistators ought to receive our pannage-dues: and in those two swainmotes the foresters, verderers, and agistators shall meet, and no others by distraint; and the third swainmote shall be held in the beginning of the fifteen days before the Feast of Saint John the Baptist concerning the fawning of our does; and at that swainmote the tenants shall meet the foresters and verderers, and no others shall be distrained to be there. Moreover every forty days through the whole year, the foresters and verderers shall meet for seeing to attachments of the forests, as well of vert [green forest vegetation supporting deer] as of venison, by the presentment of the foresters themselves and before those who are attached. And the aforesaid swainmotes shall not be holden, except in those counties where they were accustomed to be held.

### Clause 9
Every free man shall agist [to pasture livestock] his own wood in the forest as he wishes and have his pannage [the right to allow pigs to forage in woodland]. We grant also that every free-man may drive his swine through our demesne wood freely and without impediment to agist them in his own woods or anywhere else he wishes. And if the swine of any free-man shall remain one night in our forest, he shall not on that account lose anything of his for it.

### Clause 10
No man henceforth shall lose life or limb for taking our venison, but if he shall be seized and convicted of taking venison he shall be fined heavily if he has the means to pay; but if he has not the means, he shall lie in

our prison for a year and a day; and if after a year and a day he can find sureties, he shall leave prison; but if not, he shall abjure the kingdom of England.

**Clause 11**
Whatever archbishop, bishop, earl or baron shall be passing through our forest, it shall be lawful for them to take one or two deer under the view of the forester, if he shall be present; but if not, he shall cause a horn to be blown, lest it should seem like theft.

**Clause 12**
Every free-man for the future, may, without being prosecuted, erect a mill in his own wood or upon his own land which he has in the forest; or make a warren, or pond, or marl-pit, or ditch, or turn it into arable land, so that it be not to the detriment of any of the neighbours.

**Clause 13**
Every free-man shall have the eyries of hawks, sparrowhawks, falcons, eagles and herons in his own woods, and he shall likewise have the honey found in his woods.

**Clause 14**
No forester from henceforth, who is not a forester in fee-farm, giving to us rent for his bailiwick, shall take any cheminage [toll on transport in the forest], within his bailiwick; but a forester in fee, paying to us rent for his bailiwick, shall take cheminage; that is to say, for every cart two-pence for the one half year, and two-pence for the other half year; and for a horse that carries burdens, one half-penny for the one half year, and one half-penny for the other half year: and not that excepting of those who come out of their bailiwick by licence of their bailiff as dealers, to buy underwood, timber, bark, or charcoal; to carry it to sell in other places where they will: and of no other carts nor burdens shall any cheminage be taken; and cheminage shall not be taken excepting in those places where anciently it used to be and ought to be taken. Also those who carry wood, bark, or coal, upon their backs to sell, although they get their livelihood by it, shall not for the future pay cheminage. Also cheminage shall not be taken by our foresters, for any besides our demesne woods.

## Clause 15

All persons outlawed for forest offences from the time of king Henry our grandfather up to our first coronation, shall be released from their outlawry without legal proceedings; and they shall find sureties that for the future they will not trespass unto us in our forests.

## Clause 16

No castellan or other person shall hold forest pleas whether concerning vert or venison but every forester-in-fee shall attach forest pleas as well concerning both vert and venison and shall present them to the verderers of the provinces; and when they have been enrolled and put under the seals of the verderers they shall be presented to our chief forester, when he comes into those parts to hold forest pleas and before him they shall be determined.

And these liberties concerning the forests we have granted to all men, saving to the archbishops, bishops, abbots, priors, earls, barons, knights, and others, ecclesiastical as well as secular; Templars and Hospitallers, their liberties and free customs, in forests and outside, in warrens and other places, which they had previously. All these aforesaid customs and liberties which we have granted to be observed in our kingdom for as much as it belongs to us; all our kingdom shall observe, clergy as well as laity, for as much as belongs to them. Because we have at present no seal, we have caused the present charter to be sealed with the seals of our venerable father the lord Guala, cardinal-priest of St Martin, legate of the apostolic see, and of William Marshal earl of Pembroke, guardian of us and of our kingdom. Witness the before-named and many others. Given by the hands of the aforesaid lord, the legate, and of William Marshal at St Paul's, London, on the sixth day of November in the second year of our reign.

# Notes

**Introduction**
1. Matthew Paris quoted in Marc Morris, *King John*, p.286.

**Chapter One: An Investigation into Nicholaa de la Haye's Family Origins**
1. Louise Wilkinson, *Women in Thirteenth-Century Lincolnshire*, p.14.
2. Ann Williams, *The English and the Norman Conquest*, p.205.
3. *Ibid*, p.98.
4. *Ibid*, p.107.
5. Kirk, R. E. G. *The Countess Lucy: Singular Or Plural?* p.31.
6. *Ibid*, p.32.
7. Ann Williams, *The English and the Norman Conquest*, p.27.
8. GBB fol. 333v. quoted in Ann Williams, *The English and the Norman Conquest*, p.203.
9. Kirk, R. E. G. *The Countess Lucy: Singular Or Plural?* p.33.
10. Ann Williams, *The English and the Norman Conquest*, p.107.
11. Kirk, R. E. G. *The Countess Lucy: Singular Or Plural?* p.57.
12. Ann Williams, *The English and the Norman Conquest*, p.107.
13. *Giraldi Cambrensis Opera*, vol VII, Appendix B, Lincoln Cathedral Obituary, p.153, quoted in fmg.ac/MedLands.
14. KSB Keats-Rohan, *Domesday descendants, A Porsopography of persons occurring in English Documents, 1066–1166: II Pipe Rolls to Cartae Baronum*, p.496.
15. Kirk, R. E. G. *The Countess Lucy: Singular Or Plural?* p.9.
16. Ann Williams, *The English and the Norman Conquest*, pp.37–38.
17. Sir William Dugdale, *The Baronage of England after the Norman Conquest*, pp.598–599.
18. Ann Williams, *The English and the Norman Conquest*, p.107.
19. KSB Keats-Rohan, *Domesday descendants, A Porsopography of persons occurring in English Documents, 1066–1166: II Pipe Rolls to Cartae Baronum*, p.496.
20. Wace, Master Wace, his chronicle of the Norman conquest from the *Roman de Rou*, p.102.
21. *Ibid*.
22. *Ibid*, p.103, *n*. 6.
23. 'La Manche: Part 4', in *Calendar of Documents Preserved in France 918–1206*, ed. J. Horace Round (London, 1899), pp.327–351. *British History Online* http://www.british-history.ac.uk/cal-state-papers/france/918-1206/pp327-351 [accessed 28 April 2022].
24. Wace, Master Wace, his chronicle of the Norman conquest from the *Roman de Rou*, p.101–102.
25. *Ibid*, pp.235–236.
26. *Ibid*, pp.236–237, *n*. 40.
27. KSB Keats-Rohan, *Domesday descendants, A Porsopography of persons occurring in English Documents, 1066–1166: II Pipe Rolls to Cartae Baronum*, p.496.
28. *Ibid*.

29. Everson, Paul and David Stocker, *Custodians of Continuity? The Premonstratensian Abbey at Barlings and the Landscape of Ritual*, p.135.
30. KSB Keats-Rohan, *Domesday descendants, A Porsopography of persons occurring in English Documents, 1066–1166: II Pipe Rolls to Cartae Baronum*, p.496.
31. Dugdale *Monasticon* IV, Basselech Priory, Monmouth, I, p.633, quoted in fmg.ac/MedLands.
32. Bayeux (Livre noir), Tome I, XXXIV, p.41, quoted in fmg.ac/MedLands.
33. 'La Manche: Part 1', in *Calendar of Documents Preserved in France 918–1206*, ed. J. Horace Round (London, 1899), pp.249–280. British History Online http://www.british-history.ac.uk/cal-state-papers/france/918-1206/pp249-280 [accessed 28 April 2022].
34. *Ibid.*
35. *Ibid.*
36. *Ibid.*
37. *Ibid.*
38. *Ibid.*
39. *Ibid.*
40. *Ibid.*
41. *Ibid.*
42. *Ibid.*
43. *Ibid.*
44. *Ibid.*
45. *Ibid.*
46. *Ibid.*
47. *Regesta Regem Anglo-Normannorum* (1956), Vol. II, Appendix, CLXXVII, p. 353, quoted in fmg.ac/MedLands.
48. *Gallia Christiana*, quoted in Wace, Master Wace, his chronicle of the Norman conquest from the *Roman de Rou*, p.103, n. 6.
49. Kirk, R. E. G. *The Countess Lucy: Singular Or Plural?* p.56.
50. *Giraldi Cambrensis Opera*, Vol. VII, Appendix B, Lincoln Cathedral Obituary, p.153, quoted in fmg.ac/MedLands.
51. J. C. Holt, "The Carta of Richard de La Haye, 1166: A Note on 'Continuity' in Anglo-Norman Feudalism." *The English Historical Review*, vol. 84, no. 331.
52. Kirk, R. E. G. *The Countess Lucy: Singular Or Plural?* p.53.
53. *Ibid*, p.56.
54. Dugdale, Sir William, *The Baronage of England after the Norman Conquest*, pp.598–599.
55. *Ibid.*
56. Actes Henri II, Tome I, XXXIV, p.135, quoted in fmg.ac/MedLands.
57. Orderic Vitalis (Prévost), Vol. IV, Liber XII, IV, p.323, quoted in fmg.ac/MedLands.
58. J.W.F. Hill, *Medieval Lincoln*, p.87.
59. fmg.ac/MedLands.
60. Everson, Paul and David Stocker, *Custodians of Continuity? The Premonstratensian Abbey at Barlings and the Landscape of Ritual*, p.361.
61. *Ibid.*
62. *Ibid.*
63. *Ibid*, p.236.
64. *Ibid*, p.153.
65. *Ibid*, p.133.
66. *Ibid*, p.363.

67. Dugdale *Monasticon*, Vol. IV, Boxgrave Priory, II, p.645, quoted in fmg.ac/MedLands.
68. 'Aquitaine', in *Calendar of Documents Preserved in France 918–1206*, ed. J. Horace Round (London, 1899), pp.446–454. British History Online http://www.british-history.ac.uk/cal-state-papers/france/918-1206/pp446-454 [accessed 28 April 2022].
69. Everson, Paul and David Stocker, *Custodians of Continuity? The Premonstratensian Abbey at Barlings and the Landscape of Ritual*, p.361.
70. 'Aquitaine', in *Calendar of Documents Preserved in France 918–1206*, ed. J. Horace Round (London, 1899), pp.446–454. British History Online http://www.british-history.ac.uk/cal-state-papers/france/918-1206/pp446-454 [accessed 28 April 2022].
71. Everson, Paul and David Stocker, *Custodians of Continuity? The Premonstratensian Abbey at Barlings and the Landscape of Ritual*, p.136.
72. *Liber Feodorum*. The Book of Fees, Commonly Called *Testa de Nevill*, pp. 939 and 655, respectively.
73. Sir William Dugdale, *The Baronage of England after the Norman Conquest*, pp.598–599.
74. Red Book Exchequer, Part II, *Infeudationes militum…duci normanniæ…1172*, p.632. Quoted in fmg.ac/MedLands.
75. *Ancient charters, royal and private, prior to A.D. 1200*, edited by John Horace Round, pp.58–9.
76. *Ibid*, p.59.
77. J.W.F. Hill, *Medieval Lincoln*, p.87.
78. *Ibid*, p.88.
79. Jonathan Clark, Justin Garner-Lahire, Cecily Spall and Nicola Toop, *Lincoln Castle Revealed; the Story of a Norman Powerhouse and its Anglo-Saxon Precursor*, p.86.
80. J.W.F. Hill, *Medieval Lincoln*, p.88.
81. Jonathan Clark, Justin Garner-Lahire, Cecily Spall and Nicola Toop, *Lincoln Castle Revealed; the Story of a Norman Powerhouse and its Anglo-Saxon Precursor*, p.86.
82. *The Anglo-Saxon Chronicles*, translated and edited by Michael Swanton, p. 253.
83. Everson, Paul and David Stocker, *Custodians of Continuity? The Premonstratensian Abbey at Barlings and the Landscape of Ritual*, p.135.
84. *Ibid*, p.361.
85. *Ibid* and J.W.F. Hill, *Medieval Lincoln*, p.87.
86. Ordericus Vitalis, *The Ecclesiastical History of Orderic Vitalis, 1075–1143*, book XIII, p.539.
87. *Ibid*.
88. *Ibid*, p.541.
89. *Ibid*.
90. *Ibid*.
91. Matthew Lewis, *Stephen and Matilda's Civil War: Cousins of Anarchy*, p.98.
92. Vitalis, book XIII, p.541.
93. *Ibid*.
94. *The Chronicle of Henry of Huntingdon. Comprising the history of England, from the invasion of Julius Caesar to the accession of Henry II. Also, the Acts of Stephen, King of England and duke of Normandy* Translated and edited by Thomas Forester, p.274.
95. Smurthwaite, David, *The Complete Guide to the Battlefields of Britain*, pp. 68–9.
96. Henry of Huntingdon, *The Chronicle of Henry of Huntingdon* p.274.
97. *Ibid*, p.274.
98. *Ibid*, p.279.
99. Vitalis, book XIII, p.543.
100. *Ibid*. p.279.
101. *Ibid*. p.279.

102. Catherine Hanley, *Matilda: Empress, Queen, Warrior*, p.140.
103. Vitalis, book XIII, p.543.
104. Henry of Huntingdon, *The Chronicle of Henry of Huntingdon* p.279.
105. *Ibid.* p.279.
106. Catherine Hanley, *Matilda*, p.141.
107. J. Sharpe (trans.), *The History of the Kings of England and of his Own Times by William Malmesbury*.
108. Henry of Huntingdon, *The Chronicle of Henry of Huntingdon* p.280.
109. Vitalis, book XIII, p.545.
110. William of Malmesbury quoted in Catherine Hanley, *Matilda*, p.141.
111. Vitalis, book XIII, p.545.
112. *Ibid*.
113. Catherine Hanley, *Matilda*, p.150.
114. *The Chronicle of John of Worcester*, translated and edited by Thomas Forester, A.M., pp.280–281.
115. *Ibid*, p.281.
116. *Ibid*, p.282.
117. *Ibid*, p.286.
118. Paul Dalton, *Roumare, William de, first earl of Lincoln (c.1096–1155x61)*, Oxforddnb.com.
119. J.H. Round quoted in J.W.F. Hill, *Medieval Lincoln*, p.180.
120. Teresa Cole, *The Anarchy: The Darkest Days of Medieval England*, pp.255–256.
121. J.W.F. Hill, *Medieval Lincoln*, p.180–181 and Everson, Paul and David Stocker, *Custodians of Continuity? The Premonstratensian Abbey at Barlings and the Landscape of Ritual*, p.88.
122. 'Aquitaine', in *Calendar of Documents Preserved in France 918–1206*, ed. J. Horace Round (London, 1899), pp.446–454. British History Online http://www.british-history.ac.uk/cal-state-papers/france/918-1206/pp446-454 [accessed 28 April 2022].
123. *The Anglo-Saxon Chronicles*, translated and edited by Michael Swanton, p. 265.

**Chapter Two: Richard de la Haye**
1. *Giraldi Cambrensis Opera*, Vol. VII, Appendix B, Lincoln Cathedral Obituary, p.160, quoted in fmg.ac/MedLands.
2. *Ancient charters, royal and private, prior to A.D. 1200*, edited by John Horace Round, pp.58–9.
3. Kirk, R. E. G. *The Countess Lucy: Singular Or Plural?* p.9.
4. 'Appendix II', in *Calendar of Documents Preserved in France 918–1206*, ed. J. Horace Round (London, 1899), pp.529–538. British History Online http://www.british-history.ac.uk/cal-state-papers/france/918-1206/pp529-538 [accessed 28 April 2022].
5. *Ibid*.
6. *Ibid*.
7. 'La Manche: Part 2', in *Calendar of Documents Preserved in France 918–1206*, ed. J. Horace Round (London, 1899), pp.281–308. British History Online http://www.british-history.ac.uk/cal-state-papers/france/918-1206/pp281-308 [accessed 28 April 2022].
8. J.W.F. Hill, *Medieval Lincoln*, p.183.
9. *Ibid*.
10. Red Book Exchequer, Part I, p.171.
11. *Ibid*, p.75.
12. Everson, Paul and David Stocker, *Custodians of Continuity? The Premonstratensian Abbey at Barlings and the Landscape of Ritual*, p.361.

13. 'La Manche: Part 2', in *Calendar of Documents Preserved in France 918–1206*, ed. J. Horace Round (London, 1899), pp.281–308. *British History Online* http://www.british-history.ac.uk/cal-state-papers/france/918-1206/pp281-308 [accessed 28 April 2022].
14. 'La Manche: Part 3', in *Calendar of Documents Preserved in France 918–1206*, ed. J. Horace Round (London, 1899), pp.309–326. *British History Online* http://www.british-history.ac.uk/cal-state-papers/france/918-1206/pp309-326 [accessed 3 May 2022].
15. *Ibid*.
16. 'La Manche: Part 2', in *Calendar of Documents Preserved in France 918–1206*, ed. J. Horace Round (London, 1899), pp.281–308. *British History Online* http://www.british-history.ac.uk/cal-state-papers/france/918-1206/pp281-308 [accessed 28 April 2022].
17. 'La Manche: Part 4', in *Calendar of Documents Preserved in France 918–1206*, ed. J. Horace Round (London, 1899), pp.327–351. *British History Online* http://www.british-history.ac.uk/cal-state-papers/france/918-1206/pp327-351 [accessed 3 May 2022].
18. 'La Manche: Part 4', in *Calendar of Documents Preserved in France 918–1206*, ed. J. Horace Round (London, 1899), pp.327–351. *British History Online* http://www.british-history.ac.uk/cal-state-papers/france/918-1206/pp327-351 [accessed 3 May 2022].
19. *Ibid*.
20. J. C. Holt, "The Carta of Richard de La Haye, 1166: A Note on 'Continuity' in Anglo-Norman Feudalism." *The English Historical Review*, vol. 84, no. 331, Oxford University Press, 1969, pp.289–97, http://www.jstor.org/stable/564522.
21. *Ibid*.
22. Red Book Exchequer, Part I, pp.390–391.
23. *Ibid*.
24. Richard R. Heiser, 'Castles, Constables, and Politics in Late Twelfth-Century English Governance', *Albion: A Quarterly Journal Concerned with British Studies* Vol. 32, No. 1 (Spring, 2000), pp.19–36.
25. *Ibid*.
26. Jonathan Clark, *Historic Graffitti Survey: Cobb Hall, Lincoln Castle, Lincolnshire*, p.3.
27. *Ibid*.
28. J.W.F. Hill, *Medieval Lincoln*, p.96.
29. *Ibid*.
30. *Ibid*.
31. Jonathan Clark, Justin Garner-Lahire, Cecily Spall and Nicola Toop, *Lincoln Castle Revealed; the Story of a Norman Powerhouse and its Anglo-Saxon Precursor*, pp.86–88.
32. fmg.ac/MedLands.
33. 'La Manche: Part 4', in *Calendar of Documents Preserved in France 918–1206*, ed. J. Horace Round (London, 1899), pp.327–351. *British History Online* http://www.british-history.ac.uk/cal-state-papers/france/918-1206/pp327-351 [accessed 5 May 2022].
34. *Ibid*.
35. 'La Manche: Part 3', in *Calendar of Documents Preserved in France 918–1206*, ed. J. Horace Round (London, 1899), pp.309–326. *British History Online* http://www.british-history.ac.uk/cal-state-papers/france/918-1206/pp309-326 [accessed 5 May 2022].
36. *Ibid*.

37. *Ibid.*
38. Sir William Dugdale, *The Baronage of England after the Norman Conquest*, pp.598–599.
39. Robert de Torigny, II, 1169, p.12. Quoted in fmg.ac/MedLands.
40. Red Book Exchequer, Part I, p.55.
41. *Giraldi Cambrensis Opera*, Vol. VII, Appendix B, Lincoln Cathedral Obituary, p.156. Quoted in fmg.ac/MedLands.
42. Wace, Master Wace, his chronicle of the Norman conquest from the *Roman de Rou*, p.236.

## Chapter Three: Nicholaa and her Sisters

1. fmg.ac/MedLands.
2. 'Seine Inférieure: Part 1', in *Calendar of Documents Preserved in France 918–1206*, ed. J. Horace Round (London, 1899), pp.1–35. *British History Online* http://www.british-history.ac.uk/cal-state-papers/france/918-1206/pp1-36 [accessed 5 May 2022].
3. With grateful thanks to Professor Daniel Power, Professor of Medieval history at Swansea University, who very kindly shared his research on the Hommet family to fill in the blanks.
4. 'Calvados: Part 2', in *Calendar of Documents Preserved in France 918–1206*, ed. J. Horace Round (London, 1899), pp.164–189. *British History Online* http://www.british-history.ac.uk/cal-state-papers/france/918-1206/pp164-189 [accessed 5 May 2022].
5. Again, thank you to Professor Daniel Power for pointing me to this story, "Notice sur les attaches d'un Sceau de Richard Coeur de Lion." *Bibliothèque de l'École Des Chartes*, vol. 4, 1853, p.58.
6. *Ibid.*
7. Again, thank you to Professor Daniel Power for pointing me to this story
8. Léopold De Lisle, "Notice sur les attaches d'un Sceau de Richard Coeur de Lion." *Bibliothèque de l'École Des Chartes*, vol. 4, 1853, p.60.
9. *Ibid.*
10. *Ibid*, p.61.
11. *Ibid.*
12. *Ibid.*
13. *Ibid*, pp.61–61.
14. 'Parishes: Stanwick St. John', in *A History of the County of York North Riding: Volume 1*, ed. William Page (London, 1914), pp.127–134. *British History Online* http://www.british-history.ac.uk/vch/yorks/north/vol1/pp127-134 [accessed 5 May 2022].
15. 'Parishes: Easby', in *A History of the County of York North Riding: Volume 1*, ed. William Page (London, 1914), pp.51–64. *British History Online* http://www.british-history.ac.uk/vch/yorks/north/vol1/pp51-64 [accessed 5 May 2022].
16. J. M. Lee and R. A. McKinley, 'Saddington', in *A History of the County of Leicestershire: Volume 5, Gartree Hundred* (London, 1964), pp.282–287. *British History Online* http://www.british-history.ac.uk/vch/leics/vol5/pp282-287 [accessed 5 May 2022].
17. Wace, Master Wace, his chronicle of the Norman conquest from the *Roman de Rou*, pp.239–240.
18. I owe a huge debt to Professor Daniel Power for sharing his knowledge of the Fitz Erneis family.
19. Wace, Master Wace, his chronicle of the Norman conquest from the *Roman de Rou*, p.240.
20. Red Book Exchequer, Part I, pp.406 and 272.
21. *Ibid*, p.78.
22. *Ibid*, pp.156 and 140.

23. *Ibid*, p.375.
24. *The Publications of the Pipe Roll Society*, PRS, vol. 21, p.103. I would also like to express my undying gratitude to Professor Louise Wilkinson, who lent me her notes on Nicholaa de la Haye, so that I did not have to hunt through the Pipe Rolls and could go straight to the relevant references. The time I saved!
25. *Ibid*, vol. 22, p.148.
26. *Ibid*, vol. 25, p.78.
27. *Ibid*.
28. *Ibid*, vol. 26, p.111.
29. *Ibid*, vol. 27, p.8.
30. Susan M. Johns, 'Nicola de la Haie (d. 1230), landowner', Oxforddnb.com.
31. J.W.F. Hill, *Medieval Lincoln*, p.220.
32. Thanks to Professor Daniel Power for the background to Matilda's marriage.
33. Francis Blomefield, 'Taverham Hundred: Rackheath Parva', in *An Essay Towards A Topographical History of the County of Norfolk: Volume 10* (London, 1809), pp.451–453. British History Online http://www.british-history.ac.uk/topographical-hist-norfolk/vol10/pp451-453 [accessed 6 May 2022].
34. Again, thank you to Professor Daniel Power for clarifying the timing of the agreement.

**Chapter Four: Prince John**
1. Sara Cockerell, *Eleanor of Castile: The Shadow Queen*, pp.291–292.
2. Thomas K. Keefe, *Henry II (1133–89)*, Oxforddnb.com.
3. *Ibid*.
4. Marc Morris, *King John*, p.24.
5. John Gillingham, 'John (1167–1216)', Oxforddnb.com.
6. *Ibid*.
7. *Ibid*.
8. *Ibid*.
9. Giraldus Cambrensis, *The Conquest of Ireland*, translated by Frederick J. Furnival, p.134.
10. *Ibid*, p. 139.
11. *Ibid*.
12. *Ibid*, p.141.
13. *Ibid*, p.145.
14. *Ibid*, p.146.
15. *Ibid*, p.147.
16. *Ibid*.
17. *The Annals of Roger de Howden: Comprising the History of England and of other Countries of Europe from A.D. 732 to A.D. 1201*, edited and translated by Henry T. Riley, p.50.
18. Giraldus Cambrensis, *The Conquest of Ireland*, translated by Frederick J. Furnival, p.147.
19. *Ibid*, p.149.
20. *The Annals of Roger de Howden: Comprising the History of England and of other Countries of Europe from A.D. 732 to A.D. 1201*, edited and translated by Henry T. Riley, p.52.
21. Joyce Marlow, *Kings and Queens of Britain*, p.23.
22. *Ibid*, p.26.
23. Marc Morris, *King John*, p.61.
24. *Ibid*, p.74.
25. Gillingham, 'John,' Oxforddnb.com.

## Chapter Five: Nicholaa and Gerard de Camville

1. Sir William Dugdale, *The Baronage of England after the Norman Conquest*, pp.627–628.
2. Dugdale *Monasticon* V, Combe, Warwickshire, I, p.584, quoted in fmg.ac/MedLands.
3. Sir William Dugdale, *The Baronage of England after the Norman Conquest*, pp.627–628.
4. *Ibid.*
5. *Ibid.*
6. Red Book Exchequer, Part I, p.32.
7. William of Newburgh, quoted in W.L. Warren, *Henry II*, p.259.
8. Sir William Dugdale, *The Baronage of England after the Norman Conquest*, pp.627–628.
9. Douglas Boyd, *Plantagenet Princesses: The Daughters of Eleanor of Aquitaine and Henry II*, p.46.
10. Ralph of Diceto, quoted in Elizabeth Hallam, *The Pantagenet Chronicles*, p. 146.
11. Alison Weir, *Eleanor of Aquitaine: By the Wrath of God, Queen of England*, p.175.
12. Benedict of Peterborough quoted in Jacqueline Alio, *Betrothal of Joanna of England to William II of Sicily*.
13. William Farrer and Charles Travis Clay, editors, *Early Yorkshire Charters, Volume 8: The Honour of Warenne*, p.19.
14. Benedict of Peterborough quoted in Jacqueline Alio, *Betrothal of Joanna of England to William II of Sicily*.
15. *The Annals of Roger de Howden: Comprising the History of England and of other Countries of Europe from A.D. 732 to A.D. 1201*, edited and translated by Henry T. Riley, p.413.
16. Brian Golding, 'Gerard de Canville (d. 1214)', Oxforddnb.com.
17. Eynsham, Vol. I, 584, p.399, quoted in fmg.ac/MedLands.
18. A. P. Baggs, W. J. Blair, Eleanor Chance, Christina Colvin, Janet Cooper, C. J. Day, Nesta Selwyn and S. C. Townley, 'Stanton Harcourt: Manors and other estates', in *A History of the County of Oxford: Volume 12, Wootton Hundred (South) Including Woodstock*, ed. Alan Crossley and C. R. Elrington (London, 1990), pp.274–281. British History Online http://www.british-history.ac.uk/vch/oxon/vol12/pp274-281 [accessed 11 May 2022].
19. Jumièges, Tome II, CI, p.1, quoted in fmg.ac/MedLands.
20. *Rotuli Dominabus, Rotuli X, Cantebrigesire*, p.44, quoted in fmg.ac/MedLands.
21. *Ibid.*
22. *Chronica Albrici Monachi Trium Fontium* 1116, MGH SS XXIII, p.822, quoted in fmg.ac/MedLands.
23. Kennett (1818), p.154, footnote, quoted in fmg.ac/MedLands.
24. *Regesta Regum Anglo-Normannorum* (1968), Vol. III, 140, p.52, quoted in fmg.ac/MedLands.
25. Sir William Dugdale, *The Baronage of England after the Norman Conquest*, pp.627–628.
26. *Ibid.*
27. Nicholas Vincent, *Canville [Camville], Richard de (d. 1191)* (article), Oxforddnb.com.
28. Roger of Howden, *The Annals of Roger de Howden: Comprising the History of England and of other Countries of Europe from A.D. 732 to A.D. 1201*, translated by Henry T. Riley, p.146.
29. *Ibid*, p.147.
30. *Ibid*, pp.147–148.
31. *Ibid*, p.148.
32. *Ibid*, pp.148–149.
33. *Ibid*, p.149.
34. *Ibid*, p.149.
35. *Ibid*, p.151.

36. *Ibid*, p.156.
37. *Ibid*, pp.164–166.
38. *Ibid*, p.200.
39. *Ibid*, p.201.
40. *Ibid*, p.202.
41. *Ibid*, p.205.
42. *Ibid*.
43. *Ibid*, p.210.
44. *Inquisitions Post Mortem*, Vol. I, Henry III, 858, p.294, quoted in fmg.ac/MedLands.
45. Nichols (1811), Vol. IV, Part II, p.493, quoting "Inter Nova Oblata in Rot. Pip. 4 Ric I", quoted in fmg.ac/MedLands.
46. Louise Wilkinson, *Women in Thirteenth-Century Lincolnshire*, p.16.
47. *Ibid*, pp.16–17, n. 21.
48. Stephen Church, *King John: England, Magna Carta and the Making of a Tyrant*, p.40.
49. *Ibid*.
50. 'La Manche: Part 3', in *Calendar of Documents Preserved in France 918–1206*, ed. J. Horace Round (London, 1899), pp.309–326. *British History Online* http://www.british-history.ac.uk/cal-state-papers/france/918-1206/pp309-326 [accessed 3 May 2022].
51. *The Acta of the Bishops of Chichester 1075–1207*, edited by Mayr-Harting, no. 141, pp.192–193.
52. *English Episcopal Acta VI, Norwich 1070–1214*, edited by Christopher Harper-Bill, no. 310B, pp.244–245n.
53. In Latin: '*cum custodia et constabularia ca[ste]lli Lincolnie.*' Louise Wilkinson, *Women in Thirteenth-Century Lincolnshire*, p.15.
54. *Ancient charters, royal and private, prior to A.D. 1200*, edited by John Horace Round, p.91.
55. *The great roll of the pipe for the first year of the reign of King Richard the First, A.D. 1189–1190*, edited by Joseph Hunter, p.96.
56. *Ibid*.
57. In Latin: '*pro vicecomitatu Lincolnie et castello civitatis habendis*'. Louise Wilkinson, *Women in Thirteenth-Century Lincolnshire*, pp.15–16, n. 13.
58. Ingulph, *Ingulph's Chronicle of the Abbey of Croyland*, p.276.
59. *Ibid*, p.277.
60. *Ibid*, p.277.
61. *Ibid*, p.277.
62. *Ibid*, p.278.
63. *Ibid*, p.282.
64. *Ibid*, p.283.
65. *Ibid*, p.284.
66. *Ibid*, p.285.
67. *Ibid*, p.287.
68. *Ibid*, p.287–288.
69. *Ibid*, p.297.
70. *Ibid*, p.298.
71. *Ibid*, p.309.
72. J.H. Round, editor, Ancient charters, royal and private, prior to A.D. 1200, pp.92–93.
73. With grateful thanks to Professor Daniel Power, Professor of Medieval history.
74. J.H. Round, editor, Ancient charters, royal and private, prior to A.D. 1200, p.93.

75. With grateful thanks to Professor Daniel Power, Professor of Medieval history at Swansea University.
76. *Ibid.*
77. Bracton's Note Book, Vol. II, 503, p.391, quoted in fmg.ac/MedLands.

**Chapter Six: 1191**
1. Richard of Devizes, *The Chronicle of Richard of Devizes: Concerning the Deeds, of Richard the First King of England also Richard of Cirencester's Description of Britain*, edited and translated by J.A. Giles, p.23.
2. William of Newburgh quoted in Brian Golding, 'Gerard de Canville', oxforddnb.com.
3. Roger of Howden, *The Annals of Roger de Howden: Comprising the History of England and of other Countries of Europe from A.D. 732 to A.D. 1201*, translated by Henry T. Riley, pp.164–166.
4. William of Newburgh, quoted in Morris, *King John*, p.67.
5. *Ibid.*
6. *Ibid.*
7. Richard of Devizes, *The Chronicle of Richard of Devizes: Concerning the Deeds of Richard the First King of England also Richard of Cirencester's Description of Britain*, edited and translated by J.A. Giles, p.23.
8. *Ibid.*
9. *Ibid*, p.23.
10. *Ibid.*
11. Elizabeth Hallam, *The Pantagenet Chronicles*, p.210.
12. *Ibid*, p.220.
13. Ingulph, *Ingulph's Chronicle of the Abbey of Croyland*, p.283.
14. Richard of Devizes, *The Chronicle of Richard of Devizes: Concerning the Deeds of Richard the First King of England also Richard of Cirencester's Description of Britain*, edited and translated by J.A. Giles, p.23.
15. *Ibid*, p.24.
16. *Ibid.*
17. *Pipe roll 3 & 4, Richard I*, quoted in Louise Wilkinson, *Women in Thirteenth-Century Lincolnshire*, p.18.
18. Roger of Howden, *The Annals of Roger de Howden: Comprising the History of England and of other Countries of Europe from A.D. 732 to A.D. 1201*, translated by Henry T. Riley, p.225.
19. *Ibid.*
20. Richard of Devizes, *The Chronicle of Richard of Devizes: Concerning the Deeds of Richard the First King of England also Richard of Cirencester's Description of Britain*, edited and translated by J.A. Giles, p.24.
21. *Ibid.*
22. Roger of Howden, *The Annals of Roger de Howden: Comprising the History of England and of other Countries of Europe from A.D. 732 to A.D. 1201*, translated by Henry T. Riley, p.244.
23. Richard of Devizes, *The Chronicle of Richard of Devizes: Concerning the Deeds of Richard the First King of England also Richard of Cirencester's Description of Britain*, edited and translated by J.A. Giles, p.25.
24. *Ibid*, p.26.
25. *Ibid.*
26. *Ibid.*

27. Roger of Howden, *The Annals of Roger de Howden: Comprising the History of England and of other Countries of Europe from A.D. 732 to A.D. 1201*, translated by Henry T. Riley, p.227.
28. *Pipe Roll 2 Richard I*, quoted in Jonathan Clark, *Historic Graffitti Survey: Cobb Hall, Lincoln Castle, Lincolnshire*, p.4.
29. *Pipe Roll 5 Richard 1, 37*, quoted in Jonathan Clark, *Historic Graffitti Survey: Cobb Hall, Lincoln Castle, Lincolnshire*, p.
30. Jonathan Clark, *Historic Graffitti Survey: Cobb Hall, Lincoln Castle, Lincolnshire*, p.4.
31. *Pipe Roll 2 John, 64*, quoted in Jonathan Clark, *Historic Graffitti Survey: Cobb Hall, Lincoln Castle, Lincolnshire*, p.4.
32. Jonathan Clark, *Historic Graffitti Survey: Cobb Hall, Lincoln Castle, Lincolnshire*, p.4.
33. Richard of Devizes, *The Chronicle of Richard of Devizes: Concerning the Deeds of Richard the First King of England also Richard of Cirencester's Description of Britain*, edited and translated by J.A. Giles, p.22.
34. Gerald of Wales quoted in Stephen Church, *King John: England, Magna Carta and the Making of a Tyrant*, p.44.
35. Elizabeth Hallam, *The Pantagenet Chronicles*, p.220.
36. Richard of Devizes, *The Chronicle of Richard of Devizes: Concerning the Deeds of Richard the First King of England also Richard of Cirencester's Description of Britain*, edited and translated by J.A. Giles, pp.30–31.
37. Marc Morris, *King John*, p.73.
38. *Ibid*, p.80.
39. *Ibid*, p.81.
40. Gillingham, 'John,' Oxforddnb.com.
41. Marc Morris, *King John*, p.82.
42. *Ibid*, p.84.
43. William of Newburgh quoted in Marc Morris, *King John*, p.100.
44. Roger of Howden, *The Annals of Roger de Howden: Comprising the History of England and of other Countries of Europe from A.D. 732 to A.D. 1201*, translated by Henry T. Riley, p.316.
45. *Ibid*, pp.317–318.
46. *Ibid*, p.318.
47. Irene Gladwin, *The Sheriff: The Man and his Office*, p.90.
48. *Ibid*.
49. Susan M. Johns, *Haie, Nicola de la (d.1230), landowner*, Oxforddnb.com.
50. Red Book Exchequer, Part I, *Anno VI regis Ricardi, ad redemptionem eius, scutagium ad XXs*, pp.83, 84 and 93, quoted in fmg.ac/MedLands.
51. Red Book Exchequer, Part I, *Anno VIII regis Ricardi scutagium Normanniæ ad XXs*, p.100, quoted in fmg.ac/MedLands.
52. Roger of Howden, *The Annals of Roger de Howden: Comprising the History of England and of other Countries of Europe from A.D. 732 to A.D. 1201*, translated by Henry T. Riley, p.354.
53. *Ibid*.
54. *Ibid*, p.453.
55. *L'Histoire de Guillaume le Maréchale* quoted in Marc Morris, *King John*, p. 104.
56. *Ibid*, p.105.

## Chapter Seven: Lincoln Restored
1. *Historical introductions to the Rolls series*, edited by Arthur Hassall, p.257.
2. Marc Morris, *King John*, pp.105–106.

3. *Ibid*, p.107.
4. *The History of William Marshal*, translated by Nigel Bryant, p.152.
5. David Crouch, *William Marshal*, p.101.
6. Danny Danziger and John Gillingham, *1215*, p.156.
7. *Ibid*, pp.156–157.
8. Gervase of Canterbury, quoted in Marc Morris, *King John*, p.109.
9. *The History of William Marshal*, translated by Nigel Bryant, p.152.
10. Ralph of Coggeshall quoted in Marc Morris, *King John*, p.110.
11. Gervase of Canterbury quoted in Morris, *King John*, p.112.
12. Elizabeth Hallam, *The Plantagenet Chronicles*, p.262.
13. Ralph of Coggeshall quoted in Marc Morris, *King John*, p.115.
14. Bertrand de Born, quoted in J.C. Holt, *King John*, p.17.
15. Ralph of Coggeshall quoted in Hallam, *The Plantagenet Chronicles*, p.262.
16. *Ibid*.
17. *Ibid*.
18. *Ibid*.
19. Sharon Bennett Connolly, *Heroines of the Medieval World*, pp.138–143.
20. *The History of William Marshal*, translated by Nigel Bryant, p.152.
21. Roger of Howden, *The Annals of Roger de Howden: Comprising the History of England and of other Countries of Europe from A.D. 732 to A.D. 1201*, translated by Henry T. Riley, p.502.
22. *Ibid*, pp.502–503.
23. *Ibid*, p.503.
24. Ralph of Coggeshall quoted in Hallam, *The Plantagenet Chronicles*, p.268.
25. *Ibid*.
26. Jonathan Clark, Justin Garner-Lahire, Cecily Spall and Nicola Toop, *Lincoln Castle Revealed; the Story of a Norman Powerhouse and its Anglo-Saxon Precursor*, p.99.
27. *Ibid*, pp.96–99.
28. *Rotuli de Oblatis et Finibus*, 2 John, p.88, quoted in fmg.ac/MedLands.
29. Hagger (1998), p. 44, citing Pipe Roll, 2 John, p.87, quoted in fmg.ac/MedLands.
30. *Liber Feodorum. The Book of Fees, Commonly Called Testa de Nevill*, Part 1, p.272.
31. Lincolnshire Eyre 1202 https://sourcebooks.fordham.edu/seth/pleas-lincolneyre.asp.
32. Hartshorne 1850, 41, referenced in Jonathan Clark, *Historic Graffitti Survey: Cobb Hall, Lincoln Castle, Lincolnshire*, p.5.
33. *Red Book Exchequer, Part II, Inquisitiones…Regis Johannis…anno regno XII et XIII…de servitiis militum*, p.483, quoted in fmg.ac/MedLands.
34. *Red Book Exchequer, Part I*, p.171.
35. *Red Book Exchequer, Part I*, p177.
36. *Testa de Nevill, Part I*, p.192, quoted in fmg.ac/MedLands.
37. *Liber Feodorum. The Book of Fees, Commonly Called Testa de Nevill*, Part 1, p.192.
38. Sharon Bennett Connolly, *Defenders of the Norman Crown: Rise and Fall of the Warenne Earls of Surrey*, p.99.
39. *Liber Feodorum. The Book of Fees, Commonly Called Testa de Nevill*, Part 1, p.192.
40. *Ibid*.
41. Ralph of Coggeshall quoted in Hallam, *The Plantagenet Chronicles*, p.266.
42. *Ibid*, p.272.
43. Marc Morris, *King John*, p.124.
44. *The History of William Marshal*, translated by Nigel Bryant, p.153.
45. Roger of Wendover quoted in J.C. Holt, *King John*, p.18.
46. Ralph of Coggeshall quoted in Elizabeth Hallam, *The Plantagenet Chronicles*, p.278.

47. *Ibid.*
48. *Ibid*, p.280.
49. John Gillingham, 'John,' Oxforddnb.com.
50. *Ibid.*
51. *Ibid.*
52. *Ibid.*
53. Gervase of Canterbury quoted in Hallam, *The Plantagenet Chronicles*, p. 288.
54. *Ibid*, p.290.
55. John Gillingham, 'John,' Oxforddnb.com.
56. Irene Gladwin, *The Sheriff: The Man and his Office*, p.102.
57. *Ibid*, p.107.
58. *Ibid.*
59. Brian Golding, 'Gerard de Canville', oxforddnb.com.
60. J.W.F. Hill, *Medieval Lincoln*, p.98 and *n.* 4.
61. The Barnwell annalist quoted in Elizabeth Hallam, *The Plantagenet Chronicles*, p.296.
62. *Ibid*, p.293.
63. Brian Golding, 'Gerard de Canville', oxforddnb.com.
64. S. Mac Airt, *Annals of Innisfallen*, quoted in *Ibid.*
65. *Memoriale fratris Walteri de Coventria* quoted in *Ibid.*
66. Sharon Bennett Connolly, *Ladies of Magna Carta: Women of Influence in Thirteenth Century England*, p.27.
67. The Barnwell annalist quoted in Elizabeth Hallam, *The Plantagenet Chronicles*, p.296.
68. *Ibid*, p.298.
69. *Ibid*, p.300.
70. *Ibid*, p.298.
71. *Ibid*, p.302.
72. John Gillingham, 'John,' Oxforddnb.com.

**Chapter Eight: The Magna Carta Crisis**
1. Marc Morris, *King John*, p.219.
2. The Barnwell annalist quoted in Elizabeth Hallam, *The Plantagenet Chronicles*, p.305.
3. John Gillingham, 'John,' Oxforddnb.com.
4. *L'Histoire de Guillaume le Maréchale* quoted in John Gillingham, 'John,' Oxforddnb.com.
5. Louise Wilkinson, *Women in Thirteenth-Century Lincolnshire*, p.18, n. 31.
6. *Ibid*, p.18.
7. *Ibid*, p.18, n. 33.
8. Jonathan Clark, *Historic Graffitti Survey: Cobb Hall, Lincoln Castle, Lincolnshire*, p.5.
9. Coronation Charter of Henry I in bl.uk.
10. *Select Charters* quoted in Marc Morris, *King John*, p.247.
11. The Barnwell annalist quoted in Elizabeth Hallam, *The Plantagenet Chronicles*, p.308.
12. Danny Danziger and John Gillingham, *1215*, p.258.
13. Letter from Pope Innocent III, quoted in Danny Danziger and John Gillingham, *1215*, p.263.
14. Letter of 5 April 1216. Price, Rich, *King John's Letters*, Facebook Study Group, 5 April 2019.
15. Letter of 16 April 1216. Price, *King John's Letters*.
16. *Ibid.*
17. Letter of 4 February 1216. Price, *King John's Letters*.
18. Letter of 22 February 1216. Price, *King John's Letters*.

19. Letter of 23 February 1216. Price, *King John's Letters*.
20. Elizabeth Hallam, *The Plantagenet Chronicles*, p.317.
21. John Gillingham, 'John,' Oxforddnb.com.
22. J.W.F. Hill, *Medieval Lincoln*, p.200.
23. Letter of 4 September 1216. Price, *King John's Letters*.
24. Elizabeth Hallam, *The Plantagenet Chronicles*, p.317.
25. Brian Golding, 'Gerard de Canville', oxforddnb.com.
26. Sean McGlynn, *Blood Cries Afar: The Magna Carta War and the Invasion of England 1215–1217*, p.182.
27. Letter of 26 September 1216. Price, *King John's Letters*.
28. J.W.F. Hill, *Medieval Lincoln*, p.200.
29. *Rotuli hundredonum*, 1.315 quoted in Johns, 'Nicola de la Haie'; and Irene Gladwin, *The Sheriff: The Man and his Office*, p.132.
30. Letter of 28 September 1216. Price, *King John's Letters*.
31. *The History of William Marshal*, translated by Nigel Bryant, pp.185–186.
32. *Ibid*, p.186.
33. Ralph of Coggeshall quoted in Elizabeth Hallam, *The Plantagenet Chronicles*, p.320.
34. Letter of 18 October 1216. Price, *King John's Letters*.
35. Louise Wilkinson, *Women in Thirteenth-Century Lincolnshire*, p.20.
36. *Ibid*, p.19.
37. *Ibid*.
38. King John quoted in *The History of William Marshal*, translated by Nigel Bryant, pp.185–186.
39. *The History of William Marshal*, translated by Nigel Bryant, p.186.
40. Roger of Wendover, *Roger of Wendover's Flowers of History: Comprising the History of England from the Descent of the Saxons to A.D. 1235*, volume II, p.379n.
41. Ralph of Coggeshall quoted in Hallam, *The Plantagenet Chronicles*, p.320.

**Chapter Nine: 1217**
1. The Barnwell Annalist quoted in Elizabeth Hallam, *Chronicles of the Age of Chivalry*, p.26.
2. Roger of Wendover, *Roger of Wendover's Flowers of History: Comprising the History of England from the Descent of the Saxons to A.D. 1235*, volume II, p. 379.
3. John Paul Davis, *King John, Henry III and England's Lost Civil War*, p.47.
4. The Barnwell Annalist quoted in Elizabeth Hallam, *Chronicles of the Age of Chivalry*, p.26.
5. *Ibid*.
6. Roger of Wendover, *Roger of Wendover's Flowers of History: Comprising the History of England from the Descent of the Saxons to A.D. 1235*, volume II, pp. 379–380.
7. The Barnwell Annalist quoted in Elizabeth Hallam, *Chronicles of the Age of Chivalry*, p.26.
8. John Paul Davis, *King John, Henry III and England's Lost Civil War*, p.47.
9. Roger of Wendover, *Roger of Wendover's Flowers of History: Comprising the History of England from the Descent of the Saxons to A.D. 1235*, volume II, p. 380.
10. J.W.F. Hill, *Medieval Lincoln*, p.201.
11. Irene Gladwin, *The Sheriff: The Man and his Office*, p.132.
12. *Ibid*.
13. Roger of Wendover, *Roger of Wendover's Flowers of History: Comprising the History of England from the Descent of the Saxons to A.D. 1235*, volume II, p.381.
14. *Ibid*, pp.381–382.

15. *The History of William Marshal*, translated by Nigel Bryant, p.192.
16. Roger of Wendover, *Roger of Wendover's Flowers of History: Comprising the History of England from the Descent of the Saxons to A.D. 1235*, volume II, p.385.
17. Ibid.
18. *Ibid*, p.387.
19. Letter of 12 February 1217. Price, *King John's Letters*.
20. Letter of 12 February 1217. Price, *King John's Letters*.
21. Irene Gladwin, *The Sheriff: The Man and his Office*, p.132.
22. Ibid.
23. Roger of Wendover, *Roger of Wendover's Flowers of History: Comprising the History of England from the Descent of the Saxons to A.D. 1235*, volume II, p.391.
24. Kate Norgate, *The Minority of Henry III*, p.20.
25. With thanks to military historian, Julian Humphrys for helping me to work out the aims of the siege.
26. Jonathan Clark, *Historic Graffitti Survey: Cobb Hall, Lincoln Castle, Lincolnshire*, p.5 and Irene Gladwin, *The Sheriff: The Man and his Office*, p.133.
27. *The History of William Marshal*, translated by Nigel Bryant, pp.195–196.
28. Thomas Asbridge, *The Greatest Knight*, p.353.
29. Roger of Wendover, *Roger of Wendover's Flowers of History: Comprising the History of England from the Descent of the Saxons to A.D. 1235*, volume II, p.391.
30. *The History of William Marshal*, translated by Nigel Bryant, p.197.
31. Thomas Asbridge, *The Greatest Knight*, p.353.
32. David Crouch, *William Marshal*, 3rd edition, p.164.
33. Roger of Wendover, *Roger of Wendover's Flowers of History: Comprising the History of England from the Descent of the Saxons to A.D. 1235*, volume II, p.393.
34. *The History of William Marshal*, translated by Nigel Bryant, p.198.
35. Thomas Asbridge, *The Greatest Knight*, p.357.
36. *The History of William Marshal*, translated by Nigel Bryant, p.199.
37. Roger of Wendover, *Roger of Wendover's Flowers of History: Comprising the History of England from the Descent of the Saxons to A.D. 1235*, volume II, pp.394–395.
38. *The History of William Marshal*, translated by Nigel Bryant, p.200.
39. *Ibid*, p.201.
40. *Ibid*.
41. *Ibid*, p. 202.
42. *Ibid*, p.203.
43. Dr Erik Grigg, *Lincoln and the Magna Carta*, p.43.
44. J.W.F. Hill, *Medieval Lincoln*, p.205.
45. Roger of Wendover, *Roger of Wendover's Flowers of History: Comprising the History of England from the Descent of the Saxons to A.D. 1235*, volume II, p.397.
46. Elizabeth Hallam, *Chronicles of the Age of Chivalry*, p.29.

**Chapter Ten: The In-Laws**
1. Matthew Strickland, 'William Longespée [Lungespée], third earl of Salisbury (b. in or before 1167, d. 1226)', Oxforddnb.com.
2. Ibid.
3. Ibid.
4. Ibid.
5. Ibid.
6. Ibid.
7. 'Ela, Countess of Salisbury', medievalwomen.org.

8. Emilie Amt, 'Patrick Salisbury, first Earl of Salisbury [Earl of Wiltshire] (d. 1168)', Oxforddnb.com.
9. 'Ela, Countess of Salisbury', medievalwomen.org.
10. W.L. Bowles and J.G. Nicholls, *Annals and Antiquities of Lacock Abbey*, quoted in Ally McConnell, 'The Life of Ela, Countess of Salisbury', Wiltshire and Swindon History Centre, wshc.eu, 15 September 2015.
11. 'Ela, Countess of Salisbury', medievalwomen.org.
12. *Ibid.*
13. David Crouch, *William Marshal*, third edition.
14. Strickland, 'William Longespée'.
15. *Ibid.*
16. David Crouch and Anthony J. Holden, *History of William Marshal: Text and Translation*.
17. Strickland, 'William Longespée'.
18. With thanks to Rich Price for clarification of events. Rich is currently translating King John's letters.
19. Strickland, 'William Longespée'.
20. Crouch, *William Marshal*.
21. Roger of Wendover, *Flowers of History*, vol. II, translated by J.A. Giles.
22. B.R. Kemp, 'Nicholas Longespée (d. 1297)', Oxforddnb.com.
23. Fine Rolls of Henry III Project, Finerollshenry3.co.uk.
24. *Ibid.*
25. *Ibid.*
26. https://fmg.ac/Projects/MedLands.
27. Fine Rolls of Henry III Project, Finerollshenry3.co.uk.
28. William Farrer and Charles Travis Clay, editors, *Early Yorkshire Charters, Volume 8: The Honour of Warenne*.
29. Magna Carta, British Library, transcript from bl.uk.
30. Bowles and Nicholls, *Annals and Antiquities of Lacock Abbey*, quoted in McConnell, *The Life of Ela*.
31. 'Ela, Countess of Salisbury', medievalwomen.org.
32. Wilkinson, *Women in Thirteenth-Century Lincolnshire*.
33. 'Ela, Countess of Salisbury', medievalwomen.org.
34. finerollshenry3.org.uk content/calendar/roll_027.html#it003_009, 29 Oct. 1227.
35. The National Archives, Ref: WARD 2/27/94B/137.
36. *Ibid*, WARD 2/27/94B/28.
37. 'Ela, Countess of Salisbury', medievalwomen.org.
38. The National Archives, Ref: WARD 2/27/94B/146.
39. Jennifer C. Ward, 'Ela, suo jure Countess of Salisbury (b. in or after 1190, d. 1261)', Oxforddnb.com, October 2009.
40. 'Ela of Salisbury', stanfordmagnacarta.worpress.com.
41. 'Ela, Countess of Salisbury', medievalwomen.org.

### Chapter Eleven: Retirement – Eventually

1. Anonymous de Béthune quoted in Louise Wilkinson, *Women in Thirteenth-Century Lincolnshire*, p.22.
2. *Ibid*, p.21.
3. *Ibid.*
4. *Ibid.*
5. The Dunstable annalist quoted in *Ibid*, p.21.
6. Dr Erik Grigg, *Lincoln and the Magna Carta*, pp.43–44.

7. Irene Gladwin, *The Sheriff: The Man and his Office*, p.134.
8. Louise Wilkinson, *Women in Thirteenth-Century Lincolnshire*, p.23.
9. Fine Rolls of Henry III Project, Finerollshenry3.co.uk.
10. Irene Gladwin, *The Sheriff: The Man and his Office*, p.134.
11. Irene Gladwin, *The Sheriff: The Man and his Office*, p.135.
12. David Carpenter, *Henry III: The Rise to Power and Personal Rule 1207–1258*, p.21.
13. Louise Wilkinson, *Women in Thirteenth-Century Lincolnshire*, p.24.
14. Irene Gladwin, *The Sheriff: The Man and his Office*, p.135.
15. Kate Norgate, *The Minority of Henry III*, pp.147–149.
16. Louise Wilkinson, *Women in Thirteenth-Century Lincolnshire*, p.24.
17. David Carpenter, *Henry III: The Rise to Power and Personal Rule 1207–1258*, p.27.
18. Jonathan Clark, *Historic Graffitti Survey: Cobb Hall, Lincoln Castle, Lincolnshire*, p.5.
19. Pipe Rolls 2 Henry III, 94.
20. Jonathan Clark, *Historic Graffitti Survey: Cobb Hall, Lincoln Castle, Lincolnshire*, p.5.
21. *Ibid*.
22. Fine Rolls of Henry III Project, Finerollshenry3.co.uk.
23. PR 8 Henry III, 49–50.
24. Jonathan Clark, Justin Garner-Lahire, Cecily Spall and Nicola Toop, *Lincoln Castle Revealed; the Story of a Norman Powerhouse and its Anglo-Saxon Precursor*, p.106.
25. *Ibid*.
26. *Ibid*.
27. *Ibid*.
28. Fine Rolls of Henry III Project, Finerollshenry3.co.uk.
29. *Liber Feodorum*. The Book of Fees, Commonly Called *Testa de Nevill*, Part I, p.285.
30. Fine Rolls of Henry III Project, Finerollshenry3.co.uk.
31. Sir William Dugdale, *The Baronage of England after the Norman Conquest*, pp.598–599.
32. *Ibid*.
33. Fine Rolls of Henry III Project, Finerollshenry3.co.uk.
34. Louise Wilkinson, *Women in Thirteenth-Century Lincolnshire*, p.26.
35. *Ibid*.
36. Everson, Paul and David Stocker, *Custodians of Continuity? The Premonstratensian Abbey at Barlings and the Landscape of Ritual*, p.363.
37. Louise Wilkinson, *Women in Thirteenth-Century Lincolnshire*, p.26.
38. *Ibid*, p.25.
39. *Annales Monastici: Annales prioratus de Dunstaplia (A.D. 1–1297), Annales monasterii de Bermundesia (A.D. 1042–1432)*, edited by Henry Richards Luard, p.53.
40. catherinehanley.co.uk/historical-background/nicola-de-la-haye.
41. Fine Rolls of Henry III Project, Finerollshenry3.co.uk.
42. *Ibid*.
43. *Ibid*.
44. *Ibid*.
45. Louise Wilkinson, *Women in Thirteenth-Century Lincolnshire*, p.20.
46. *The History of William Marshal*, translated by Nigel Bryant, p.204.

**Chapter Twelve: The Legacy of Nicholaa de la Haye**
1. Thomas of Walsingham, Thomae Walsingham Historia Anglicana, edited by H.T. Riley, in part one of Chronica Monasterii Sancti Albani, pp.148–9.
2. Brindle and Sadraei, Conisbrough Castle, pp.30–31.
3. Conisbrough Court Rolls, dhi.ac.uk/conisbrough/index.html.
4. Hunter's South Yorkshire II: Deanery of Doncaster II quoted in Fairbank, 'The Last Earl of Warenne and Surrey', p.213.

5. Calendar of Close Rolls, 1313–18, p.575 quoted in *Ibid*, p.195.
6. Rees, Calendar of Ancient Petitions, No. 8830, 14 June 1318, pp.296–297.
7. Vita Edwardi Secundi quoted in Spinks, Edward II The Man, p.149.
8. *Ibid*, pp.149–50.

### Appendix A: The 1215 Magna Carta
1. Danny Danziger and John Gillingham, *1215*, pp.285–299; Marc Morris, *King John*, pp.299–311; David Starkey, *Magna Carta: The True Story Behind the Charter*, pp.160–251; H. Summerson et al, translator, *Magna Carta*, The Magna Carta Project, http://magnacarta.cmp.uea.ac.uk/read/magna_carta_1215, accessed 13 March 2019.

### Appendix B: Enforcers of Magna Carta – The Twenty-Five
1. Danny Danziger and John Gillingham, *1215*, pp.298–299; Matthew Strickland, '*Enforcers of Magna Carta (act, 1215–1216)*', oxforddnb.com.

### Appendix C: The Charter of the Forest 1217
1. Dan Jones, *Realm Divided: A Year in the Life of Plantagenet England*, pp.271–277; National Archives, nationalarchives.gov.uk/education/resources/magna-carta/charter-forest-1225-westminster.

# Bibliography

**Primary Sources**

*Ancient charters, royal and private, prior to A.D. 1200*, edited by John Horace Round, Pipe Roll Society, London, 1888.

*Annales Monastici: Annales prioratus de Dunstaplia (A.D. 1–1297) Annales monasterii de Bermundesia (A.D. 1042–1432)*, edited by Henry Richards Luard, Longmans, London, 1866.

Carlin, Martha and David Crouch (eds and trans), *Lost Letters of Medieval Life: English Society, 1200–1250*, University of Pennsylvania Press, Pennsylvania, 2013.

Carpenter, David, *Henry III: The Rise to Power and Personal Rule 1207–1258*, Yale University Press, Yale, 2021.

Carpenter, David, *Magna Carta* (translated with a new commentary), Penguin Random House, London, 2015.

Anderson, A.O. and M.M.O Anderson (eds), *Chronicle of Melrose 731–1270*, 1936.

Bryant, Nigel, translator, *The History of William Marshal*, The Boydell Press, Woodbridge, 2016.

*Chronicles of the Reigns of Stephen, Henry II and Richard I*, Nabu Press, 2012.

Crawford, Anne (ed and trans), *Letters of Medieval Women*, Sutton Publishing, Stroud, 2002.

Crouch, David and Anthony J. Holden (eds), *History of William Marshal: Text & Translation (II. 10032–end)*, Anglo-Norman Text Society from Birkbeck College, 2002.

Dronke, Peter, *Abelard and Heloise in Medieval Testimonies*, Glasgow, University of Glasgow Press, 1976.

*English Episcopal Acta VI, Norwich 1070–1214*, edited by Christopher Harper-Bill, Oxford, 1990.

*Florentii Wigorniensis monachi chronicon ex chronicis*, edited by B. Thorpe, English Historical Society, (1849).

Fine Rolls of Henry III Project, Finerollshenry3.co.uk.

Gervase of Canterbury, *The Deeds of Kings*, edited by W. Stubbs, in *The Historical Works of Gervase of Canterbury*, Rolls Series, 1880.

*Gesta Regis Henrici Secundi Benedicti Abbatis: The Chronicle of the Reigns of Henry II and Richard I A. D. 1169–1192: Known Commonly Under the Name of Benedict of Peterborough*, edited by William Stubbs, Longmans, 1867.

Giraldus Cambrensis, *The Conquest of Ireland*, translated and edited by Frederick J. Furnival, Early English Text Society, London, 1896.

*Historical introductions to the Rolls series*, edited by Arthur Hassall, Longmans, Green and Co., London, 1902.

Ingulph, *Ingulph's Chronicle of the Abbey of Croyland*, edited by Henry T. Riley, H.G. Bohn, London, 1854.

John of Salisbury, *The Letters of John of Salisbury*, edited by W.J. Miller, S.J. Butler, H.E. Butler and revised by C.N.L. Brooke, Thomas Nelson and Sons, London, 1955.

*Liber Feodorum. The Book of Fees, Commonly Called Testa de Nevill*, H.M. Stationery Office, London, 1920.

Mackay, A.J.G. (ed), *The Historie and Chronicles of Scotland…by Robert Lindesay of Pitscottie*, 3 vols, Scottish Text Society, 42–3, 60 (1899–1911).

*Magna Carta*, British Library, transcript from bl.uk.

National Archives; nationalarchives.gov.uk/education/resources/magna-carta/charter-forest-1225-westminster/.

Ordericus Vitalis, *The Ecclesiastical History of England and Normandy*, edited by H.G. Bohn, London, 1853.

Paris, Matthew, Robert de Reading and others, *Flores Historiarum*, volume III, edited by Henry Richards Luard, H.M. Stationary Office, 1890.

Price, Rich, *King John's Letters*, Facebook Study Group, 20 June 2016 onwards.

Ralph of Coggeshall, *The English Chronicle*, edited by J. Stevenson, in *Chronicon Anglicanum*, Rolls Series, 1875.

Ralph of Diceto, *Images of History*, edited by W. Stubbs, in *The Historical Works of Master Ralph of Diceto*, Rolls Series, 1876.

Richard of Devizes, *Chronicle*, Objective Systems Pty Ltd., ebook, 2008.

Richard of Devizes, *The Chronicle of Richard of Devizes: Concerning the Deeds of Richard the First King of England also Richard of Cirencester's Description of Britain*, edited and translated by J.A. Giles, London, 1841.

Roger of Wendover, *Roger of Wendover's Flowers of History: Comprising the History of England from the Descent of the Saxons to A.D. 1235*, volume II, edited by J.A. Giles, H.G. Bohn, London, 1849.

Rotulus Cancellarii: vel, Antigraphum magni rotuli pipæ de tertio anno regni Regis Johannis, Great Britain Exchequer, 1833.

Round, J.H., editor, Ancient charters, royal and private, prior to A.D. 1200, Public Record Office, London, 1888.

Rymer, T. (ed), *Foedera, conventions, literae*, Record Commission, edition li, 144, London, 1816–69.

Sawyer, P.H., *Anglo-Saxon Charters: An Annotated List and Bibliography*, Royal Historical Society Guides and Handbooks (1968).

Sharpe, J. (trans), *The History of the Kings of England and of his Own Times by William Malmesbury*, Seeleys, 1854.

Shirley, W.W. (ed), *Royal and other Historical Letters*, Rolls Series, Chronicles and Memorials, London, 1862–6.

Stow, John, *The Annales of England: The Race of the Kings of Brytaine after the received Opinion since Brute, &c*, G. Bishop and T. Adams, London, 1605.

Strachey, J. (ed), *Rotuli parliamentorum ut et petitiones, et placita in parliamento*, 6 vols (1767–77).

Summerson, H. et al (trans), *Magna Carta*, The Magna Carta Project, http://magnacarta.cmp.uea.ac.uk/read/magna_carta_1215, accessed 13 March 2019.

*The Acta of the Bishops of Chichester 1075–1207*, edited by Mayr-Harting, The Canterbury and York Society, 1964.

*The Anglo-Saxon Chronicles*, translated and edited by Michael Swanton, revised edition, Phoenix Press, London, 2000.

*The Annals of Roger de Howden: Comprising the History of England and of other Countries of Europe from A.D. 732 to A.D. 1201*, edited and translated by Henry T. Riley, H.G. Bohn, London, 1853.

*The Autobiography of Giraldus Cambrensis*, edited and translated by H.E. Butler, 1937, archive.org.

*The 'Barnwell' Annals* (anon), edited by W. Stubbs, in *The Historical Collections of Walter of Coventry*, Rolls Series, 1873.

'The Chronicle: 1187–1214', in *Annales Cestrienses Chronicle of the Abbey of S. Werburg, at Chester*, edited by Richard Copley Christie, London, 1887, pp. 36–49; British History Online http://www.british-history.ac.uk/lancs-chesrecord-soc/vol14/pp36-49 [accessed 1 May 2019].

*The Chronicle of John Florence of Worcester with the two continuations*, translated and edited by Thomas Forester, A.M. (London; Henry G. Bohn, 1854).

*The great roll of the pipe for the first year of the reign of King Richard the First, A.D. 1189–1190*, edited by Joseph Hunter, Exchequer, London, 1844.

*The Publications of the Pipe Roll Society*, Pipe Roll Society, London, 1884–1925.

*The Red Book of the Exchequer*, Part I, edited by Hubert Hall, Exchequer, London, 1896.

*The Red Book of the Exchequer*, Part III, edited by Hubert Hall, Exchequer, London, 1896.

Thomas of Walsingham, *Thomae Walsingham Historia Anglicana*, edited by H.T. Riley, in part one of *Chronica Monasterii Sancti Albani*, vol. 4, Rolls Series, 1863–4.

Thompson, Doug (trans), *Royal Letter 763a*, douglyn.co.uk/Braose.

Thomson, Doug (trans), *Royal Letter 763b*, douglyn.co.uk/Braose.

Trivet, Nicholas, *Annales Sex Regum Angliae*, edited by T. Hog, 1845.

Van Houts, Elisabeth M.C. and Rosalind C. Love (eds and trans), *The Warenne (Hyde) Chronicle*, Clarendon Press, Oxford, 2013.

Wace, *Master Wace, his chronicle of the Norman conquest from the Roman de Rou*, with notes and illustrations by Edgar Taylor, W. Pickering, London, 1837.

White, Hugh (trans), *Ancrene Wisse: Guide for Anchoresses*, Penguin, Harmondsworth, 1993.

William of Malmesbury, *Chronicles of the Kings of England, From the Earliest Period to the Reign of King Stephen, c. 1090–1143*, Perennial Press, ebook, 2016.

William of Malmesbury, *Chronicles of the Kings of England, From the Earliest Period to the Reign of King Stephen, c. 1090–1143*, edited by John Sharpe and J.A. Giles, H.G. Bohn, London, 1847.

Yonge, C.D. (trans), *Medieval Sourcebook: Matthew of Westminster: Simon de Montfort's Rebellion 1265*, excerpt from Matthew Paris, *The Flowers of History*, sourcebooks.fordham.edu.

**Secondary Sources**

*6 Facts about Magna Carta* (article), historyextra.com, 22 August 2018.

*A History of the County of Rutland: Volume 2*, Victoria County History, London, 1935.

Abulafia, D.S.H., *Isabella [Elizabeth, Isabella of England] (1214–1241)* (article), Oxford Dictionary of National Biography, Oxford University Press, online edition, 23 September 2004.

Adams, George Burton, *The History of England from the Norman Conquest to the Death of John*, public domain, ebook.

Alio, Jacqueline, *Betrothal of Joanna of England to William II of Sicily* (article), academia.edu, 2016, accessed January 2020.

Altschul, Michael, *Clare, Richard de, sixth earl of Gloucester and fifth earl of Hertford* (article), Oxford Dictionary of National Biography, Oxford University Press, online edition, 23 September 2004.

Ambler, Sophie, *Advisers of King John* (article), Oxford Dictionary of National Biography, Oxford University Press, online edition, 28 May 2015.

Ambler, Sophie, *Henry III's Confirmation of Magna Carta in 1265* (article), magna carta research.org, March 2014.

Ambler, Sophie, *Simon de Montfort's 1265 Parliament and Magna Carta* (article), thehistoryofperliament.wordpress.com, 20 January 2015.

Amt, Emilie, *Salisbury, Patrick, first Earl of Salisbury [Earl of Wiltshire]* (article), Oxford Dictionary of National Biography, Oxford University Press, online edition, 23 September 2004.

Archer, T.A., revised by Michael Altschul, *Clare, Gilbert de, fifth earl of Gloucester and fourth earl of Hertford* (article), Oxford Dictionary of National Biography, Oxford University Press, online edition, 23 September 2005.
Asbridge, Thomas, *The Greatest Knight: The Remarkable Life of William Marshal, the Power behind Five English Thrones*, Simon & Schuster, London, 2015.
Ashley, Maurice, *The Life and Times of King John*, George Weidenfield and Nicolson, London, 1972.
Ashley, Mike, *A Brief History of British Kings and Queens*, Constable & Robinson Ltd., London, 2014.
Ashley, Mike, *The Mammoth Book of British Kings & Queens*, Robinson, London, 1998.
Baker, Darren, *The Two Eleanors of Henry III: The Lives of Eleanor of Provence and Eleanor de Montfort*, Pen & Sword History, Barnsley, 2019.
Baker, Darren, *With All For All: The Life of Simon de Montfort*, Amberley, Stroud, 2015.
Barrow, Julia, *Briouze, Giles de (c. 1170–1215), bishop of Hereford* (article), Oxford Dictionary of National Biography, Oxford University Press, online edition, 26 May 1216.
Bartlett, Robert, *England Under the Norman and Angevin Kings, 1075–1225*, Oxford University Press, Oxford, 2000.
Bartlett, W.B., *Richard the Lionheart: The Crusader King of England*, Amberley, Stroud, 2018.
Bateson, Mary, *Medieval England 1066–1350*, Lecturable, ebook.
Bémont, Charles and Gabriel Monod, *Medieval Europe, 395–1270*, Lecturable, ebook, 2012.
Blackburn, Robert, *Britain's Written Constitution* (article), bl.uk/magna-carta, 13 March 2015.
Boyd, Douglas, *Eleanor, April Queen of Aquitaine*, Sutton Publishing, Stroud, 2004.
Boyd, Douglas, *Plantagenet Princes: The Sons of Eleanor of Aquitaine and Henry II*, Pen and Sword, Barnsley, 2021.
Boyd, Douglas, *Plantagenet Princesses: The Daughters of Eleanor of Aquitaine and Henry II*, Pen and Sword, Barnsley, 2020.
Brand, Paul, *Bigod, Hugh (b. in or before 1220, d. 1266)* (article), Oxford Dictionary of National Biography, Oxford University Press, online edition, 3 January 2008.
Brindle, Steven and Agnieszka Sadraei, *Conisbrough Castle, English Heritage Guidebook*, English Heritage, London, 2015.
Brooks, Richard, *The Knight who Saved England, William Marshal and the French Invasion, 1217*, Osprey Publishing, Oxford, 2014.
Burke, John and John Bernard Burke, *A Genealogical and Heraldic Dictionary of the Peerages of England, Ireland and Scotland*, Henry Colburn, London, 1846.
Campbell, Bruce, *Britain 1300* (article), History Today, Volume 50 (6), June 2000.
Cannon, John, editor, *The Oxford Companion to British History*, Oxford University Press, Oxford, 1997.
Carol, *Eleanor of Leicester: A Broken Vow of Chastity* (article), historyofroyalwomen.com, 28 February 2017.
Carpenter, David, *Revival and Survival: Reissuing Magna Carta* (article) bl.co.uk/magna-carta/articles, 13 March 2015.
Castor, Helen, *She-Wolves: The Women who Ruled England before Elizabeth*, Faber and Faber, London, 2010.
Cawley, Charles, *Foundation for Medieval Genealogy*, fmg.ac/MedLands, accessed 22/04/2022.
Chadwick, Elizabeth, *Clothing the Bones: Finding Mahelt Marshal* (article), livingthehistoryelizabethchadwick.blogspot.com, 7 September 2008.
Chadwick, Elizabeth, *Roger Bigod Earl of Norfolk circa 1140–1221* (article), thehistory-girls-blogspot.com, 24 November 2018.

Chadwick, Elizabeth, *Roger Bigod II Earl of Norfolk* (article), livingthehistoryelizabethchadwick. blogspot.com, 12 June 2009.
Church, Stephen, *King John: England, Magna Carta and the Making of a Tyrant*, Pan MacMillan, London, 2015.
Clark, Jonathan, *Historic Graffitti Survey: Cobb Hall, Lincoln Castle, Lincolnshire*, Lincolnshire County Council, Lincoln, 2008.
Clark, Jonathan, Justin Garner-Lahire, Cecily Spall and Nicola Toop, *Lincoln Castle Revealed; the Story of a Norman Powerhouse and its Anglo-Saxon Precursor*, Oxbow Books, Oxford, 2021.
Cockerill, Sara, *Eleanor of Castile: The Shadow Queen*, Amberley, Stroud, 2014.
Cole, Margaret Wren, *Llywelyn ab Iorwerth: The Making of a Welsh Prince*, Phd thesis, ethos. bl.uk, January 2012.
Cole, Teresa, *The Anarchy: The Darkest Days of Medieval England*, Stroud, Amberley, 2019.
Connolly, Sharon Bennett, *Defenders of the Norman Crown: Rise and Fall of the Warenne Earls of Surrey*, Pen and Sword, Barnsley, 2021.
Connolly, Sharon Bennett, *Heroines of the Medieval World*, Amberley, Stroud, 2017.
Connolly, Sharon Bennett, *Ladies of Magna Carta: Women of Influence in Thirteenth Century England*, Pen and Sword, Barnsley, 2020.
Corvi, Steven J., *Plantagenet Queens and Consorts: Family, Duty, Power*, Amberley, Stroud, 2018.
Cross, Peter, *The Lady in Medieval England 1000–1500*, Sutton Publishing, Stroud, 1998.
Crouch, David, *Breteuil, Robert de, fourth earl of Leicester* (article), *Oxford Dictionary of National Biography*, Oxford University Press, online edition, 24 September 2004.
Crouch, David, *Marshal, William [called the Marshal], fourth earl of Pembroke (c. 1146–1219)* (article), *Oxford Dictionary of National Biography*, Oxford University Press, online edition, 24 May 2007.
Crouch, David, *William Marshal*, 3rd edition, Routledge, Abingdon, 2016.
Dalton, Paul, *Roumare, William de, first earl of Lincoln (c.1096–1155x61)* (article), *Oxford Dictionary of National Biography*, Oxford University Press, online edition, 23 September 2004.
Danziger, Danny and John Gillingham, *1215: The Year of Magna Carta*, Hodder & Stoughton, London, 2004.
Davis, H.W. Carless, *England under the Normans and Angevins 1066–1272*, Lecturable, ebook.
Davis, John Paul, *King John, Henry III and England's Lost Civil War*, Pen & Sword, Barnsley, 2021.
Davis, William Stearns, *A History of France from the Earliest Times to the Treaty of Versailles*, The Riverside Press, Cambridge Massachusetts, 1919.
De Lisle, Léopold. "Notice sur les attaches d'un Sceau de Richard Coeur de Lion." *Bibliothèque de l'École Des Chartes*, vol. 4, 1853, pp.56–62, http://www.jstor.org/stable/42994225. Accessed 5 May 2022.
Dodd, Gwilym and Alison K. Hardy, editors, *Petitions from Lincolnshire c.1200–c.1500*, Lincoln Record Society, Woodbridge, 2020.
Duducu, Jem, *Forgotten History: Unbelievable Moments from the Past*, Amberley, Stroud, 2016.
Dugdale, Sir William, *The Baronage of England after the Norman Conquest*, quod.lib.umich. edu. Accessed 15/03/22.
Duruy, Victor, *History of the Middle Ages*, Lecturable, ebook, 2012.
Eales, Richard, *Ranulf III [Ranulf de Blundeville], sixth earl of Chester and first earl of Lincoln* (article), *Oxford Dictionary of National Biography*, Oxford University Press, online edition, 4 October 2008.

*Ela, Countess of Salisbury* (article), medievalwomen.org.
Epistolae, *Eleanor of England* (article), epistolae.ctl.columbia.edu/women.
Epistolae, *Isabel of Angoulême* (article), epistolae.ctl.columbia.edu/women.
*Eva Marshal*, Revolvy.com, accessed 13 March 2019.
Everson, Paul and David Stocker, *Custodians of Continuity? The Premonstratensian Abbey at Barlings and the Landscape of Ritual*, Heritage Trust of Lincolnshire, Sleaford, 2011.
Farrer, William and Charles Travis Clay, editors, *Early Yorkshire Charters, Volume 8: The Honour of Warenne*, Cambridge University Press, Cambridge, 2013 edition, first published 1949 *Biography*, Oxford University Press, online edition, 23 September 2004.
Flanagan, M.T., *Clare, Isabel de, suo jure countess of Pembroke (1171x6–1220)* (article), *Oxford Dictionary of National Biography*, Oxford University Press, online edition, 23 September 2010.
Ford, David Nash, *Matilda de St Valery, Lady Bergavenny (c. 1153–1210)* (article), berkshirehistory.com, 2003.
Fraser, Antonia, *The Warrior Queens: Boadicea's Chariot*, George Weidenfeld & Nicolson Ltd., London, 1993.
Gardiner, Juliet and Neil Wenborn, editors, *History Today Companion to British History*, Collins & Brown, London, 1995.
Gillingham, John, *John (1167–1216)* (article), *Oxford Dictionary of National Biography*, Oxford University Press, online edition, 23 September 2010.
Gladwin, Irene, *The Sheriff: The Man and his Office*, Victor Gollancz, London, 1974.
Golding, Brian, *Canville [Camville], Gerard de (d. 1214)* (article), *Oxford Dictionary of National Biography*, Oxford University Press, online edition, 28 September 2006.
Goubert, Pierre, *The Course of French History*, Routledge, London, 1991.
Grant, Lindy, *Eleanor of Aquitaine* (article), *BBC History Magazine*, August 2016.
Green, Mary Anne Everett, *Lives of the Princesses of England from the Norman Conquest*, Volume 1, Longman, London, 1857.
Green, Mary Anne Everett, *Lives of the Princesses of England from the Norman Conquest*, Volume 2, Longman, London, 1857.
Grey, Madeleine, *Four Weddings, Three Funerals and a Historic Detective Puzzle: A Cautionary Tale* (article), 2014, https://biography.wales/article/s12-JOAN-TYW.
Grigg, Erik, *1217: the Battle of Lincoln*, Lincoln BIG, Lincoln, 2017.
Grigg, Erik, *Lincoln and the Magna Carta; Being an account of Lincoln's 1215 Magna Carta, the 1217 Battle of Lincoln and Lincoln's 1217 Charter of the Forest*, Ed's Music, Lincoln, 2019.
Hallam, Elizabeth, editor, *Chronicles of the Age of Chivalry*, Tiger Books, Twickenham, 1995.
Hallam, Elizabeth, *Eleanor, Countess of Pembroke and Leicester (1215?–1275)* (article), *Oxford Dictionary of National Biography*, Oxford University Press, online edition, 23 September 2004.
Hallam, Elizabeth, editor, *The Plantagenet Chronicles*, Tiger Books, Twickenham, 1995.
Hanley, Catherine, *Louis: The French Prince who Invaded England*, Yale University Press, Yale, 2016.
Hanley, Catherine, *Nichola de la Haye* (article), catherinehanley.co.uk.
Hanley, Catherine, *The Battle that Saved England* (article), historiamag.com, 20 May 2017.
Hanna-Black, Sara, themortimersblog.wordpress.com.
Heiser, Richard R., 'Castles, Constables, and Politics in Late Twelfth-Century English Governance', *Albion: A Quarterly Journal Concerned with British Studies* Vol. 32, No. 1 (Spring, 2000), pp.19–36, https://www.jstor.org/stable/4053985.
Hill, J.W.F., *Medieval Lincoln* Cambridge University Press, Cambridge, 1948.
Hilliam, David *Kings, Queens, Bones and Bastards: Who's Who in the English Monarchy from Egbert to Elizabeth II*, The History Press, Stroud, 2008 (first published 1998).

Hilton, Lisa, *Queens Consort: England's Medieval Queens*, Orion Books, London, 2008.
Holt, J.C., *King John*, Historical Association, London, 1963.
Holt, J. C. "The Carta of Richard de La Haye, 1166: A Note on 'Continuity' in Anglo-Norman Feudalism." *The English Historical Review*, vol. 84, no. 331, Oxford University Press, 1969, pp.289–97, http://www.jstor.org/stable/564522.
Huizinga, J. *The Waning of the Middle Ages*, 4th edition, The Folio Society. London, 2000.
Hume, David, *The History of England, Volume I*, public domain, ebook.
*Joan, Lady of Wales (c.1191–1237)* (article), englishmonarchs.co.uk, 2004.
Jobson, Adrian, *English Government in the Thirteenth Century*, Boydell Press, Woodbridge, 2004.
Johns, Susan M., *Alice [married name Alice de Lusignan] suo jure countess of Eu* (article), *Oxford Dictionary of National Biography*, Oxford University Press, online edition, 23 September 2004.
Johns, Susan M., *Briouze, Loretta de, countess of Leicester (d. in or after 1266)* (article), *Oxford Dictionary of National Biography*, Oxford University Press, online edition, 28 September 2006.
Johns, Susan M., *Haie, Nicola de la (d. 1230), landowner* (article), *Oxford Dictionary of National Biography*, Oxford University Press, online edition, 23 September 2004.
Johns, Susan M., *Warenne, Isabel de, suo jure countess of Surrey (d. 1203)* (article), *Oxford Dictionary of National Biography*, Oxford University Press, online edition, 2004.
Jones, Dan, *The Plantagenets: The Kings Who Made England*, Kindle edition, Harper Collins, London, 2013.
Jones, Dan, *Realm Divided: A Year in the Life of Plantagenet England*, Head of Zeus, London, 2015.
Jones, Dan, *What Was Magna Carta and Why Was it Significant?* (article), hitoryhit.com, 15 June 2018.
Jones, Michael, *Eleanor [Eleanor of Brittany] suo jure duchess of Brittany* (article), *Oxford Dictionary of National Biography*, Oxford University Press, online edition, 3 January 2008.
Jones, Terry, *Terry Jones' Medieval Lives*, BBC Books, London, 2005.
Keats-Rohan, KSB, *Domesday descendants, A Porsopography of persons occurring in English Documents, 1066–1166: II Pipe Rolls to Cartae Baronum*, Boydell Press, Suffolk, 2002.
Keefe, Thomas K., *Henry II (1133–89)*, *Oxford Dictionary of National Biography*, Oxford University Press, online edition, 3 January 2008.
Kemp, B.R., *Longespée, Nicholas* (article), *Oxford Dictionary of National Biography*, Oxford University Press, online edition, 27 May 2010.
Kirk, R. E. G. (Richard Edward Gent). The Countess Lucy: Singular Or Plural? Exeter, 1889, www.archive.org.
Koenigsberger, H.G., *Medieval Europe 400–1500*, Longman, New York, 1987.
Kramer, Kyra Cornelius, *The Jezebel Effect: Why the Slut Shaming of Famous Women still Matters*, Ash Wood Press, Indiana, 2015.
Labarge, Margaret Wade, *A Small Sound of the Trumpet; Women in Medieval Life*, Penguin Books, Middlesex, 1086.
Lacroix, Paul, *Medieval Life: Manners, Customs and Dress During the Middle Ages*, Arcturus, London, 2011.
Laffin, John, *Brassey's Battles: 3,500 Years of Conflict, Campaigns and Wars from A–Z*, Brassey's, London, 1995.
Lawless, Erin, *Forgotten Royal Women: The King and I*, Pen & Sword Books, Barnsley, 2019.
Lewis, Matthew, *Henry III: The Son of Magna Carta*, Amberley, Stroud, 2016.
Leyser, Henrietta, *Medieval Women: A Social History of Women in England 450–1500*, Phoenix, ebook, 2013.

Lloyd, Simon, *Longespée, Sir William* (article), *Oxford Dictionary of National Biography*, Oxford University Press, online edition, 27 May 2010.
Maddicott, J.R., *Montfort, Simon de, eighth earl of Leicester (1208–1265)* (article), *Oxford Dictionary of National Biography*, Oxford University Press, online edition, 3 January 2008.
*Magna Carta*, salisburycathedral.org.uk.
Magna Carta Project, magnacartaresearch.org.
*Magna Carta Quotations*, magnacarta800th.com.
McConnell, Ally, *The Life of Ela, Countess of Salisbury* (article), Wiltshire and Swindon History Centre, wshc.eu, 15 September 2015.
McGlynn, Sean, *Blood Cries Afar: The Magna Carta War and the Invasion of England 1215–1217*, The History Press, Stroud, 2015, ebook.
Marlow, Joyce, *Kings & Queens of Britain*, 6th edition, Artus Publishing, London, 1979.
Martindale, Jane, *Eleanor, suo jure duchess of Aquitaine (c.1122–1204)* (article), *Oxford Dictionary of National Biography*, Oxford University Press, online edition, May 2006.
Matthew, Donald, *King Stephen*, Hambledon and London, London, 2002.
Mcglynn, Sean, *King John and the French Invasion of England* (article), *BBC History Magazine*, Vol. 11, no. 6, June 2010.
Messer, D.R. (2018), *Joan (Siwan) (died 1237), princess and diplomat* (article), *Dictionary of Welsh Biography*, https://biography.wales/article/s12-JOANTYW-1237, 19 Aug 2019.
Morris, Marc, *A Great and Terrible King: Edward I and the Forging of Britain*, Windmill Books, London, 2009.
Morris, Marc, *From Friendly Neighbours to Bitter Enemies* (article), *BBC History Magazine*, Vol. 9 no. 3, March 2008.
Morris, Marc, *How Important was Magna Carta?* (article), historyhit.com, 24 September 2018.
Morris, Marc *King John: Treachery, Tyranny and the Road to Magna Carta*, Windmill Books, London, 2015.
Mount, Toni, *A Year in the Life of Medieval England*, Amberley, Stroud, 2016.
Mundy, John H., *The High Middle Ages 1150–1309*, The Folio Society, London, 1998.
Musgrove, David, *100 Places that Made Britain*, BBC Books, London, 2011.
Nelson, Jessica A., *Isabella, Countess of Norfolk* (article), magnacarta800th.com.
Nelson, Jessica, *Isabella [Isabella Bigod]* (article), (article), *Oxford Dictionary of National Biography*, Oxford University Press, online edition, 13 September 2018.
Newcomb, Charlene, *John's Man in Lincoln: Gerard de Camville* (article), englishhistoryauthors.blog.uk, 4 October 2015.
Nichols, John A., *Warenne, Isabel de [married name Isabel d'Aubigny], countess of Arundel* (article), *Oxford Dictionary of National Biography*, Oxford University Press, online edition, 23 September 2004.
Norgate, Kate, *The Minority of Henry III*, MacMillan & Co., London, 1912.
Norton, Elizabeth, *She Wolves: The Notorious Queens of England*, The History Press, Stroud, 2008.
Oliver, Neil, *The Story of the British Isles in 100 Places*, Penguin Random House, London, 2018.
Ormrod, W.M., *English Historical Review* (article), December 2015.
Patterson, Robert B., *Isabella, suo jure countess of Gloucester (c. 1160–1217)* (article), *Oxford Dictionary of National Biography*, Oxford University Press, online edition, 2004.
Power, Eileen, *Medieval Women*, Cambridge University Press, Cambridge, 1975
Prestwich, J. O. "The Military Household of the Norman Kings." *The English Historical Review*, vol. 96, no. 378, Oxford University Press, 1981, pp.1–35, http://www.jstor.org/stable/568383.

Phillips, Charles, *The Illustrated Encyclopaedia of Kings and Queens of Britain*, Hermes House, Leicestershire, 2011.
Power, Eileen, *Medieval English Nunneries c. 1275–1535*, Cambridge University Press, London, 1922.
Price, Rich, *King John's Letters*, Facebook Study Group, 20 June 2016 onwards.
Ramirez, Janina, *Julian of Norwich: A Very Brief History*, London, SPCK Publishing, 2016.
Rees, William, editor, Calendar of Ancient Petitions Relating to Wales (Thirteenth to Sixteenth Century), Cardiff, University of Wales Press, 1975.
Ridgeway, H.W., *Munchensi, Warin de* (article), Oxford Dictionary of National Biography, Oxford University Press, online edition, 23 September 2004.
Robertson, Geoffrey, *Magna Carta and Jury Trial*, (article), bl.uk/magna-carta, 13 March 2015.
Ross, David, *Scotland: History of a Nation*, Lomond Books Ltd., Broxburn, 2014.
Saul, Nigel, *Geoffrey de Mandeville* (article), magnacarta800th.com.
Scott, W.W., *Ermengarde [Ermengarde de Beaumont] (1233)* (article), Oxford Dictionary of National Biography, Oxford University Press, online edition, 23 September 2004.
Scott, W.W., *Margaret, countess of Kent* (article), Oxford Dictionary of National Biography, Oxford University Press, online edition, 23 September 2004.
Scott, W.W., *William I [known as William the Lion] (c. 1142–1214)* (article), Oxford Dictionary of National Biography, Oxford University Press, online edition, 23 September 2004.
Seward, Desmond, *The Demon's Brood*, Constable, London, 2014.
Soden, Iain, *The First English Hero; The Life of Ranulf de Blondeville*, Amberley, Stroud, 2021.
Southern, R.W., *The Making of the Middle Ages*, 4th edition, The Folio Society, London, 1998.
Stacey, Robert C., *Bigod, Roger, fourth earl of Norfolk* (article), Oxford Dictionary of National Biography, Oxford University Press, online edition, 23 September 2004.
Stacey, R.C., *Divorce, Medieval Welsh Style*, (article), *Speculum*, Volume 77, issue 4 October 2002, University of Chicago Press.
Starkey, David, *Magna Carta: The True Story Behind the Charter*, Hodder, London, 2015.
Strickland, Matthew, *Enforcers of Magna Carta (act, 1215–1216)* (article), Oxford Dictionary of National Biography, Oxford University Press, online edition, 22 September 2005.
Strickland, Matthew, *Longespée [Lungespée], William, third earl of Salisbury* (article), Oxford Dictionary of National Biography, Oxford University Press, online edition, 27 May 2010.
Stringer, Keith, *Alexander II (1198–1249)* (article), Oxford Dictionary of National Biography, Oxford University Press, online edition, 23 September 2004.
Stringer, Keith, *Joan (1210–1237)* (article), Oxford Dictionary of National Biography, Oxford University Press, online edition, 23 September 2004.
Swaton Parish Council, *The History of Swaton* (article), swaton.org.uk.
The Historier, *The Treaty of Kingston: On this Day and on this Spot?* (article), anhistoriersmiscellany.com, 12 September 2017.
Thompson, S.P., *Mary [Mary of Blois], suo jure countess of Boulogne (d. 1182), princess and abbess of Romsey* (article), Oxford Dictionary of National Biography, Oxford University Press, online edition, May 2014.
Tickhill Castle Guide Leaflet, *Lords of the Honour of Tickhill*, author unknown, 2017.
Tranter, Nigel, *The Story of Scotland*, ebook, 4th edition, Neil Wilson Publishing, 2011.
Turner, Ralph V., *Aubigny, William d', [William de Albini], third earl of Arundel* (article), Oxford Dictionary of National Biography, Oxford University Press, online edition, 23 September 2004.
Turner, Ralph V., *Briouze [Braose], William de (d. 1211)* (article), Oxford Dictionary of National Biography, Oxford University Press, online edition, 28 September 2006.
Vincent, Nicholas, *Canville [Camville], Richard de (d. 1191)* (article), Oxford Dictionary of National Biography, Oxford University Press, online edition, 23 September 2004.

Vincent, Nicholas, *Feature of the Month: May 2015 – A Glimpse of London, May 1216* (article), The Magna Carta Project, magnacarta.cmp.uea.ac.uk, May 2015.
Vincent, Nicholas, *From the Tower: John Sends a Coded Message to His Queen* (article), The Magna Carta Project, magnacartaresearch.org, accessed 19 May 2019.
Vincent, Nicholas, *Isabella [Isabella of Angoulême], suo jure countess of Angoulême (c. 1188–1246)* (article), Oxford Dictionary of National Biography, Oxford University Press, online edition, 5 January 2006.
Vincent, Nicholas, *John Deals with Loretta de Braose and Isaac of Norwich* (article), The Magna Carta Project, magnacarta.cmp.uea.ac.uk.
Vincent, Nicholas, *King John's Blood Lust* (article), BBC History Magazine, April 2019.
Vincent, Nicholas, *King John's Evil Counsellors (act. 1208–1214)* (article), Oxford Dictionary of National Biography, Oxford University Press, online edition, 4 October 2008.
Vincent, Nicholas, *Lacy, John de, third earl of Lincoln* (article), Oxford Dictionary of National Biography, Oxford University Press, online edition, 23 September 2010.
Vincent, Nicholas, *Richard, first earl of Cornwall and king of Germany* (article), Oxford Dictionary of National Biography, Oxford University Press, online edition, 3 January 2008.
Vincent, Nicholas, *Tournaments, Ladies and Bears* (article) and *The Magna Carta Project* (article), magnacartaresearch.org, accessed 27 November 2018.
Vincent, Nicholas, *Warenne, William de, fifth earl of Surrey [Earl Warenne]* (article), Oxford Dictionary of National Biography, Oxford University Press, online edition, 23 September 2004.
Walker, R.F., *Marshal, William, fifth earl of Pembroke (c. 1190–1231)* (article), Oxford Dictionary of National Biography, Oxford University Press, online edition, 22 September 2005.
Ward, Jennifer C., *Lacy [née Quincy], Margaret de, countess of Lincoln* (article), Oxford Dictionary of National Biography, Oxford University Press, online edition, 3 January 2008.
Warren, W.L., *Henry II*, new edition, Yale University Press, New Haven, 2000.
Waugh, S.L., *The Lordship of England: Royal Wardships and Marriages in English Society and Politics, 1217–1327* (article) (1988).
Weir, Alison, *Britain's Royal Families: The Complete Genealogy*, 2nd edition, Pimlico, London, 1996.
Weir, Alison, *Eleanor of Aquitaine: By the Wrath of God, Queen of England*, Jonathan Cape, London, 1999.
West, F.J., *Burgh, Hubert de, earl of Kent (c. 1170–1243)* (article), Oxford Dictionary of National Biography, Oxford University Press, online edition, 3 January 2008.
Whittle, Elisabeth, *Abergavenny Castle* (article), castlewales.com, 1992.
*Why Magna Carta Matters* (article), historyextra.com, 23 January 2013.
Wilkinson, Louise, *Isabella of Angoulême, wife of King John* (article), magnacarta800th.com.
Wilkinson, Louise, *Isabel of Gloucester, wife of King John* (article), magnacarta 800th.com.
Wilkinson, Louise, *Joan, daughter of King John* (article), magnacarta800th.com, 2016.
Wilkinson, Louise, *Women in Thirteenth-Century Lincolnshire*, Boydell, Suffolk, 2007.
*William Marshal, Earl of Pembroke* (article), englishmonarchs.co.uk, 2004–2018.
*William de Warenne, 5th earl of Surrey* (article), howlingpixel.com.
Williamson, David, *Brewer's British Royalty*, Cassell, London, 1996.
Wilson, Derek, *The Plantagenets*, Quercus, London, 2011. *The Woes of King John Parts I and II* (article), weaponsandwarfare.com, 7 June 2016.
Wright, James, *A Palace for Our Kings: The History and Archaeology of a Mediaeval Royal Palace in the Heart of Sherwood Forest*, Triskele Publishing, London, 2016.
Yonge, Charlotte M., *History of France*, D. Appleton and Company, New York, 1882.

# Index

Alexander II, King of Scots 107, 115, 119, 149, 182
Alexander III, Pope 3, 48
Alexander of Lincoln, Bishop of Lincoln 17, 18
Adelice, or Alice, wife of Richard de Camville 54, 57-58
Adeliza of Louvain 13, 58
Anjou 27, 28, 35, 46, 48, 51, 75, 90, 91, 92, 93, 94, 95, 101, 104,
Arthur, Duke of Brittany 46, 63, 76-77, 81, 89, 90, 91, 94, 95, 101-103, 143
Aubigny, William d', Earl of Arundel 13, 68
Audemar, Count of Angoulême 95, 96

Barlings Abbey 3, 12-13, 14, 16, 28, 36, 100, 159, 169
Barnwell annalist, chronicler 102
Berengaria of Navarre, Queen of England 65-66, 84, 89
Bigod, Hugh, third Earl of Norfolk 19, 149, 185
Bigod, Ralph 139
Bigod, Roger, second Earl of Norfolk 139, 185
Bigod, Roger, fourth Earl of Norfolk 149-150
Blanche of Castile, Queen of France 94-95
Blanche of Lancaster 169
Blanchelande Abbey 11, 28-29, 34, 36, 39
Bloet, Robert de, Bishop of Lincoln 15
Blois, Henry of, Bishop of Winchester 21
Blundeville, Ranulf de, Earl of Chester and Lincoln 14, 125-126, 128, 131-132, 135, 136, 145
Bolingbroke, Lucy of, Countess of Chester 2, 15, 23, 25, 32, 33, 72
Bouvines, battle, 1214 111, 139, 143
Braose, Matilda de 14
Braose, William (II) de, third Lord of Bramber xiv, 103, 107, 111, 113, 143

Brattleby viii, 1, 11, 14, 16, 37, 40, 44, 54, 80, 88, 100, 154, 162
Bréauté, Faulkes de 129, 132, 135-136, 144, 155-156
Burgh, Hubert de, justiciar and Earl of Kent xiv, 100, 118, 127, 140, 145, 148, 150, 154-156, 158, 171

Camville-les-Deux-Églises 67, 75
Camville, family 67-68, 70
Camville, Adelice de, mother of Gerard 57
Camville, Gerard de 43, 44, 53, 54, 58, 68, 69-70, 71-73 74, 75, 76, 79-81, 87-88, 96, 98, 99, 105-106, 112, 159
Camville, Idonea de 44, 75, 98, 117-118, 146-147, 154, 160-162
Camville, Millicent de, stepmother of Gerard 58
Camville, Richard de, brother of Gerard 57, 58, 59-63, 65, 66-67, 68
Camville, Richard de, father of Gerard 54-55, 57, 69, 159
Camville, Richard de, son of Gerard and Nicholaa de la Haye 44, 97-99, 117, 129, 146, 158, 160
Chapel, Iwun (Eudo, Eudes) al 4-6, 10
Charter of the Forest, 1217 138, 186
Chinon Castle 47, 51, 90, 91, 103
Clare, Gilbert de, Earl of Gloucester and Hertford 20, 185
Clare, Richard de, Earl of Gloucester and Hertford 185
Colswein (Colsuan, Kolsweinn) de Lincoln 1-3, 10-12, 14-16, 26, 31, 33
Constance, Duchess of Brittany 46, 101
Coutances, Walter de, Archbishop of Rouen 78, 80-81, 84, 91
Crowland Abbey 70-73, 120
Crowland Chronicle 71, 79

Edmund Crouchback, Earl of Lancaster 163
Ela, Countess of Salisbury 98, 117, 122, 140-143, 146, 147-151, 163

Eleanor of Aquitaine, Queen of England 25, 45-46, 47-48, 65, 76, 84, 87, 90, 92, 94, 103, 140
Eleanor of Brittany 103
Eleanor of England, Queen of Castile 46, 94, 100, 101, 103

Fitz Erneis, Matilda, Nicholaa's daughter 43-44, 88-89, 97
Fitz Erneis, Ralph 41
Fitz Erneis, Robert 40-42
Fitz Erneis, Robert II 41
Fitz Erneis, Robert III 41
Fitz Erneis, Robert IV 41
Fitz Erneis, William 40, 42-44, 88
Fitzpatrick, William, Earl of Salisbury 140, 141
Fitz Peter, Geoffrey, Earl of Essex 71, 73, 78, 143
Fitzwalter, Robert, magnate 108, 110, 127, 134, 137, 185
Fontevrault Abbey 47, 48, 51, 90, 100

Gant, Gilbert de, Earl of Lincoln, rebel baron 119, 120, 121, 126, 128
Geoffrey of Anjou 27, 140
Geoffrey, son of Henry II and Duke of Brittany 46, 47, 49, 51, 101
Geoffrey, illegitimate son of Henry II and Archbishop of York 52, 76, 83, 87, 139
Gerald of Wales, chronicler 49-50
Gernon, Ranulf de, Earl of Chester 15-16, 17, 18, 20-21, 23, 25, 26, 33, 82
Glanville, Ranulf de, justiciar 49, 69

Haye family 4, 5, 6, 11, 12, 13, 15, 16, 24, 25, 34, 54, 67, 68, 70, 73, 74, 75, 79, 98, 100, 106, 154
Haye, Cecilie (Cecilia) de la 3, 7, 10-12, 26, 29
Haye, Gila (Gille) de la 37, 38-39, 42, 70, 73, 74, 75
Haye, Isabel de la 37, 39, 40, 73-74, 75
Haye, Nicholaa de la viii, ix, xiv-xv, 1, 13, 28, 30, 33, 37, 40, 41, 42, 43-44, 48, 53, 54, 65, 67, 68-70, 73, 74, 75, 76, 79-80, 82-83, 86, 88-89, 91, 96, 97-98, 99-100, 106, 112, 116-117, 118, 119, 120-121, 122, 126, 128-129, 130, 134-135, 145, 146, 147, 148, 152-154, 155-156, 157, 158-161, 162-163, 169, 170

Haye, Ralph (Ranulf) de la, son of Robert 3, 11, 12-14, 16, 28, 29, 30, 68, 159, 169
Haye, Ralph, son of Ralph 30, 120
Haye, Ralph de la, seneschal for Count of Mortain 3-4, 5-6
Haye, Richard de la 1, 3, 7, 11, 12, 14, 16, 24, 25-27, 28, 29, 30, 31-33, 34, 35-36, 37, 70, 75, 88, 99, 100, 106
Haye, Robert de la 1, 3-4, 5-7, 10, 11, 13, 14, 15-16, 17, 24, 25, 26, 33, 70, 76
Henry, archbishop of Dublin 110, 171, 184
Henry VI, Holy Roman Emperor 62, 85, 86
Henry I, King of England 4, 6, 7, 10-11, 13, 15, 25, 26, 27, 38, 39, 40, 45, 52, 57, 58, 107, 113
Henry II, King of England xiii, 12, 14, 22, 23-24, 25, 27-28, 29-30, 33-34, 35, 38, 39, 42, 44, 45-48, 49, 50-51, 54-56, 58, 67, 68, 70, 71, 72, 90, 97, 98, 101, 103, 107, 121, 124, 134, 139-140, 180, 181
Henry III, King of England viii, ix, xiv, 44, 47, 67, 118, 122, 124, 125-126, 128, 131, 134, 138, 139, 145, 148, 150, 152, 154, 155, 157, 158, 160, 161, 170
Henry of Blois, Bishop of Winchester 21
Henry of Huntingdon, chronicler 18, 19, 20
Henry V, 'the Lion', Duke of Saxony 55
Henry, the Young King 14, 35, 46, 56
Hommet, Richard du 37-39, 70, 75
Hommet, William du 37, 68, 70, 75
Hugh of Avalon, Bishop of Lincoln 81, 91, 97, 171

Innocent III, Pope 102, 104, 105, 109, 110, 114-115, 124, 172
Isaac Comnenus 65, 66-67
Isabella of Gloucester, Countess of Gloucester 48, 52, 85, 95-96, 110, 148
Isabella of Scotland, princess 149
Isabelle d'Angoulême, Queen of England and Countess of Angoulême 95-96, 100, 103, 111, 126

Joan, Lady of Wales 107
Joan, Queen of Scots 111
Joanna, Queen of Sicily and Countess of Toulouse 42, 46-47, 55-57, 61-62, 65, 77
Joan of Bar, Countess of Surrey 164

Joan, dowager Countess of Lincoln 168
John, King of England viii-ix, xiii-xv, 39, 40, 41, 43-44, 45-53, 65, 72-75, 76-78, 79-82, 83-85, 86-88, 89-90, 91-96, 97, 99-104, 105, 106-109, 110-114, 115-124, 125-127, 130, 139-140, 141, 142-146, 152-154, 158, 159, 161, 162, 170, 186, 188

La Haye-du-Puits 1, 4, 5, 7, 14, 28, 67, 74
Lacey, Alice de, Countess of Lincoln and Salisbury ix, 13, 151, 162-163, 164, 165, 167-170
Lacey, Henry de, Earl of Lincoln 147, 151, 162-163
Lacy, Hugh de, Lord of Meath 49, 50, 107
Lacy, John de, Earl of Lincoln 151, 185
Lacy, Margaret de, Countess of Lincoln (Margaret de Quincey) 13, 147, 151, 162, 163
Langton, Stephen, Archbishop of Canterbury 104-105, 110, 124
Le Mans 9, 51, 91-93
Leopold, Duke of Austria 85
Lincoln,
   bishop of 15-16, 17, 18, 33, 81, 91, 154, 169, 171
   castle viii-ix, xiv, 2, 3, 4, 10, 14-16, 17, 18, 23-24, 25, 27, 32, 33, 36, 37, 42, 44, 45, 68, 69-70, 76, 79, 80, 81-82, 87, 91, 97-99, 106, 112, 118-119, 120-121, 126, 128, 129, 130, 131-138, 144-146, 152, 153, 154, 155-156, 157-158, 159, 161, 162-163, 168, 170
   cathedral 3, 10, 18, 25, 35, 96, 97, 134, 152, 159, 160
   city xv, 1, 2, 3, 10, 12, 15, 17, 18, 19, 21, 23-24, 27-28, 32, 36, 40, 72, 73, 76, 79, 80, 81, 86, 87, 96-97, 98-99, 100, 105, 106, 112, 116-117, 118-120, 121, 126, 128, 129, 130, 131-138, 146, 152, 154, 156, 158, 159, 170
   First Battle of, 1141 19-22
   Second Battle of, 1217 ix, 83, 116, 131-138, 145, 146, 152, 153, 156, 161, 170
Lincolnshire viii-ix, xiv, 1, 3, 4, 10, 12-14, 15, 17, 20, 24, 25, 28, 31, 33, 35, 37, 39, 40, 42, 44, 45, 55, 67, 70, 79, 88, 91, 98-99, 106, 119, 121, 122, 138, 140, 146, 148, 152, 153, 154, 155, 157, 158, 160, 161, 162, 168-169
Llywelyn ap Iorweth, Prince of Gwynedd 107, 108, 113, 115, 143, 147, 182
London 22, 28, 72, 83, 84, 97, 105, 106, 113-115, 118, 125, 127, 137-138, 144, 154-155, 174, 177, 191
Longchamp, William de, Bishop of Ely, Justiciar xiv, 53, 72, 74, 76-84, 87, 88, 141, 162
Longespée, Nicholas, Bishop of Salisbury 146
Longespée, William, first Earl of Salisbury viii, xiv, 44, 98, 110-111, 117-118, 122, 132, 136, 138, 139-140, 142-149, 150, 153-155
Longespée, William II, second Earl of Salisbury 75, 98, 117, 146-147, 148, 150-151, 154, 160, 162
Longespée, William III 147, 151
Louis (prince, future Louis VIII, King of France) viii, xiii, 94-95, 111, 115, 118-119, 123-124, 125, 126-131, 134, 138, 145, 153, 159
Louis VII, King of France 46-48
Louis IX, King of France 147
Lusignan, Geoffrey de 102
Lusignan, Hugh Le Brun (IX) de, Count of La Marche 95, 100, 102, 111
Lusignan, Hugh (X) de, Count of La Marche 111

Macwilliam, Guthred, Scottish pretender 106-107
Magna Carta viii, xiii, xv, 45, 104, 107, 114-115, 124, 126, 138, 144, 148, 150, 152, 161, 171, 185
Malregard, Ralph 8
Mandeville, Geoffrey de, Earl of Essex and Gloucester 110, 185
Marc, Philip, Sheriff of Nottingham viii, 112, 116, 122, 128, 130, 180
Marshal, John 132, 134, 171
Marshal, William, first Earl of Pembroke ix, xiv, 78, 90, 92, 103, 112-113, 123-124, 125-128, 130-138, 140, 143, 145, 152, 155, 161, 170, 171, 187, 191
Marshal, William, second Earl of Pembroke 128, 132, 145, 150, 185

Matilda, Countess of Gloucester 21
Matilda, Duchess of Saxony 46, 55-56, 134
Matilda, Empress and Lady of the English 12, 16, 18, 21-23, 34, 45, 52, 138, 140
Matilda of Boulogne, Queen of England 22
Meschin, Ranulf le, Earl of Chester 7
Mirebeau 47, 101-102, 143
Muriel, wife of Iwun al Chapel 4-6
Muriel, wife of Robert de la Haye 1, 3, 7, 10-12, 14-17, 25-26

Nonant, Hugh de, Bishop of Chester 72
Norham, treaty of 106
Nottingham, city, castle 15, 26, 28, 48, 52, 79, 80, 81, 87, 88, 108, 116, 128

Otto IV, Emperor of Germany 108, 110, 111, 143, 144, 131, 138, 141, 179

Pandulf, papal legate 171, 184
Patrick, Earl of Salisbury 140
Philip II Auguste King of France xiii, 51, 62, 84, 86-87, 89, 91, 93-95, 96, 100-101, 102-103, 109, 110, 111, 115, 124, 142, 143-144
Picot 1, 2, 3, 10-11, 12, 15, 26, 33

Quincy, Saher de, Earl of Winchester 134, 185

Rainauld, Count of Boulogne 107, 110
Redvers, Baldwin de, earl of Devon 33, 35
Richard, Bishop of Coutances 29
Richard, Earl of Cornwall 147
Richard the Lionheart, King of England xiv, 37-38, 39, 45-46, 57, 59, 62, 65-67, 69-70, 72-74, 76-78, 83-90, 91-92, 101-102, 124, 139-142, 180-181, 188
Roger of Howden (Hoveden) 50, 56, 59-62, 65-66, 80-81, 88, 90
Rollos (or Roullours), William de 39-40, 75
Rollos family 39-40
Ros, Matilda de, sister of Gerard de Camville 58
Rouen, Normandy 29, 30, 37, 56, 63, 68, 72, 78, 80, 81, 90, 91, 93, 102, 103

Roumare, William de, Earl of Lincoln 15-17, 23-24, 33, 55, 72
Runnymede 114, 144, 183

Sablé, Robert de, Grand Master of the Knights Templar 59-61, 63
Sancho I, King of Portugal 59-60
Serland, Geoffrey de 122, 128, 129, 130, 134
St Jean, Thomas de 8
Stephen, King of England 26
St John, Roger de 7, 10-12

Taisson, Raoul I 41
Taisson, Raoul II 41
Talbot, William 142
Tickhill, honour and castle, Yorkshire 52, 79, 80, 81, 86, 88
Tosney, Ida de, Countess of Norfolk 139
Turstain Halduc (Richard) 30, 34

Vernon, Matilda de 1, 28, 33-34, 36, 37, 39-40
Vernon, William de
Vescy, Eustace de, magnate 108, 110, 186

Walter, Hubert, Archbishop of Canterbury 86, 87, 90, 92, 104
Warenne, Beatrice de, heiress 100
Warenne, Hamelin de, fourth Earl of Warenne and Surrey 56, 87
Warenne, John de, seventh Earl of Surrey 164-167, 168
Warenne, William de, first Earl of Warenne and Surrey 11
Warenne, William de, third Earl of Warenne and Surrey 19-20
Warenne, William de, fifth Earl of Warenne and Surrey xiv, 113, 119, 128, 143, 145, 148, 151, 155, 171
William of Huntingfield 152-153, 158, 185
William of Ypres 19-20, 22
William I, the Conqueror, King of England and Duke of Normandy 1-2, 3, 4-6, 8, 31, 41, 45, 76, 107, 140
William II, King of Sicily 56-57, 61-62, 77
William the Lion, King of Scots 87, 93, 94, 96-97, 106, 143, 182